Elhaz Ablaze

A Compendium of Chaos Heathenry

Elhaz Ablaze: A Compendium of Chaos Heathenry

Copyright © 2018 to the respective creators.

Published under the auspices of Elhaz Press.

ISBN:
978-0-692-98471-0 (Print)
978-0-692-98474-1 (eBook)

All rights reserved. No part of this book, in part or in whole, may be reproduced, transmitted, or utilized in any form or by any means, electric or mechanical, including photocopying, recording, or by any information storage or retrieval system, without express permission in writing from the creators of this text, except for brief quotations in articles, books, and reviews.

Find *Elhaz Ablaze* on the web at **www.elhazablaze.com**

Chaos Heathenry embraces and seeks to be inclusive of all races, genders, sexualities, and identities.

The creators of this book reserve the right to freely disagree with one another, and perhaps even with themselves. Our quoting and referencing of sources in this text should not be taken as uncritical endorsements.

MichaELFallson Artist Statement: Included in this book are images of the swastika. In Thor's name, I am endeavouring to reclaim this symbol from fascists, who I have directly fought both physically and artistically since my late teenage years. My artistic contributions should be taken as a declaration of war against spiritual ignorance and racists/fascists.

The similarity of this book's creators to actual people, living or dead, is entirely coincidental. This may be a work of fiction.

Discordian Disclaimer: This Text is Dangerous, Use it at Your OWN RISK.

Contents

Welcome — 7

Introduction: Why We are Here — 9
   Matthew Hern

Introduction: Eveline's Question — 14
   Heimlich A. Laguz

The Marriage of Heathenry and Chaos Magic: a Dagazian Paradox that Gave Birth to a Bastard Child — 21
   Matthew Hern

Bronze Gods — 43
   Klintr O'DubhGhaill

Ancestors: the Good, the Bad, the Funky — 47
   Lonnie Scott

What is Ancestor Worship? — 61
   Heimlich A. Laguz

Chaos Heathenry: Incompleteness and Elegance — 69
   Heimlich A. Laguz

Kalos Sthenos — 95
   Klintr O'DubhGhaill

Beyond Belief: Toward a Dogma-Free Rational Heathenism — 101
   Sweyn Plowright

"Everything Fornicates All the Time:" an Ancient Pattern that Journeys Far — 121
   Matthew Hern

Pine Ranger Love Song   **139**
    MichaELFallson

Chaos Heathen Results Magic   **141**
    Heimlich A. Laguz

Chaos, *Wyrd*, and the Left Hand Path   **173**
    Matthew Hern

"Not a War but a Rescue Mission:" Heathenry, Gnosis, & Liberation   **187**
    VI

Arete   **201**
    Klintr O'DubhGhaill

Experiencing Thor   **207**
    Heimlich A. Laguz & Arrowyn Craban Lauer

On *Participation Mystique*   **221**
    Heimlich A. Laguz

Academic Sources   **229**
    Sweyn Plowright
    Additional suggestions by Rig Svenson & Heimlich A. Laguz

Sources for Inspiration   **236**

Gratitude   **248**

About the Creators   **252**

Index   **261**

Artwork

By MichaELFallson

Berzerkergang	6
Wood Thing	8
Odin as Shiva as Odin	20
Merry Met	42
LOVE	46
Hel's Home	60
Dance of Sleipnir (The Smashing of the Fascia)	68
ForestFaceFallson	94
HappyHound	100
Pine Ranger	138
Goddess of Summer	140
Eternity Three	172
Elektrik Vitki	186
Ullr's Gift	200
Thursjoy	206
Sunna	220

By Arrowyn Craban Lauer

ALL Father	**Cover Art**
Portrait of an Owl	228

By Mark Morte

Untitled	120

Berzerkergang, MichaELFallson

Welcome

Do you know the warm progress under the stars?
Do you know we exist?
Have you forgotten the keys to the Kingdom?
Have you been born yet and are you alive?
Let's reinvent the gods, all the myths of the ages
Celebrate symbols from deep elder forests.

– Jim Morrison

In the spirit of ancient hospitality
We bid thee welcome.
Be welcome in our chaos halls
Be welcome in our temple of spontaneity!
No boundaries will we accept
Of what you appear, what parts you bear,
What shape your soul, what folk you hail.
We decline the need to buttress weak spines
With arbitrary divides, or rigid lines in the sand.
No!
Be welcome in the halls of Chaos Heathenry,
And the less thou dost conform – the better.

Wood Thing, MichaELFallson

Introduction One: Why We are Here
Matthew Hern

"Philosophy separates thee person from thee Mass. Exit all legends. Enter thee laws of magick."
– Genesis P. Orridge, Psychick TV

"Create your own current."
– Peter "Sleazy" Christopherson (Coil), during our conversation in Berlin, 2005

Nothing exists in isolation. Everything, every religion, philosophy, tradition, scientific discovery, or idea originates in a certain historical and cultural context, no matter how original or new. Chaos Heathenry is no exception. The two ideas or currents that Chaos Heathenry unites, transforms, and transcends into something new are Chaos Magic and Heathenry. Both these currents came into contemporary form during the 1970s, though at that time no such names were given to them. Both currents were reactions to, or products of, their own time, and both had ideological predecessors.

Chaos Magic

Chaos Magic relied heavily on Aleister Crowley's "93rd Current" of Thelema and on Austin Osman Spare's Zos Kia Cultus. It was an attempt to break free from the rigidity and dogmatism of 19th century Ceremonial Magic of the Golden Dawn type, which still dominated much of occult practice and theory in the 1970s. Simultaneously, Chaos Magic was a child of the postmodern zeitgeist of the 1960s-80s and tried to incorporate the emerging ideas of Chaos Theory and quantum physics into its model of magic.

Scholars agree that occultism as a coherent *Weltanschuung* came into existence in 1875 (the term *l'occultisme* appears for the first time in Jean-Baptiste Richard de Randonvilliers' 1842 *Dictionnaire des mots nouveaux*, in an article by A. de Lestrange about "*Ésotérisme chrétien*"), with the founding of the Theosophical Society by Blavatsky and Olcott. Its origins are to be found in mesmerism, spiritualism, Renaissance magic lore, and Rosicrucian and Free Masonry myths, underpinned by a neo-Platonic framework. It represented an attempt to reconcile the older esoteric currents of Renaissance Magic – think Marsilio Ficino, Giovanni Pico della Mirandola, or Agrippa von Nettesheim – with the new discoveries of modern science.

Marsilio Ficino and Giordano Bruno could still believe that their magic accorded with the newest discoveries of their age as well as with the most ancient philosophy of the pagan theologians. But with the rise of "the cold shower of philology" (Joscelyn Godwin) in the 17th century, the discoveries of the Enlightenment era in the 18th century, and the forcefully emerging power of modern science in the 19th century, the old dream was over. The occultist woke up in a world in which the sacred, ancient 'occult sciences' of astrology, alchemy, and magic were suddenly superstitions of unenlightened, foolish, deluded philosophers who did not know the 'laws of nature' yet.

Thus the rise of Occultism, beginning with Blavatsky, popularly reformulated by Crowley in his "magick = science" equation, and continuing with Peter Carroll's Chaos Magic to the present day, is the attempt to explain magic in scientific terms, to reconcile magic (read: 'superstition') with science (read: 'truth'). Occultism sees itself as using 'laws of nature' not yet discovered by modern science, manipulating 'occult' – that is, hidden – 'laws' to affect the world (or so the story goes). The theories of magic devised by the occultists of the 19th and 20th centuries are narratives that embody the attempt to use (the newest) scientific theories to explain magic. When the dominant scientific paradigm changes, so change the occult theories. A nice feature of this approach is that it allows the educated, intellectual, contemporary person to engage in magical experiments without feeling like some backward-thinking fool who missed the news that magic does not exist.

Heathenry

The Heathen approach or mindset is very different from this occult framework of 'scientific sorcery,' and indeed trades on its Romantic aura. I believe that many Heathens feel a certain discomfort with some aspects of the modern world. Since the rise of science and its accompanying scientific revolutions during the last three centuries there have always been reactions to this modern project of progress and secularization. The German Romantic movement, the *Lebensphilosophie*, the 'Kosmiker' circle (consisting of Klages, Schuler, George, etc., with their anti-intellectualist "pagan Eros"), the reform movements of the early 20th century, and other European intellectuals that were connected by the Swiss Eranos School (such as Carl Gustav Jung and Mircea Eliade) all tried in different ways to redress the shocks of the modern world, with its rational reductionism, technocratic exploitation, atheism, 'displacement of man,' and the "disenchantment of the world," as Max Weber put it so aptly.

Heathenism, I assume, is a successor of these German Romantic and anti-modernist movements. It expresses a profound discomfort with modernity and attempts to re-sacralize nature and defend the nobility of the human spirit as the descendant of a divine origin. The Heathen movement, I think, expresses a deep yearning for an ancestral religion, one that enables us to see the holiness of nature and create a deep bond with the divine source behind the wonders of the visible world. Thus do I trace it to the same spiritual root as the intellectual German movements just mentioned.

Yet the Romantic current within Heathenry can also be contested, as may be seen in Sweyn Plowright's idea of a "Rational Heathenism," which emphasizes the role of the Enlightenment in the European history of ideas. This view could be seen as a necessary (and perhaps complementary) compensation for the irrational, dogmatic, and fanatic fights within the cultic milieu of neo-pagan and Heathen groups. It is an anarchic power, one which substantiates Chaos Heathenry's radical critique of any claim to absolute authority over pagan or spiritual issues. Here then we must acknowledge also the American Transcendentalists like Emerson and 'the Father of American Psychology,' William James, who represent a radical empiricism that remains open to spiritual experience. It is not by chance that James' radical empiricism influenced Vivekananda, who in turn directly influenced Crowley's famous doctrine, "the method of science – the aim of religion," which valorizes personal, experiential revelation over mediated, authoritative dogmas camouflaged as unquestioned 'truths.'

In the 1970s there existed no Heathen handbooks, no Thor's hammers in esoteric shops, and there was no one to ask how to become a Heathen. Everything had to be invented out of scratch, based on the material available, such as the *Eddas* or the stimulating works of Tolkien. Despite the barren lacuna of a millennium of Christianity in Europe, Heathenry stresses tradition, the past, and evokes a historical continuity via the link of the ancestors and the heroic tales of their deeds. Its emphasis on the past and ancestral lineage need not lie in ethnocentrism but in a Romantic impulse, a desire for security in a world in which all old certainties are lost, consumed by the uprooting of modernity. That said, it is rather ironic that the profoundly modernist notion of 'race,' a product largely of 19th-century (pseudo-) scientific materialism, is evoked by contemporary Heathens of the folkish brand to 'defend' a supremely Romantic, anti-materialistic cause. The line between reclaiming the past and inventing it anew is perilously thin.

Chaos Heathenry

Both Chaos Magic and Heathenry are reactions to the "disenchantment of the world" and modernity. While Chaos Magic embraces the postmodern signs of disintegration in a magical gnosis of 'sex and death' and focuses on the future, Heathenry tries to resist the symptoms of cultural disintegration with a return to spiritual roots and a focus on the past. Chaos Heathenry is the bastard offspring of these antagonistic currents, an attempt to break free from the limiting perspectives that constrain both Chaos Magic and Heathenry, while still incorporating and extracting the best of each.

The binding thread of Chaos Magic and Heathenism is simply this: orthopraxy (right action) trumps orthodoxy (right belief). Chaos Magic doesn't care what your beliefs are, it cares about whether your magical practice is done well, e.g., that it works. The ancient Heathens didn't have any requirements about what one should believe or not believe; to them what mattered was how one lived, whether one honored the divine forces of the world appropriately. Dogmatic belief is an invention of Christianity which has been continued over into this nihilistic modern age. Chaos Heathens will have none of such foolishness (and this is part of why the authors of this book freely and happily contradict each other and themselves).

Another main feature that binds Chaos Magic and Heathenry into Chaos Heathenry is an embrace of the world – not shunning it, not hiding in the woods from the bad, modern world. Living in the modern world and living an authentic spirituality is another dance with Chaos, where right action and perfect spontaneity need to marry one another. No matter what they tell you, after you learn the ancient lore, you apply the runes in today's real world and make your own thing out of it. What can be done with runes fully depends on the mind and the intentions of the one using them.

We do not believe that the "nothing is true" gnosis of Chaos Magic is always a liberating force; it easily loses itself in the "epistemological hypochondria" (Clifford Geertz) of postmodernity and cultural relativism. Nonetheless, it promotes the necessary freedom of movement to experiment with magical techniques and to deal with the postmodern condition of late capitalist societies in an open-minded way. Heathenry takes all too often the shape of a dogmatic, conservative, stubborn dwarf who wants to keep 'the gold' all for himself. But our vision is rather of the spiritual, courageous Viking, who travels the world – inner and outer – to find new treasures and to experience new horizons of spirit and the Unknown. Heathenry and our ancestral tradition is our harbor to which we always return, but we are yearning for the distance of the limitless ocean.

Thus our magic is informed by both currents, Chaos Magic and Heathen alike, as we attempt to create a new synthesis. We are setting sail on our dragon ships and, like Óðinn, we dare anything and everything in our quest for wisdom and knowledge.

Introduction Two: Eveline's Question
Heimlich A. Laguz

If you do not express the truth of your soul you will sicken in body and mind. Words that need to be spoken are not spoken. Questions that need to be asked are not asked. Thoughts and feelings that emerge unbidden are dismissed to the underworld with ringing imprecations. That which the soul spontaneously presents to the ego is buried in contempt and distrust. When we suppress and deny the moving serpent of inspiration (which means 'breathing in'), we become calcified, hardened, filled with bile and hatred and self-pity. Misery.

The rigid application of socially constructed rules is therefore disastrous for the flexible, sinuous, amoral, delight-filled spirit that wants to be channeled by each of us. To be sure, some kind of social structure is necessary and advantageous, however the tendency too often is to make that structure into a psychic straight-jacket. The result is profound pathology.

To illustrate these concerns I would like to share a little of the life story of my grandmother, Eveline. Among other things, in doing so I hope that in some way I do honor to her memory.

As a small child, Eveline pondered deep existential questions. At the age of six she asked her mother "what are we?" – surely one of the more profound questions that can be asked! In response her mother hushed her, glossed her over, shamed Eveline for her questioning spark. And with no opportunities to explore her question, she eventually let its living flesh become compressed into coal by action of psycho-geological forces.

Indeed, Eveline's life gave her little opportunity to heed and explore the inner call of spontaneous questioning, of wonder, of magic. Victim to layers of manipulation, deceit, violence, all the trappings of patriarchal abuse, of living with an alcoholic, brutal husband, of raising a clutch of sons in the raw days of rural Australia – there was precious little time for the nurturing of her soul.

In her later years some reprieve was offered in the form of travel and genealogy studies. Yet that vast potential she showed as a six year old, asking a question that many adults never think to ask, was not allowed to flourish.

Worse, she became deeply harmed by that repression and oppression. Lodged in her throat, lodged in her heart, shoved back down into her bowels, Eveline's youthful question turned to poison because it was not allowed to germinate and bloom. She became a curious mix of tendencies. An endless kaleidoscope of health problems emerged from her chronically overstressed system, and with them a bevy of psychosomatic symptoms, the sequelae of profound psychological trauma.

As such, she often retreated into a fortress of self-pity, dissolving into a sea of tears and loneliness and that curious kind of egocentrism in which one breaks oneself down instead of building oneself up (I can say this because I inherited the same attitude and have had to work very hard to recognize, own, and dismantle it). Yet she also became a Dragon – her very namesake in fact – a vindictive person, willing to tear down others in order to claw back some semblance of self-esteem.

And all of this because the social norms into which she was thrust taught her to suppress the intense *numina* of her questioning spirit; because those social norms sanctified the starvation of her intellect, sanctified her husband's violence and meanness, sanctified even the edge of contempt that some of her own family members expressed at her funeral. Eveline was taught to be a victim, and the lesson consisted in regular cauterization of her spiritual, intellectual, and emotional spontaneity from a young age. Was there ever a safe place for her to be vulnerable, to open into the joyous mystery that waited within the never-found answer to her question, "what are we?"

As an undergraduate philosophy student I was introduced to Martin Heidegger's 'question of the meaning of Being,' and how this initially led to his inquiry into the Being of human beings. One day I told Eveline about my studies into the Being of human beings. She animated in a way I had never seen; it was that day she told me about her childhood question. Heidegger argued that the essence of human nature is *care*, and it was lovely to explore the implications of this answer with her.

For I too am driven by the question, "what are we?" and from there into "what is Being?" Like Heidegger I see question marks where others see only periods and exclamation points. I received this "quest to question" (Lasher Keen) as an inheritance from Eveline. Where the seed within her was cast onto barren ground, mine received enough nourishment that, in broken fits, it began to grow. In some ways my contribution to this book is the fruit of the tree that grew from the seed that she bequeathed to me. I hope that she will be pleased.

In telling Eveline's story, I described how the suppression of her spontaneous curiosity caused terrible physical and psychological symptoms, as well as setting her on the path of a lifetime of oppression, marginalization, denial, and illness (of her children, only my father ever displayed unwavering care for her, though to be fair she was good at driving people away).

Why do I emphasize this continuum of spontaneous inspiration – social support or suppression – psychophysical dysfunction? Because when we look at the Indo-European traditions of Tantra and Buddhism, we find that they are technologies of liberation that achieve their means by working through the body. By becoming sensitive to its spontaneity, gently releasing the layers of armor, scar tissue, that a lifetime of hard knocks (physical, emotional, spiritual) can inscribe into its flesh.

In their distilled, technical practice, Tantra and Buddhism go beyond external directives, socially constructed rules, arbitrary but absolute dictates of who and what we 'must' be. They teach us to heed our own organismic wisdom, to heed Eveline's question, "what are we?" They defy conventions because they answer to a higher law, that of impermanent, impersonal spontaneity. In all of this, they are profound healing traditions.

Had Eveline been offered the chance to study, say, *Vipassana* meditation, she may well have created a very different life for herself. Or, for that matter, the opportunity to get psychotherapy, or even a regular massage. Yes, she *did* heal herself somewhat with her genealogical studies, but they were not enough.

At their best, Tantra and Buddhism are a tremendous threat to any kind of constrictive social order. The various ways they have been institutionalized and watered down over the centuries – only to resurge again and again in their original expression – expose the patriarchs' (meant in the broadest possible sense) desire to keep them contained, to keep the lid on the djinn's bottle.

This is not to say that Tantra and Buddhism require us to be iconoclasts (S. N. Goenka might disagree). Indeed, their embodied, vulnerable, spontaneous, practical, non-dogmatic essence can actually deepen and further the trappings of social, religious, and political constructs. If the water is flowing easily into these constructs they remain supple and beautiful; when the river is dammed, we are left with the kind of cultural drought to which Eveline was abandoned.

All of these considerations bring me to the purpose of these remarks, which is to define Chaos Heathenism. Very simply, *Chaos Heathenism is Heathenism that remembers it has a body.* From the body comes the spontaneous curiosity, delight, and inspiration that led Eveline to wonder "what are we?" The body is inarticulate, it is often outmaneuvered by our word-bound egos and cultures. It therefore needs loving attention. Chaos Heathenism is the lover of the spiritual essence that is the well-spring of Heathenism, but which Heathenism all too readily denies.

By that I mean that Heathens are as addicted to absolute, arbitrary rules and social constructs as any other group. We are terrified of anything mysterious, complex, subtle, surprising. We want to hunker down into whatever anachronistic, unwitting parody of the ancient Heathens we can cobble together (most painfully evident when one sees the all-too-modern misogyny, racism, homophobia, transphobia, classism, ableism, etc., that circulates in some Heathen communities). Once installed in our dogmatic, cowardly bunkers, we take pot-shots at ourselves and anyone else who differs from our rigid notions. The fact that our own ideas tend to change over time we deny; so easily we allow ourselves to become both hypocrites and reactionary misers.

Chaos Heathenry makes its harbor in good, solid reconstructionist practice. But the purpose of a harbor is to make a home for ships, and the purpose of ships is to sail the infinite sea of mystery that is the cosmos. The root of our cultural trappings is the spontaneous body-wisdom, and we make a home for that wisdom however we may, using whatever metaphors might be appropriate.

This may make it seem as though Chaos Heathenism endorses some kind of lazy, eclectic neopaganism or occultism, smeared with a Heathen veneer. Quite the opposite! We do not seek out whatever looks good in the spiritual supermarket. Rather, *we heed the call and visitation of spontaneous life in whatever form it chooses to present itself.* We take seriously the notion that we humans are a small slice of a very large pie, and we discipline ourselves to remain open to the horizons of our ignorance. We venerate mystery, the very mystery that we literally embody.

Consider my foregoing comparisons to Tantra or Buddhism in their full application. Chaos Heathenism approaches spirituality from an Indo-European mindset, which is to say, a mindset which seeks to forge dynamic equilibrium between spontaneous inspiration and the religious/cultural forms this inspiration generates. We need both. We refuse to dam the river of inspiration just because it occasionally floods and sweeps away all our pitiful human artifice. Indeed, we worship the river precisely because it *does* sweep away our arbitrary constructions of ego, and belief, and habit, and assumption. How else will we have the chance to do better next time?

If Heathenism cannot heed Eveline's question – "what are we?" – then it will become like every other ossified institution. It will be just like Christianity, just like capitalism, just like the institutions of science (as opposed to the idea of science as such). It will become mired in rules of control and definition, rather than debating the terms of reference themselves.

In particular, we have seen many unfortunate attempts to define Heathenry as a religion of *exclusion* – examples might include 'no creativity,' 'no questions,' 'no curiosity,' 'no innovation,' 'no admitting to (ubiquitous) cultural hybridity,' 'no people of color.' Even open-minded investigation into the past – reconstructionism used with a conscious sense of the need for modern, practical adaptation and elaboration – is often discouraged (ironically, often by those who appeal to some backward-projected 'history' of isolative bigotry).

This exclusionary stance channels energy into a rigid outer shell; meanwhile the inner world lies abandoned and becomes a sterile waste. The exclusionary obsession – in part a frantic attempt to silence the question "what are we?" – leads us to destroy the living, pulsing heart of Heathenry, the very thing that we think we are protecting. No surprise, then that Chaos Heathenry necessitates the cultivation of an intuitive sense for detecting irony.

What is the answer to Eveline's question? What are we? What is the answer to my or Heidegger's question – what is the meaning of Being? We conclude that *mystery* is the only fitting answer, and our strange journey into mystery must begin by sensitizing ourselves to our vulnerability, our curiosity, our strangeness, our fundamental unintelligibility. Chaos Heathens strive to keep Heathenry honest by being open in every field of expression. Otherwise, our religion will become a junk yard of meaningless superstitions, just like so much of the Christian faith that conquered it one thousand years ago.

Being open requires self-trust and self-love. These are precious commodities. We have to learn how to love ourselves as we are, without abstraction, qualification, or caveat. The paradox is well known: change only occurs on the condition of accepting that which we wish to change, just as it is. As human beings we are assaulted on all sides by forces that encourage us to distrust and undermine ourselves. Self-love is not easy to achieve.

Thankfully we are guided by gods, ancestors, and spirits. My own grandmother's sacrifices and suffering laid magical seeds within me. My fellow *Elhaz Ablaze* creators all have their own versions of this magical inheritance, leading us to both converge and diverge in our experiences and outlooks. We are not alone in this Quixotic project we call life – and we will live up to the inner call of the spontaneous ocean of chaos, just as we will faithfully honor the port and harbor of the Heathen domain.

It is fitting to conclude by quoting part of Tool's song "Lateralus:"

I embrace my desire to
feel the rhythm, to feel connected
enough to step aside and weep like a widow
to feel inspired, to fathom the power,
to witness the beauty, to bathe in the fountain,
to swing on the spiral
of our divinity and still be a human.

With my feet upon the ground I lose myself
between the sounds and open wide to suck it in,
I feel it move across my skin.
I'm reaching up and reaching out,
I'm reaching for the random or whatever will bewilder me.
And following our will and wind we may just go where no one's been.
We'll ride the spiral to the end and may just go where no one's been.

Spiral out, keep going.
Spiral out, keep going.
Spiral out, keep going.
Spiral out, keep going.

Odin as Shiva as Odin, MichaELFallson

The Marriage of Heathenry and Chaos Magic: A Dagazian Paradox[1] that Gave Birth to a Bastard Child

Matthew Hern

Setting the Stage

Do I contradict myself? I embrace multitudes.
– Walt Whitman

Odin is the Chaos Magician of traditional Northern European belief who dares anything and everything in his quest for wisdom and knowledge.
– Ian Read

This essay is an attempt to present a few impressions of my involvement with Germanic magic and to contextualize the birth of Chaos Heathenry in the complex web of the cultural, social, and psychological developments of the 21st century: namely globalization, late capitalism, and the Internet. Beside this bigger frame, which impacts each one of us who lives in this world, I will also mention a few recent developments in the esoteric subcultures and occultism of the postmodern era that so profoundly influence our magic. I do this from the perspective of a scholar-practitioner, who graduated in Religious Studies at the Universiteit van Amsterdam; I am someone who has studied these things as a spiritual seeker as well as within an academic context. Do not expect some dry, 'objective,' academic text, but rather a very subjective account of how our own magical background and the Kali Yuga state of the world has contributed to the birth of Chaos Heathenry.

---

[1] The term 'Dagazian Paradox' is taken from Jon Sharp's Masterwork for the Rune Gild and PhD thesis *Looking For Mr. Wednesday*. It describes the nature of the rune ᛞ Dagaz and simultaneously the mysterious, mystical nature of Odin's mind himself: that two contradicting ideas/concepts/thoughts/things/agents are united in a higher synthesis, which gives birth to a 'third thing' that partakes in both and simultaneously transcends them.

I am not attempting to give answers to all the questions I raise; rather I want to merely point my finger at them, so that the many mothers that gave birth to Chaos Heathenry become visible, and the shades of my approach to Germanic magic can be perceived for a short moment in the far distance. I have chosen this approach for presenting Chaos Heathenry because I am rather perplexed by the low level at which many who claim to follow the ways of their pre-Christian ancestors are operating and arguing, with their half-knowledge, claims to authenticity, political agendas, isolationism, retro-romanticism, and a small-heartedness that is shown in racist statements, as if they have some right to dictate just who Odin and *Runa* may call. As if they knew what *Óðr* or who Odin is, or how true Mysteries reveal themselves to an individual human being...

Consciousness is God is Nothing

There is no god and this is exactly our God.
– Ian Read

That is why I begin with the proposition that religion (and even more so the term spirituality) cannot be really defined, as magic cannot be, neither among practitioners nor among academics. There exist multitudes of definitions of each by academics and magicians, but not one is agreed upon by all. Émile Durkheim tried to explain religion as a social phenomenon, while magic, he claimed, was performed solitary. There is something to this, but obviously he was disproved by many ethnologists, who documented communal magic performed in tribes. To separate religion and magic completely is not possible either, as many Catholics should know, though they almost always neglect this knowledge. Furthermore, there has always been a conflict in Religious Studies between those who claim that religion can only be studied 'objectively' by those who are irreligious (like Durkheim, Mauss, and Freud), and those who believe that religion can only be understood by someone who has had actual religious experiences (like Otto, Eliade, and Jung).

Though I believe that both approaches are necessary to understand all aspects of religion, I definitely belong to the latter, phenomenological school, which explains religion as a *sui generis* phenomenon; religion exists because the Divine exists, and a human being is a *homo religiosus*. More than that: humans are ecstatic beings, who will never fulfill their complete potential until they experience states of Higher Consciousness. Transformation and ecstasy, illumination and inspiration, creativity and Self-exploration, meditation and world(s)-expeditions, these are at the core of human consciousness, which – according to the myths of our forefathers and foremothers – is a Gift of the God who Himself represents these qualities: Óðinn, Woden, or Wotan.

This is also true of another major deity of the wider, older Indo-European tradition: Shiva. Shiva is considered in Tantric Shaivism as the embodiment of (enlightened) 'pure Consciousness.'[2] "The greatest living German poet,"[3] Rolf Schilling, said in his poetic genius and divine intuition that Odin is Shiva's "divine brother."[4] In Kashmir Shaivism the Divine – represented by the deity Shiva – is present to everything. It is nothing but pure Consciousness, the fullness of absolute I-Consciousness or *purnahanta*.[5] However, with regard to Ian Read's statement quoted above there is a mystical paradox present here: this divine I-Consciousness is now here and yet nowhere to be found. This divine state is a Void, a Nothingness, a state of in-betweeness, which cannot be fully grasped:

> *In Kashmir Shaivism this void is precisely found in all the in-between states – the most important and yet not easy to catch being the void between breathing in and breathing out. And in this in-between is found the pure consciousness, the thought-free state:* nirvikalpa...[6]

"There is no god where I am" was also one of Crowley's statements in his *Book of the Law* and it indicates a state in which one becomes this divine "I Am." It is not a passive state, in which you "receive" or perceive God; rather the receiver, the giver, and the gift given are One, not separate. This Mystery is encoded in the rune ᚷ Gebo, too. In this state there is no god; you are God. The Indian mystic and a contemporary representative of the *philosophia perennis* tradition, Ravi Ravindra, explains that the state of 'I AMness' reflects a non-

---

2 David Frawley 2015: *Shiva – The Lord of Yoga.*

3 Quoting Ian Read.

4 Rolf Schilling 2012: *Lingaraja.*

5 See Bettina Bäumer: p. 4, in Bäumer and Dupuche 2005: *Void and Fullness.*

6 Bäumer 2005: p. 3.

dual state of Consciousness.[7] This state is not transferable and has various names in different traditions. It refers to an awakened state of Consciousness that has been described as 'The Witness,' a luminous mirror-mind that is one with everything witnessed; a still point of is-ness around which everything turns, changes, transforms, and comes into being; an openness that transmits a radical freedom to man by partaking in what the German mystic Meister Eckhart called the Eternal Now ("*das ewige Nun*"), becoming one with the witnessed eternity hidden as emptiness, or in-betweeness, or nothingness.

This *No-Thingness* is the secret door through which we enter the Divine. The mystical path of contemplation is actually a very dynamic and disruptive process that tears us apart from the womb of the world. All mystics knew this and never believed in 'big daddy up there,' but rather thought and taught in parables, allegories and symbolic understanding of the Word and Nature, where they found the "Signature of All Things," as Jakob Böhme called it. The mystic's transformation is an active Becoming and a motionless Being, a process and a state of mind; in short a state which is paradoxical and cannot be grasped by intellectual reflection, nor pinned down by logic. These things can only be transmitted by symbols, signs, and secrets to those who have the right mind to decode them in a state of Higher Consciousness.

> *...[B]eyond the literal stands the metaphorical: the viewed object is not there to represent itself, but some other, deeper meaning that cannot be communicated in words. In this case the symbol is a means of experiencing the eldritch world, the numinous, essentially a personal experience that is not transferable. At this point the seen symbol provides access to the unconscious, the collective, and the cosmic.[8]*

When Odin in his Yggdrasil-Ordeal sacrificed himself to himSelf – *sjálfr sjálfúm mér* – he reached that ecstatic state of pure I-Consciousness, a mysterious paradoxical state that cannot be expressed verbally without contradictory statements, as Odin's words themselves are truly paradoxical. How can he sacrifice himself to Himself, and why? The paradox actually is that this pure I-Consciousness is only experienced when it is emptied of all 'I-ness.' The root of

---

7 See Ravi Ravindra 2004: *The Gospel of John in the Light of Indian Mysticism.*

8 Nigel Pennick: 2014: *The Book of Primal Signs: The High Magic of Symbols.*

that pure I-Consciousness is actually a Void, a 'No-Thing,' which indeed is the opposite of what the word 'nothing' connotes in common language:

> *It can be given no coherent definition, hence it is No-Thing, Nothing. It is every potential and possibility which we have within ourselves but have not yet made manifest. Thus it is all that...implies the omnijective[9] perspective...[W]e ourselves contain this Absolute and are Nothing, for our Essence is not bound by the Universe.*[10]

Thus there is no god, but actually this is exactly our God: Odin, who plays with Ginnung and shapes the worlds according to the deeper structures of Consciousness. This Ginnung is the Void or what Chaos Magicians call Chaos, a magically charged void that pre-existed the universe as we know it and which still and always will permeate the very fabric of the cosmos. This is the reason why magic is possible, because the universe is made of 'void-stuff,' which makes galaxies explode and quantums appear out of 'nothing' and disappear into 'nothing.' The *creatio ex nihilo* idea of the Christian Church Fathers appears rather naïve compared to the concepts that the pagans were using.[11]

Hence Odin is a profoundly mystical, magical, and mysterious deity that represents Consciousness; only those who are prepared to go through the same trials and ordeals as He did can truly know Him. Many might profess that they worship Odin and call themselves Odinists or Ásatrúar, but in truth they only worship the archetypal Christian 'father figure' in 'pagan' disguise; in practice Odin is not a god for many, but for the rare few. This is reflected in the fact that in Heathen times there were not many places named after Odin, but after other more popular gods like Thor, who were closer to the realities of most people. Odin was never a popular god, even though he later became the All-Father. There is no reason to assume that anything has changed about this today. This point is further indicated by the fact that most Heathens nowadays

---

9 The omnijective perspective is a paradoxical state of Higher Consciousness, where the subjective and objective 'reality' or separation is transcended, a state of Consciousness that is called *samadhi* in ancient Indian Yoga philosophy.

10 Michael Kelly 2009: *Apophis*, p.172.

11 Christian mystics and magicians like Pseudo-Dionysius the Areopagite, Meister Eckhart, Nicholas of Cusa, Marsilio Ficino, and Pico della Mirandola got the idea quite right, but all of them were influenced in one way or another by the pagan philosophies.

deny the dark, grim, and deceitful nature of Odin and shy away from the ambiguity and disturbing aspects of the Bolverkr. Odin is a God of magicians.

Are You a Heathen or are You Still LARPing?

At the core we deal with Consciousness and its altered as well as higher states, which can reveal mystical insights into the true nature of reality and the Soul. According to Edred Thorsson the Aesir, of whom Odin is the Lord, are the Gods of Consciousness. So someone who is Ásatrú[12] – true or loyal to the Aesir – must first and foremost be loyal to the forces of Consciousness in himself/herself and actively pursue a lifestyle and live by principles that increase Consciousness in himself/herself and the world. This is what the Aesir represent! But whoever tries to do this over a longer period of time will know how hard, how demanding this process is, how unconscious forces in both self and world create resistances to the process of growth, how we fall 'asleep' again and again, how crisis and Need-Fire spur individuation, how, ultimately, visible traits of Self-Transformation must be the consequence in our lives.

Thus, someone who engages in nothing more than LARPing (live action role playing) by wearing Viking-era clothes and shouting "Odin!" whilst raising a horn filled with mead might think themselves *Ása trú*; in actuality such a one is only skimming the spiritual and religious surface of Heathenry. This needs to be said because those from the Ásatrú community who might say that Chaos Heathenry is silly, inauthentic, or not in accordance with historical practice first need to do some Work on the Self and engage in the catastrophic and troublesome process of *sjálfr sjálfúm mér* before waving their swords and registering their protest.

The Postmodern Condition

Chaos Heathenry came into being in reaction to many psychological factors and social circumstances. It is a bastard child of the postmodern condition's best and worst aspects. To generalize about the influences that shaped the creators of the term Chaos Heathen: our generations (generations X and Y) have been profoundly brainwashed by the dominance and constant presence of media, mindfuck, and mediocrity as never seen before in human history. We

---

12 A name from the 19th century that many Germanic Heathens use nowadays to describe their religion.

met because of the Internet, not because we come from the same place. We grew up in Eastern blocks behind the Iron Curtain or in Australia. We smoked dope and did 'shrooms' in search of spiritual experiences and wisdom at age 15. We were exposed to the nihilism and decadence of consumerism, popular culture and its empty, meaningless, mindless trash – what Adorno dubbed "the consciousness industry"[13] – that were delivering false promises and delusions to our young minds. We served in the army or fully rejected it. We have lived in cities and are no 'Heathens' from the countryside and farms (what the term actually denotes). We have masturbated and copulated ourselves into ecstasy and shot sigils into the Ginnung or the Chaos or Void to practice 'magick' that we learned from Spare or Crowley or Carroll or Thee Temple ov Psychick Youth. We traveled to India and Brazil and the USA and England to meet our true love or enlightenment or our Masters.

In short: we practice magic on our own terms. That's our style of magic, and it drew on many sources suddenly available in the age of the Internet. We were raised in a world that has gone mad, without borders, without 'the old securities' of belonging to one place, culture, or traditional religion. With our personal computers we suddenly had access to the formerly secret 'occult knowledge' of all humankind within the brief span of a mouse click. In a time in which we destroy our own sacred Earth, which we humans inhabit with a myriad of living organisms that came out of a stunning process of billions of years of evolution, the standard school book pretends that this is the peak of human civilization. A world that has shrunk to a 'global village,' in which we can communicate with each other in every moment and visit each other within hours despite living on different continents. A world in which a financial elite rules and has separated from its peoples and nations whilst destroying nature and cultures and worshipping only money in order to establish a world in which everyone is eating the same food, wearing the same clothes, listening to the same music, watching the same movies – all the while pretending to promote 'individualism' and 'diversity.'

"Like pigs they are linked together, like pigs in a sausage roll, they all think they're individuals, they all think they're free,"[14] but to the seeker this 'One

---

[13] See Adorno & Horkheimer 1944: *Dialectic of Enlightenment*, as well as Marcuse 1955: *Eros and Civilization*.

[14] Douglas P. in the song "Unconditional Armistice" (Death In June).

World' dream, where everybody drinks Coca-Cola and makes 'selfies' of themselves, appears rather as a nightmare. Our own culture, which has long ago forsaken the Old Ways and "sealed up the wells,"[15] seems to turn into a worse reality than any science fiction dystopia ever created. Where big companies successively seize control and lead to a postdemocratic era, in which the market-value has replaced all other values, dominates every aspect of our societies and lives, and has permeated into our very psyches. It is this rampant, epidemic addiction to distraction – "these weapons of mass distraction" (Andrew Holecek) – that is the destructive signature of the darkness of our age. "Constant shallowness leads to evil" (John Balance). Magic and meditation, creativity and art, modern psychotherapy and ancient wisdom, these are our shields of spiritual self-defense and the weapons for Self-integration and an authentic life.

When we were born, landing on the moon was already old hat. Whether we like it or reject it, whether we confront ourselves with this reality or try to escape from it, ultimately does not matter: this is the time in which Chaos Heathenry came into being. This postmodern, pluralistic age has brought new ideas, developments, and possibilities. Chaos Heathenry is a blossom in this pluralistic flowering: mutate and survive. Chaos Heathens are like the heroes in *Watchmen* and *X-Men*, "mutants and mystics" (Jeffrey J. Kripal) who cannot resist the evolutionary impulse in the unfolding of Spirit in nature and culture.

Cultural Roots as Keys to Magic

In contrast to those who claim that with Ásatrú they are defending the 'white race,' contributors to this book embrace cross-cultural marriages with partners from India or Brazil or the USA. To us seeing the connections between cultures, celebrating their differences, and cultivating an attitude of openness, inclusiveness, and generosity is promoting the spirit of Heathenry. The argument between left-wing and right-wing factions, between Universalist and Folkish Ásatrú, is the typical disease of the 'white man' with his categorizations and -isms. Universalists tend to deny the differences between cultures, the fact that ethnicity and language have a huge impact on our identity or 'cultural self,' and may be guilt-ridden by the sins of our colonialist past. Folkish Heathens all too often reduce the Heathen discourse to genetics and the notion that choice

---

15 Ian Read in the song "Malediction" (Current 93).

of religion is determined 'by your blood;' they get caught up in *'Blut und Boden'* ideologies and identify with those aspects of European culture that they prefer, while neglecting other aspects like the Enlightenment era or the crimes committed against indigenous peoples by our colonial ancestors.

The attempt to reduce Heathenry to a political vehicle is unworthy of the honest impulse to find the spiritual heritage of our ancestors. And: we like to identify our ancestors only with certain historical eras (like the Viking era or the Icelandic sagas), but deny the long past of our ancestry that certainly includes and originates in non-Germanic DNA once you go the long way back in prehistory. Having said DNA: the biological reductionism that has invented the category of race and along with it racism is a small-minded view of the *conditio humana*; these categories are an intellectual product of 19th-century science.

I am not denying that there are differences between ethnicities, it is in plain view, go to Tamil Nadu or open a book on anthropology. But the reduction of humans to their 'race,' as well as the conclusion via pseudoscientific arguments that this determines one's spiritual path is – I'm sorry – not capable of holding ground in any serious intellectual debate. This is Christian fundamentalism in Ásatrú disguise. It is a narrow-minded view, the child of a modernist *Weltanschauung* that Heathens more usually claim to deny. The German Romantic movement, of which Ásatrú is ultimately a grandchild, was a revolt against this materialistic modernism that so many Folkish Heathens otherwise say they despise. Culture is not a neat box to be conserved forever, but an ongoing process of differentiation and incorporation of 'foreign' elements. In other words: culture is a dynamic process. The belief that it can be 'conserved' by re-enacting the past in Viking clothes or demanding that whites only copulate with whites is a naive if not vulgar conception.

Having said the necessary, let us focus on what we must preserve, learn anew, and soak into our very Souls: the 'deep lore' of the Northern Tradition. With this knowledge we can change the direction of our *wyrd* and create links to our ancestral past, which is never lost; it is a profound aspect of our Soul that we need to reawaken. Only this can lead to a new, deep Understanding and a clear direction. By rituals that we ourselves invent, based on our Understanding of the holy Lore, or by rituals like the Rune Gild Moon Workings, in which one watches the full moon and meditates on it as a link with one's ancestors, we can gain deeper, wider insights that open up the seeker's Soul to become more and more aware of the land that surrounds us, the place to which we belong.

This land is not only the material world but a magical link to the concepts, runes, and powers bequeathed to us in the ancient Lore of ancestral wisdom. In this way we can reconnect with the Gods and Goddesses, the *Ljóssalfar* and Wights, the *landvættir* and our own ancestral Dead. By reawakening them we can call on them to support our Work and thus change the tragic *wyrd* of our peoples. By strengthening our Souls in such a powerful way we can determine our direction and destiny in the world. Those things that you were made to believe were 'superstition' (*Aberglaube* in German) can bring forth the actual Heathen religion and magic of our own ancestors. Our work to recover this magical heritage has millions of implications and creates a certain turmoil in the Soul and an urgency to change one's lifestyle. The tragic dimension of the fate of our Heathen ancestors is not won by ideological debates, but by hard magical Work that changes the Soul. What we, as our ancestors' descendants, have lost is not won by delving deeply into sentimentality and wishful thinking, but by staying focused and effective in this (post)modern world. This soul-work is of paramount importance.

Soul-Lore and the *Fylgja*

The concept of Germanic Soul-Lore I have basically taken from Edred Thorsson's works *Runelore*, *A Book of Troth*, and *The Nine Doors of Midgard*. As far as I can tell Thorsson in turn derived it from a mixture of intuition, a deep exploration of Germanic Heathen Lore, and from elements of the work of C. G. Jung.[16] I mainly learned to apply it through a course I took at Arcanorium College that was taught by Ian Read.[17] Further insights stem from my work with the *Aegishjálmúr* curriculum by Michael Kelly. All that said, the following interpretation of the Soul-Lore is mine.

That our ancestors had a systematic teaching of Soul-Lore is rather unlikely, but that they possessed a great knowledge of what we call the 'Soul' is undeniable.[18] Their ideas about the Soul, I assume, were diverse and differed

---

[16] Thorsson has indicated that my hypothesis is correct; for more see his article "Toward an Archaic Germanic Psychology" (1983) published in the *Journal of Indo-European Studies*, in which he explains his approach to Soul-Lore (personal communication).

[17] Which was based to a great degree on the work developed by Ingrid Fischer.

[18] To those who doubt this I refer to Jan de Vries' *Altgermanische Religionsgeschichte*, 2 vols. 1935 and 1937.

from tribe to tribe, as well as changing over the centuries. This must be kept in mind. As with every model, the idea is not to take things literally and dogmatically stick to them, but to see the model as a dynamic, moving process, and to use it in creative and self-transformative ways. To quote Robert Anton Wilson, who quoted Korzybski: "the map is not the territory." It is important to remember that in many traditions the emptying of concepts constitutes an essential aspect of spiritual experience; we must not understand these concepts in a frozen, fixed framework. Rather we must make the serious attempt to find the meaning that is lying behind, below, and beyond them.

Wode, or *Óðr*, stands for the ecstatic, divine, inspired part of the Soul, which always dwells in *Ásgàrðr* and is one of the ninefold parts, eternal and immortal. Most of our life we are unaware of it and normally we only become conscious of it for very short moments, experiencing only glimpses of it, which in most cases are triggered by circumstances we are unable to purposely recreate. Some individuals certainly experience it in overwhelming ways through chemognostic sacraments (psilocybin, mescaline, LSD, etc.), and maybe here lies the danger for those who think that the drugs *make* the experience happen, when in fact they only act as cataclysmic gate-openers to those realms of the Soul or Consciousness that exist independently and which can in truth be accessed without any outer means. The aim must obviously be to cultivate this part of the Soul and to be able to stay aware of it, so that it can lead oneself towards higher truths and deeper mysteries.

The *Hughr* is in many ways the structuring, analytical, investigative, observing faculty, mostly identified with the intellect. The *Myne* represents the imaginative, visionary, intuitive part of the Soul that brings forth images, symbols, signs, patterns, feelings, and omen-like occurrences. The *Hughr* and *Myne* are of course Odin's two ravens Huginn and Muninn.

Ian Read calls the *Wode*, *Hughr*, and *Myne* the core-triad. This is so because all three must be developed in a careful and balanced way so that the runic learning can happen in a holistic process without bringing imbalance to the psyche. Too much *Wode* will simply consume you, your everyday personality won't be able to handle the overwhelming 'information,' and psychosis or worse would be the result. An overdeveloped *Hughr* will make you question everything – the typical academic – or you simply will accumulate a lot of knowledge that you can't put into action; the armchair scholar or the book-learning occultist who knows everything in theory but nothing in reality. If the

Myne is overdeveloped and the *Hughr* is undeveloped one will be confronted with endless images and patterns that will lose coherence. The result in most cases is the occult 'master of the astral planes' or the New Age dolphin channeler, who flies off into cuckoo fairy tale land, seeing everywhere coincidences, secret messages, and magic at work without being able to manifest any real results. So, in a nutshell: The core-triad needs to be developed harmoniously for the seeker to have a meaningful learning process.

Another essential part is the *Fylgja*, which embodies the 'following spirit,' a mysterious half-autonomous entity that is inherited over a succession of generations and which is a great source of power. It can be to some extent compared with Crowley's conception of the Holy Guardian Angel. At least this would explain why he made the Holy Guardian Angel the central aim of his magical system. This entity exists in one way or another in most indigenous, so-called 'primitive' magical traditions, and is known in Western occult lore under many names, like *Augoides* or *Daemon*. Under the latter names it somewhat combines or merges with the *Wode*-Self concept. The best account I have read on this subject in a non-Germanic context was the Work of the 'Fourth Head' in Michael Kelly's *Apophis*[19] as well as Julian Vayne and Greg Humphries' illuminating remarks on the Holy Guardian Angel entity.[20] The core idea is that contact with this entity enables the seeker to have access to profound magical information and it works as a guide for the magician henceforth. This part is also immortal, but it can survive without the individual Consciousness of oneself. It simply attaches to the next member of the family line. Unfortunately, it can remain unconscious to the individual for their entire life. The *Fylgja*, also known as the Fetch, is present at our birth and at our death; it is a powerful ally.

The next part of the Soul is the *Ek* and in my understanding it is one's everyday personality, which needs to function well so that it can deal intelligently with, and make meaningful use of, the other Soul parts.

The *Önd* is the cosmic breath or life-force that animates the Soul. Other cultures have made an art form of this part of the Soul and achieved real mastery over it. The Indians call it *prana* in Hindu Yoga philosophy, the

---

19 Michael Kelly 2009: *Apophis*.

20 Julian Vayne & Greg Humphries 2005: *Now That's What I Call Chaos Magick*.

Chinese *Chi*, the Japanese *Ki*, and in modern times Reichenbach called it Od-Kraft and Wilhelm Reich Orgon. Stanislav Grof made use of it in his Holotropic Breathing or Rebirthing. I experienced it through Dave Lee's teachings of Connected Breathwork.[21] This force can heal, vitalize, and integrate traumatic experiences from the past.

The *Hamr* is conceived as the subtle force which shapes magical and physical forms and has been compared to the 'astral body' in Western occult lore. Actors can make good use of it as they have the ability to appear as 'different faces' or personalities to the audience. When a person dies, *Önd* and *Hamr* immediately disappear, which can be seen on dead people, whose faces lose all expression as if they were not anymore the same person. All that is left to the visible eye is a dead, inanimate body.

Which brings us to the physical part of the Soul, the *Lyke*, which is a very magical and powerful tool as long as we live in this world. The body is a wondrous, wonderful product of nature, created over millions of years of evolution. The mysteries of the Flesh can reveal profound knowledge and the body has a wisdom of its own, encoded in its very structures of cells, atoms, subatoms, and all the magic of which it is made. However we are not just our bodies, which ultimately disintegrate and return to the mother womb from whence they came.

A further aspect in Soul-Lore is the *Sàl*, the shade, a kind of immaterial shell that sometimes is seen as a ghost after death, for example the deceased perhaps appearing to a family member. It has no personality or intelligence and disintegrates after death, returning to Hel. This part of the Soul is probably what – at least the honest – spiritualists were working with in the 19th century and which they mistook for the Soul and used as an argument for life after death in their fight against the rising materialism of their era. Blavatsky recognized their mistake and founded her Theosophy to find deeper answers to these strange phenomena. Many accounts of postmortem manifestations are known in Germanic lore and actually the whole 'Zombie fad' of our days (*The Walking Dead*, etc.) is a profoundly Germanic theme of the *Wiedergaenger* and other related topics. It is a deeply Germanic conception and not just related to Voudoun as many would assume. Rune graves were often created so that the

---

21 Dave Lee: *Connected Breathwork* (with CD).

Wiedergaenger, the awakened dead, would not return. Such occurrences are reported through all of human history in many cultures and are the stuff of which ghost stories are made.

The last aspect of the Soul that needs to be mentioned, and which is very essential, is the *Hamingja*. Often translated as 'luck,' it is actually one's charisma and the power to make things happen. All honorable deeds and conscious actions increase the *Hamingja*, whilst unconscious ones decrease it. It is a mysterious concept that can be studied further in Jan de Vries' works.

Work with the Soul-Lore has profound implications; such work has the ability to completely transform our outlook on reality and identity. It is very powerful Work and one of the major aims of Germanic magic, in my estimation, is the discovery and exploration of those aspects of the Soul that are immortal, so that a conscious reincarnation, or as Michael Kelly would put it, *Remanifestation*, can occur. Instead of getting lost in futile ideological and political debates, this Work can really lead to a continuation of the 'folk soul,' if such a concept fascinates you.

Many models of modern psychology appear rather dull and one-dimensional compared to the Soul-Lore, with the exceptions of Depth and Transpersonal Psychology. Magic is not an aim in itself. After you have experimented with sorcery, results magic, and transformed your personal world into accordance with your deeper desires and personality, the extra bit of money, sex, or healing don't do the job anymore. It is time to move towards the higher goals of magic, which are Self-Transformation, Illumination, and Immortality. Soul-Lore is a perfect way to enter those realms.

The Mysteries of the Gay Cunt

The magic of our ancestors was not for the faint-hearted. Magic was always regarded as something dangerous, deceitful, and awe-inspiring. The image of the dark and ambiguous that surrounds magic predates Christianity's claim that magic was invented by the devil. When you think of Thoth or Hermes or Odin – all considered to be the Gods of magicians, poets, and the written word – you will see that they are associated with alphabets, the invention of writing. Nowadays writing is not a big deal for most people living in the West. But language is the manifestation of Consciousness and the ability to encode messages in written form was considered as a magical thing in itself in societies where most were illiterate. So the association of alphabets with magic came rather naturally to the ancestral Heathens.

It might surprise the ordinary Heathen that our ancestors have hidden two forbidden words in their ABC. I remember my own disbelief when I discovered a certain wordplay within the Futhark. Actually I was told this by a Rune-Master. Consider the name Futhark. It is like the ABC of our modern alphabets. Don't forget that in the Younger Futhark the 6th rune, Kaun, is also used for the 'G' sound, so it is FUTh-ARG(r). And FUTh means something particular in Old Norse. FUTh today is still reflected in the vulgar German word *Fotze*, which means 'cunt.' *Argr* in this case is another forbidden word, namely 'gay,' the adjectival term used to accuse someone of being *ergi*.

> *I have often wondered that the literate portion of the archaic Northern European population, learning their ABCs as it were, began with two utterly forbidden, naughty words. I cannot imagine this would not have raised an eyebrow or two, or evoked a chuckle. If one examines some of the other associations in Medieval society between literacy, bawdiness, and general scallywaggery (I am thinking here of the dozens of ribald, oversexed, and rambunctious "clerkes" found throughout Chaucer's verse, for example), then perhaps we are seeing a trope that extends to rune-using cultures as well. A cursory examination of some of the more secular runic inscriptions might tell us something about the character, preoccupations, and sense of humor prevalent among those who could read runes. That in the Viking-era the phrase "FUTh-AR(G)," like "ABC," became shorthand for the whole alphabet suggests some interesting things about the earthiness of Rune-using cultures.[22]*

As far as our Gods are concerned: Odin was *ergi*, Loki (as a mare!) slept with a stallion, and Thor wore women's clothes. I think the implications are clear, as far as the Rune-Masters of yore are concerned. The conservative agendas of homophobia and racism so prevalent within parts of contemporary Ásatrú show the bigotry and small-mindedness of Christian values, rather than real Germanic Heathen ones. Our ancestors seem to have been far more

---

22 Ristandi (personal communication).

transgressive and open-minded than the general Heathen bloke today.[23] I think all those people who consider themselves Germanic Heathens, but who would deny such connections in the runic mysteries, must face the fact that they know nothing about the nature of Odin and those who truly follow his Path.

"Steps Along the Lonely Path Where Waits the Eight-Legged Steed"[24]

The initiatory steps of the seeker on the runic Path consist of a search for the meaning of the runes, to literally seek the runes and their outer manifestation in the form of the various Futhark alphabets. This basically happens by studying academic books and esoteric works on the runes, as well as the myths and sagas.[25] I still consider Edred Thorsson's book *Runelore* the best of the modern esoteric runic texts, and Klaus Düwel's *Runenkunde* as the best introduction from an academic point of view (interestingly Edred was a doctoral student of Düwel in the early 1980s). The student derives the meaning of the runes by meditating on them, on their shapes, names, numbers, position in the Futhark, and the relationships between them. Most important certainly are the rune poems themselves that ultimately should be studied also in their original languages. Many runes are hidden in these poems.

Studying the runes and the Futharks in such a thorough way, the seeker finally realizes that the runes in the shape of the Futharks have an inner dimension that the shapes, numbers, and names of the individual runes never reveal. Behind the runes (the meaning of the staves) are far deeper runes (mysteries that lead beyond the Futharks). These 'deeper runes' are the mysteries of the tradition itself, those that manifest themselves through folk religion (myths, stories, songs, poems, sayings, customs, etc.) in the form of *Siðr*,[26] and those

---

23 It must be said that the historical Heathens, who were no Rune-Masters, were not very sympathetic towards homosexuality. Rather cruel laws existed in the Viking era. But the educated Heathen of the postmodern age doesn't need to accept or revive every stupid belief or custom of their ancestors. Rather we should take what was best in them and continue to spin the threads of *Wyrd*, so that the noble is passed on. This is true tradition.

24 Ian Read in the song "Dragons in the Sunset" (Fire + Ice).

25 See the chapters on academic sources and inspirational sources at the end of this book.

26 *Siðr* is not *Seiðr*, the latter being a technique of Germanic trance-work that, according to the lore, Freyja taught Óðinn.

that manifest themselves through philosophy in the form of *Arfr*.[27] *Arfr* stands for the transcendent Tradition, the *philosophia perennis* if you like, a set of universal and eternal ideas that are common to all spiritual traditions and are accessible through initiation into them. However, *Arfr* represents an abstract, philosophical, universal conception of Tradition, similar to the concept of Tradition as formulated by René Guénon and Julius Evola. *Siðr* denotes then the particular expression of that transcendent Tradition as it manifests in the unique way of each culture in their symbolism, mythology, and customs. The runic student must know the *Siðr* of the Germanic tradition and incorporate it into his practice, but must also study the *Arfr*, the higher philosophy and universal principles behind the Germanic tradition. Only in this way will the runic student come to understand and respect the esoteric expression of that perennial wisdom in all cultures – from Tantra to Sufism – and thus be able to appreciate the unique and special expression of that ancient wisdom as handed down by their own ancestors.

This occult knowledge is hidden in folktales, folk songs, poems, sayings, symbols, and customs of European lore, and is passed down to us in mysterious ways. This can be something that 'grandma used to do,' or other folk beliefs and practices that came to be considered as superstition. These mysteries have been explored in quite a fascinating manner in the works of Nigel Pennick, certainly a Master in his own right. However, once the outer and inner runes have been studied beyond the Futharks and beyond what you can read in books or be taught by other Masters, the realization dawns on the seeker that beyond all mysteries there is an Ultimate Mystery that will never be penetrated by any human thought or mind. It is the sense of the Occult or Hidden itself, deeply ingrained in the depths of the structures of the Soul and the Cosmos itself that the seeker is striving to tap into and manifest in their life. This is the realm of 'tangled hierarchies' and where the world itself becomes or reveals itself as *Runa*, the *mysterium tremendum et fascinans*, as Rudolf Otto used to call it. This is the moment where we do not only 'do' magic, but where we 'are' magic, where everything can turn into this wondrous stream of beauty, awe, and ecstasy.

---

[27] Both terms and the ideas associated with them are taken from a "Radio Free Runa" talk that Edred gave in the early 2000s. They might be available at his web page seekthemystery.com.

The Chaos Heathen as the "Runic Anarch"

Having discussed the lonely and heroic Path of the runic initiate there remains one area, which I rather look down upon, to address. It is often associated with runes and Heathen cultural heritage, and therefore needs to be dealt with: the domain of the political. I think it is clear to anybody who has followed my musings so far that in my view the philosophical implications of the Runic Path have nothing in common with Nazis, racism, or 'black magic.' Yet it appears to me that those who begin to explore the tradition might get blocked or stopped by the association of runes with political ideas, mostly of the right-wing spectrum. All of us exist in this world and we have a responsibility, for the sake of our spiritual heritage, to address this. Ultimately, however, our spiritual tradition won't be saved by political agendas, but by magical Work.

Especially unfortunate to me are attempts to bond spiritual heritage, especially Ásatrú, to the political domain. Models that try to link the spiritual sphere to the political state include Plethon's *Laws*, or in recent times, Evola's *Revolt against the Modern World*, which basically argues that society should reflect a supposedly divine or universal hierarchy. Plethon and Evola both try to base the notion of a hierarchical state on appeals to the eternal principles of an ancient wisdom, the *philosophia perennis*.[28] Such ideas may sometimes tempt the young, who search for alternatives to modern mass societies and vulgar materialism. The interested reader can research these writers further, but I note that their ideas have always remained theoretical, i.e. fantasies; attempts to implement such ideas into political realities, such as Evola's case in fascist Italy, have only led to disappointments. This reinforces that these conceptions are, at bottom, flawed.

Beyond questioning the desirability of such supposedly traditional concepts, I want to point out that the seeker of runic mysteries who follows such

---

[28] The term itself was coined by Agostino Steuco in 1540, so it wasn't known to Plethon himself, who lived in the 14th and 15th centuries, when the Byzantine Empire was falling. He rather thought of it as a *prisca theologia*, a first theology, that was transmitted from Zoroaster to other pagan initiates like Pythagoras and Plato. It was later transformed into the conception of a perennial and "hidden" philosophy, the *philosophia perennis* and the *occulta philosophia* respectively.

phantoms will be distracted from the real Quest and led astray. It is my own conviction that to connect a political agenda with Ásatrú does a disservice to the tradition. Political ideas and religion should be separated (as we know since the Enlightenment era) and they are *fata morganas* in the desert of a world devoid of spiritual meaning. The great German writer, Ernst Jünger, who as a young man in the turbulent years of the Weimar Republic believed in a radical political vision as a solution to Germany's problems, admitted later its futility. Therefore he developed in his mature years the concept of the Anarch. The Anarch is a metaphysical concept of a sovereign individual, who forms a bond around something concrete rather than ideal, and achieves therefore an intellectual and spiritual freedom that is not bound by outer circumstances and the political *zeitgeist*. In our case the bond that we create around something concrete is our magical practice and the folk beliefs of our ancestors. Jünger wrote:

> *For the anarch, little has changed; flags have meaning for him, but not sense. I have seen them in the air and on the ground like leaves in May and November; and I have done so as a contemporary and not just as a historian. The May Day celebration will survive, but with a different meaning. New portraits will head up the processions. A date devoted to the Great Mother is re-profaned. A pair of lovers in the wood pays more homage to it. I mean the forest as something undivided, where every tree is still a liberty tree. For the anarch, little is changed when he strips off a uniform that he wore partly as fool's motley, partly as camouflage. It covers his spiritual freedom, which he will objectivate during such transitions. This distinguishes him from the anarchist, who, objectively unfree, starts raging until he is thrust into a more rigorous straitjacket.*[29]

The Anarch is related to anarchism, Jünger said, in the same manner as is the monarch to monarchism. The Anarch is their own sovereign. They are an individual who does not dance to the tunes of others, for the Anarch plays their own flute. The Chaos Heathen to me corresponds to the concept of the Anarch, creating a personal territory, vision, and *Weltanschauung*, untouched by the lowlands of the political. Our freedom hinges on the creativity of the individual, on the clarity and strength of our vision, on our *Hamingja* and the stirrings of

---

29 Ernst Jünger: *Eumeswil*.

the *Wode*-Self, the eternal flame of Consciousness; for whereas these are eternal, political systems and ideas change endlessly. Thus the Anarch is a profound metaphor for someone who maintains – untouched by the confusions and distractions of the *zeitgeist* – a poise and an inner freedom that is informed by the individual's divine spark.

Closing the Stage

When we come into this world we are not aware of the Great Mystery that gave birth to us, nor do we understand the forces that weave our lives in the endless patterns that create the web of our reality. The task is to awake, to become conscious, "to take *Wyrd* in our hands and to reclaim our might."[30] This might is the power of our Soul that is connected to and permeated by the divine *Òðr* or *Wode* gifted to us by the *Ginnregin*. It is our birthright, our duty that binds us eternally to the realms of *Ásgárðr*, it is our true and only freedom. Those who dare to walk in the footsteps of the cunning and deceitful Masked One, whose hand can guide us but not help us, must tread paths that lead to mysterious and unknown terrain. Just like in the movie *The Stalker* (Andrei Tarkovsky, 1979), the landscape constantly changes and it is hard to tell what is illusion and what is permanent.

Once we step outside of our comfort zone and our known world we are faced with an unsolvable, paradoxical Mystery which permeates the very fabric of this infinite reality. Some choose to explain it away with the terminology of materialistic scientism, others worship it as God and try to win its favor with prayers, others are confronted with inexplicable experiences and turn to occultism or some esoteric belief. The pagan religion of our ancestors had its own answer. It consists not only of dead languages, weird staves, and forsaken Gods; it is a heritage that will serve us as a priceless treasure and a map consisting of signposts, keys, doors, and paths toward higher spiritual truths that deal with that Ultimate Mystery – *Runa*. For those who still do not appreciate why they might need this old religion of their ancestors, why not just use any map or paradigm or just invent 'chaos-magically' your own? I quote the Hindu philosopher Ram Swarup (1920-98), an important intellectual figure of independent India's first half-century:

---

30 Sweyn Plowright, in the song "Fokstua Hall" (performed by Fire + Ice, album *Midwinter Fires*).

There was a time when the old Pagan Gods were pretty fulfilling and they inspired the best of men and women to acts of greatness, love, nobility, sacrifice, and heroism. It is, therefore, a good thing to turn to them in thought and pay them our homage. We know pilgrimage, as ordinarily understood, as wayfaring to visit a shrine or a holy place. But there can also be a pilgrimage in time and we can journey back and make our offerings of the heart to those Names and Forms and Forces which once incarnated and expressed man's higher life...The peoples of Egypt, Persia, Greece, Germany, and the Scandinavian countries are no less ancient than the peoples of India; but they lost their Gods, and therefore they lost their sense of historical continuity and identity...What is true of Europe is also true of Africa and South America. The countries of these continents have recently gained political freedom of a sort, but...if they wish to rise in a deeper sense, they must recover their soul, their Gods...If they do enough self-churning, then their own Gods will put forth new meanings in response to their new needs...If there is sufficient aspiration, invoking, and soliciting, there is no doubt that even Gods apparently lost could come back again. They are there all the time.[31]

In this spirit I conclude my Chaos Heathen musings on the Northern Path of magic, myth, and mystery, on which we can regain our Soul and strive for Becoming more than we are. *"Werde, der Du bist!"* – "Become who you are!" (Johann Gottlieb Fichte).

---

[31] Ram Swarup 1980: *The Word as Revelation.*

Merry Met, MichaELFallson

Bronze Gods
Klintr O'DubhGhaill

I'm going to tell you a little story. I'm not going to quote academic sources because I hate footnotes and, besides, I'm at least half Irish. So, why let the footnotes get in the way of a good story?

About five or ten thousand years ago, depending on where you want to draw the starting line, there lived a group of people who we now call the Proto-Indo-Europeans. We don't know exactly what the Proto-Indo-Europeans called themselves but there were probably several names, as there would have already been more than one tribe. In the nineteenth and early twentieth centuries we called the Proto-Indo-Europeans "Aryans," though that name has long since fallen out of favor. That's only half a shame since, even though Aryan is much easier to type than Proto-Indo-European, Aryan is now a poisoned word and the identification of all Indo-Europeans as Aryan was based on historically inaccurate information anyway. Aryan more properly refers to the Indo-Iranians, who are just one branch of the Indo-European family.

We don't know exactly where the Proto-Indo-Europeans came from either. One of the old theories is that they came from Ancient Persia or Northern India, hence the misidentification of all Indo-Europeans as Aryans. Some alternative theories would place their homeland in Ireland, Germany, or Scandinavia. These geographically extreme theories are probably motivated by politics more than anything else. Modern scholarship seems to agree that the true homeland of the Proto-Indo-Europeans was somewhere near the Black Sea. Eastern Europe, Southern Russia, and Anatolia (modern Turkey) are all plausible possibilities. The most dominant theory currently is the Kurgan Hypothesis, which would place the *Urheimat* on the Pontic Steppe, from whence came Conan's Cimmerians and the villain of the 1986 *Highlander* film. I tend to instinctively favor the Anatolian Hypothesis, myself, not because I actually know enough about archaeological linguistics to have a serious opinion but because Anatolia feels right from a mythological perspective. Troy was located in Anatolia. A lot of European nations have at one time or another claimed descent from the Trojans and the earliest written records we have of an Indo-European people (the Hittites) also came from there. Of course, it is entirely possible that they originally came from further north.

Regardless of exactly where they began, we do know that the Indo-Europeans started to branch out during the Bronze Age, several thousand years BCE. Those who would become the Aryans headed east into Persia and India. Others headed north into Russia and west into Europe. In China, the Middle East, and Africa, Indo-European migrations made headway but were eventually absorbed into the general population. In India, Persia, Russia, and Europe – they conquered. The Proto-Indo-Europeans became the cultural, linguistic, and mythological ancestors of most European nations, a large chunk of Asia, and all of modern civilization. The mystic heights of Hinduism, Buddhism, Greco-Roman Philosophy, and modern Science all have their roots in the religion of the Proto-Indo-Europeans. But...our ancestors were not always so civilized.

The Indo-Europeans didn't conquer half the world with kind thoughts and sweet words. There was an awful lot of raping, pillaging, and human sacrifice along the way. The Indo-Europeans rode chariots, carried expensive new bronze weaponry, and followed an aggressively militaristic, patriarchal, and expansionist war cult. And, at the cutting edge of every invasion, marched an elite troop of undead werewolf warriors.

The original werewolves were the young warrior-class boys (and sometimes girls) of the tribe. They were separated from their families, when they reached a certain age, and sent away for a prolonged period of military training in the forests, mountains, and border regions. Initiation into the wolf pack may have originally included the eating of human flesh and drinking of human blood. Later, human flesh was replaced by the heart of a wolf or some other great beast. The blood was replaced with mead, hemp, soma, or some other intoxicating liquor. Symbolically, these boys (and girls) were considered to be dead. No longer children and not yet adults, they existed outside the laws of humanity. They lived like animals, hunting and scavenging for their food. They dressed themselves in furs and rags, let their hair grow wild, painted their faces, and wore ferocious animal masks. In general, the Young Wolves comported themselves like the beasts they were meant to be. The Wolves patrolled the border regions, acting as lightly armed recon scouts and guerilla fighters. They raided neighboring territories and occasionally seized land. The Wolves carried spears and knives but were usually forbidden shields or armor. They were lightly armed because the Pack needed to be quick moving and agile, but the lack of armor in battle also provided for an extra test of courage. In addition to a minimum age requirement, the killing of an adult male in close combat was usually a pre-requisite for graduation from the Wolf Pack into full adult membership of the Tribe.

Adult warriors fought as chariot-borne Cavalry and Heavy Infantry. As experienced fighters and proven killers, armed with full length bronze-tipped spears, swords, and battle-axes, bearing shields and armour, they must have smashed through all primitive resistance like gods among men. These were the landowners – the only real citizens of the tribe – and their entire social system was set up to support and perpetuate the taking of more and better land. They would seize more land, so that they could feed more children, so that they could raise more warriors, so that they could seize more land. The bronze clad Indo-Europeans built a cultural, religious, and linguistic empire from India to Ireland.

Some warriors, however, would never grow up. Some would fail the test of adulthood – otherwise it wouldn't have been much of a test. Others would die trying and be honored for doing so. A small percentage, it seems, would voluntarily forsake initiation into adult citizenship. These few became the Berserkers and Centaurs. Young Wolves forever, they were the true elite. Full time warriors, dedicated to battle as though it were a religious calling, they would serve as guerilla shock troops, royal bodyguards, and teachers to the next generation of the Wolf Pack. Modern day elite forces such as the Navy SEALs and Green Berets are actually the inheritors of a tradition that extends back to the original Bear Shirts and Wolf Heads at the beginning of time.

Eventually, our ancestors settled down. They seized and held ground, wherever they went, and then they married into the local population. The Indo-Europeans adopted native traditions and ideas, absorbed elements of the local language and culture into their own – and became wiser for having done so. Hinduism and Buddhism are traditions sprung from the ancient well of Indo-European Paganism, merged with the native practices of the Indian subcontinent. Greek and Roman Philosophy sprang from a swirling brew of Indo-European, Native European, Egyptian, and Near Eastern Paganism. Even Christianity, usually decried as a foreign imposition by those who favor the Elder Gods, can actually be traced back to ideas that began in Greece and Persia as much as Egypt and Israel. Our ancestors became civilized – but some of us will never become civilized. Some of us still remember the Old Gods, from the days before the Jesus myth. Some of us yearn to go back even deeper; to run with the Wolves and ride, like the Bronze Gods, through the forests of Indo-Europa.

Love, MichaeELFallson

Ancestors: the Good, the Bad, the Ugly
Lonnie Scott

Self Discovery and Awareness

Once upon a time there was no Internet. There was no vast Sea of Google such as we swim in today. If you wanted anything Pagan, Occult, or Heathen-related then you were going to spend a lot of time in the New Age section of bookstores. That left you wondering why anything worth reading was always on the bottom shelf, in a corner tucked between alien abduction stories and almanacs. The big box book stores dotted the landscape. I was lucky to have a Waldenbooks in the local mall, and a New Age store an hour away. The local choices were pretty limited unless you wanted Wicca 101 books. The New Age store offered a wider variety of options tucked between incense burners and deity statues.

When the Internet started firing up for the general public it was all chat rooms, mailing lists, and creepy glitter-bombed websites. I never knew what book to read. I ended up collecting anything I could get my hands on. Amazon reviews were years away, and the online groups couldn't even agree whether to burn a sigil or not, so forget getting a good book recommendation. I took it all in. Chaos Magic, Egyptian magic, Druidism, Satanic Bible, Thee Temple ov Psychick Youth (TOPY), *Necronomicon*, and all things Pagan. You end up with a lot of garbage going into a young, open mind. Years of research and practice help flush out the crap. You can only hope there are hidden nuggets in what remains.

The summer I turned seventeen was the game changer. I went from taking notes to experimenting. That was the year I found myself studying *Liber Null & Psychonaut*. It was the first time I felt compelled to take magical action. I had a clear course to build the skills of sorcery. That was the same summer I started studying Runes. Bindrunes became sigils with deeper meaning and force. That was the bridge, using ancient practices to suit modern needs, that I was searching for in all those books. I was learning more about myself, and gaining skills to shape my own mind.

The floodgates to good information opened up. It wasn't just a Heathen and Pagan fever burning in my brain. I wanted to know as much as possible about all things weird, strange, unusual, and Occult. I developed a fascination with Buddhism and meditation. I fell in love with some Egyptian Deities, Hypnosis, NLP, Witchcraft, the weird, paranormal, and all the theories of the tiny bits in our multiverse. I was well on the way to a very eclectic blend of ideas and talent. I didn't know what I was, but I knew what I wanted. I was hunting magic and wisdom. I wanted to know occult secrets and bring them into the light of modern usage. Ultimately, I wanted skills that produced real results.

Now, the Internet is a global network that reveals the world's secrets in seconds. The gatekeepers are either gone or powerless. The wisdom of all ages is laid bare for anyone to find. Chat rooms crumbled into online forums that eventually morphed into Facebook groups. Tribes started forming around shared passions for every possible niche in all matters mundane and magical.

Type 'Heathen ' or 'Asatru' into Google or Facebook. You will quickly find out there are different factions within modern Heathenry. You'll find everything from Norse-inspired Wicca to the most strict Reconstructionists. Arguments rage over authenticity, lore, Vikings, Runes, practices, and skin color. The various communities will accept and reject members on a variety of matters. Rejection based on race is a sad reality among the worst groups. Fingers wave and accuse others of not being Heathen. Myths are taken too literally. Loki becomes some form of Christian-themed Asatru Devil. Be warned: the online communities seem to be where magic and mystery go to die.

My arrival into Heathenism came with a wary eye. I always felt like the odd kid out in Heathenism. I don't fantasize about being a Viking any more than I desire to live the life of a 3rd-century farmer. The history of all the Germanic, Norse, and Anglo-Saxon Heathen lands are fascinating, but I just won't be imprisoned by a world that isn't my own. I wanted to know about their magic, cosmology, myths, folktales, and all their wonderful weirdness. I wanted to know why the ancient Heathens practiced magic as they did, and what they desired as the result. I wanted to know how I could adapt it all to be effective today.

Discovery was on the horizon.

Elhaz Ablaze. A website created by rune magicians exploring Northern Mysteries, Seidhr, Western Magic, Tantra, Eastern techniques, and Chaos Magic in the pursuit of Gnosis. Chaos Heathens.

Heimlich A. Laguz, one of the site's authors, said that modern Heathenism should be more about Psychological Reconstruction, which he described as "[u]nderstanding the worldview of the old Heathens: the importance of *wyrd*, time, interconnection, sacredness, hospitality, gift giving, and reciprocity...over and above particular debates about exactly what clothes were worn when or the like."

Understanding concepts allows us to build a bridge from the deep past to the present day. Our work becomes relevant within the historical narrative. We can address our needs without worrying if it's exactly as our ancestors would address the problem. This self awareness is liberating.

We can turn to multiple sources of wisdom to shape our path. The cornerstone of our approach as Chaos Heathens is within the worldview of understanding the timeless influence of *wyrd*, how we can shape it, and the reciprocity of offerings and relationships.

My own work has uncovered the influence our ancestors have on us through time, both biologically and spiritually. The good news is your ancestors are powerful spiritual allies in life and magical pursuits. The bad news is your ancestors require work. You're going to have to visit grandma once in a while. You're going to do homework. You're going to create a real relationship. The funky news is that even science knows your ancestors passed on more than just eye color. They might also be responsible for your shitty attitude.

I developed an approach to Ancestor Healing that works within a Heathen worldview and adheres to Heathen principles while using techniques from various fields. Trance, offerings, and meditation make ancestor work richer and more rewarding. It is not enough to raise a toast to the ancestors. You must develop awareness of their presence in your life and even in your behavior.

Ancestor Awareness

Ancestor work is one aspect of the occult that crosses all borders and boundaries. Cultures worldwide have some form of tradition that honors ancestors. It's important to recognize our past. Ancestral awareness is recognizing the reciprocal relationship between you and your ancestors. They have a great influence on your life whether you like it or not.

The great achievements of the past are ours as much as the pain and suffering of each individual along the line. There is no room to choose what affects us. It's woven straight into our DNA, physically and spiritually. The important realization is that we also exist within a generational play that has neither a true beginning nor ending. The actions of the past weigh on your mindset just as your actions will weigh on generations to come. These choices flow through time like a stream through the land. All who touch the waters will be affected by its force.

This is not a fatal view of destiny. You can grab *wyrd* in your own hands and shape the outcome of your influence. First, you must uncover what needs to be healed. This will require virtue and conviction. To know the past is to turn a mirror on your own shadow. You're not always going to like what you find. You must have courage to face the truth. You must also keep working with perseverance to achieve your goal. There is wisdom to be gained in your work. That knowledge will enable you to heal what's broken, and allow you to pass on health and wisdom to your descendants.

Lineage

To develop ancestor awareness, you must first know where you come from. Your lineage is your family down through the ages. Each generation back through time. Lineage can also be those who have lived and died in your community, as well as those who were important figures in your path. Understanding your lineage will connect you to your past. You'll uncover family secrets, and come to know the struggles your ancestors faced that led to you. Begin researching your ancestry through genealogy resources. Keep track of names, places, dates, and stories on a family tree. There are places online you can pay small fees to access records for generations further back in time. Ask around in your extended family if there are family bibles or if research has already been done on documenting your family tree. Talk to your living grandparents or their siblings. Find out what stories they remember about their childhood and their grandparents. You will start to see patterns.

I was surprised to see so many important religious figures on my family tree. Pick a branch. You'll see church founders, religious leaders, and wandering priests. I found a few rumored witches, midwives, and one possible link to a crusader. I've felt a very strong pull into spiritual searching from an early age. Research into my lineage taught me that it's a calling in my blood. I've also discovered stories of war and famine. Immigration struggles, land theft, and farmer after farmer just trying to live a good life. These are all the people that lived, migrated, and made sure their children survived so that one day I might live. The least I can do is thank them for the life I was given.

Your lineage is also influenced by the Mighty Dead. These are the people that influenced your life while not being part of your family tree. I'm a martial artist so I recognize the influence of Bruce Lee, Helio Gracie, and Ed Parker. Each one of those men broke the status quo and developed arts that I practise and philosophies I admire. As a Pagan and Heathen, I honor the influence of ancient heroes, and more recent pioneers that have passed into the next world. The same can be said for the major influences in my professions of hypnosis, meditation, and Tarot. Even as a bartender, I always raise a glass in honor of those rebels that kept the drinks flowing in the Prohibition era. Recognize those men and women who made your various hobbies and skills possible with their own bravery and sacrifice.

Ancestor Communication

I dreamed of my great-grandmother the night she died. We were having a conversation about all the memories that made us laugh. I realized all the many memories of times with her that were buried. It was a joy to relive them all. She radiated the power of a family matriarch that loves her whole clan. I was surprised to learn of her death when I awoke the following morning. She was a strong woman. I think she was visiting all of her loved ones before she crossed over to the next world.

Your ancestors will find ways to communicate to you through dreams and visions. Start keeping a dream journal and look for messages. It might be a family crest, the smell of your grandma's homemade noodles, or a spirit right in front of your face. A dream journal will improve your dream recall and increase your awareness of your ancestors in your life.

You may also communicate with your ancestors through divination. This method will produce the best results once you've started a reciprocal relationship with your ancestors. Start an ancestor altar, or at least acknowledge them in your daily offerings. Some people put together a display of family photos, while others represent their ancestors with a tree. You'll find many diverse ways to make a place special for your ancestors. I include my ancestors in my daily offerings as part of my overall spiritual practice. Choose a method and start honoring your ancestors every day.

I communicate with my ancestors through divination in two ways. First, I use a specific ancestor spread with Tarot that I can use any place at any time. My ancestral spread I use with Tarot can be adapted to Runes or other forms of divination. The questions I ask in the spread are:

1. What opens the way for my ancestors?
2. Where do my ancestors manifest in my life now?
3. What is their message for me now?
4. How can I understand or hear this link/message?
5. How can I bring my ancestors' power into my daily life and improve the relationship?
6. The outcome of this work.

The second method I use is sortilege (divination by drawing lots) after an offering. I draw one Rune or Tarot card to see how the gift was accepted. I may draw one more for clarification. This establishes a consistent two way communication with you and your ancestors. You're building a reciprocal relationship and strengthening the bonds you've made with your ancestors.

Breaking Negative Influence

You should be in the daily habit of honoring your ancestors at this point. Communication is established, and offerings are made. This is important because you're going to start noticing trends in your lineage.

My own father was a drunk when I was a kid. He had serious anger problems that turned into beating me and inflicting psychological abuse. Whiskey acted as fuel for a fire already out of control. I grew up scared to speak my mind, and terrified of sleeping too deeply. I had my own anger issues in my teens as a result of all the fear in my childhood. It took a lot of internal work to get where I am today.

As my understanding of spirituality grew, my understanding of my father started to improve. He stopped drinking somewhere in my late teens. He made an attempt to be a grandfather to my kids. The damage was done with me, but I could see he was trying to be a better man. I would never have noticed those changes if I had failed to confront my own anger.

Self awareness is the first step. Start paying attention to your own stress responses. Are you likely to experience depression or anxiety? Do you overreact to your own anger? Are you quiet, withdrawn, or scared? These are all mindsets that were influenced by your ancestors and your environment.

Epigenetic research has discovered the amount of time your great-grandparents were held with love and affection can imprint a positive influence in your genes. The reverse is also true. Childhood neglect, abuse, and trauma can all imprint a negative influence on descendants. Double that influence from the environment of your own childhood.

My father was the product of an affair. His own father never had anything to do with us. We didn't even get his last name. Dad grew up in a town with a multitude of cousins that he couldn't really call family. He was blocks away from his own dad that he couldn't know in any meaningful way. That's a good building block for anger, and a terrible reference for being a good father later in life. It's not an excuse for how my dad acted. It's an influence.

That same influence of anger and substance abuse awakened in me. The seed was planted from previous generations, and my environment of fear provided fertile soil for growth. My early teen years were full of repressed rage and hate. Those feelings belonged to me, but I didn't choose them for myself. I learned how to be both angry and afraid. Those lessons were handed down from my father from his own experience of neglect, fear, and anger as a kid.

I was faced with two choices. I could ignore the problem and allow it to fester and grow; that road was filled with fights, anger, depression, and fear of being alone. That's the direction I was scared to walk. My other choice would be to face the problem. I could understand what happened to me, beat the monster, and choose how I would express my emotions in a healthier manner. It turns out that all the time I spent exploring the occult in my teens was like downloading techniques to adjust mindsets. I already had the tools necessary to navigate the darkness in my mind.

The two most important tools in my practice are meditation and offerings. I use trance, runes, and many other forms of divination and magic in my practice. None of those skills would be possible without my daily meditation and offerings. I must give credit to Jason Miller, of the Strategic Sorcery Course, for making me realize that all else flows from those skills.

We've already covered the importance of offerings to build a relationship with your ancestors. Now we'll cover meditation.

Meditation in a Chaos Heathen Minute

I first encountered meditation in my early teens. I believe it is the single greatest skill any human being can practice. There is no better way to know your own mind and discern what's influencing your emotions and thoughts.

I'm unaware of any record in the lore indicating that ancient Heathens taught or practiced meditation, although I have my suspicions. I also know of no place in the lore where ancient Heathens took antibiotics, ate Chinese food, or drove cars. I have seen a lot of evidence in the lore and history that shows our ancestors were both practical and innovative, and the magically inclined were willing to assimilate skills from other cultural influences.

We know meditation has enormous benefits. It's a shield wall against stress, anxiety, and depression. It's been shown to improve memory, concentration, relaxation, empathy, and sleep. Meditation has also been shown to reduce the risk and symptoms of chronic pain, cancer, blood pressure, heart disease, and other illnesses. That's the short list. Research reveals more benefits to meditation every day.

Chaos Heathenism builds a mindset of magical action. Your world is going to come alive. You'll get closer to your ancestors, and the spirits who inhabit the land, waters, and sky. You'll reach out to divine powers. You'll even deal with souls still wrapped in flesh, just as you are, who want to influence your mind.

You must be able to recognize when you've lost yourself in random thoughts, worry, anxiety, and daydreaming. Your mind is on autopilot most of your waking hours. You lose yourself in your thoughts, you have sudden uncontrolled reactions, assumptions, and limiting beliefs, and most of your life you never stop to question any of it.

Here's a quick exercise.

Close your eyes for 30 seconds. Don't think of anything while your eyes are closed. Nothing. Not one thought.

Go.

Frustrated? A normal functioning human brain is like a hurricane at sea. There's a lot of noise on the surface. You're being distracted by daydreams, worry, fears, hopes, ideas, song fragments, and the chorus of random thoughts that pass by without pause. You don't even notice how crazy the activity in your mind is until you try to ignore it.

Don't worry. All is not lost.

Exercise Two.

Close your eyes for another 30 seconds. This time I want you to keep track of every single thought racing through your head. That should be easier than thinking of nothing, right?

Go.

I'm guessing that didn't work so well. It's okay. You're normal. Well, you're as normal as a person who would want to read a book about Chaos Heathenism could be. And we love you for it. Moving on...

You've just learned a valuable insight into your own mind.

There's a lot of nonstop noise between your ears. You can't make it stop, and you can't track all of it as it happens. That hurricane of random thoughts is stealing your awareness. The next time you're in the shower, go ahead and check to see if you're actually in the shower. There's no doubting that you might physically be in the shower, but your mind is probably at work, off worrying about something that happened last night, or lost somewhere else in time.

Your awareness is out of control. We can fix that.

Exercise Three.

You can do this exercise with your eyes open, however closing your eyes will shut out several distractions. Sit with a posture that allows you to breathe easily. You can also do this laying down, but be aware you might fall asleep. I also recommend setting a timer for at least 5 minutes.

- Rest your attention on your breath. You may pay attention to your breath as it flows in and out, or the rise and fall of your chest, or simply say to yourself "in" on your inhale and "out" on your exhale.

- There will be distractions in your environment. Your mind will also begin to wander as you start wondering if you're doing it right, what you'll have for dinner, and suddenly you'll realize your mind is off on a trip. This is normal. Simply return your awareness to your breath.

- You haven't done anything wrong. There is no judgment here. Don't beat yourself up when you realize you're distracted. Breathe in. Breathe out. Rest in the moment. Repeat.

- You're meditating.

That's the easy explanation of how to meditate. Focus on your breath, detach from thoughts, and be nice to yourself when you get distracted. You shouldn't listen to any spirits during meditation. You don't even give the Gods an audience. You're in meditation. The time you set aside for meditation needs to be for meditation.

You'll find meditation relaxing on some days and excruciating on other days. It's important to make meditation as vital as eating in order to create the habit. Pick a space in your home that you can use consistently. Choose a time that allows you to take a few minutes for yourself. The rewards of meditation are ongoing as you practice.

Meditation can also be done walking. You can meditate on your emotional state. You can meditate on sounds. Meditation can be any activity that utilizes focused awareness to change your overall state. What I've taught you is called a Core Meditation. It's the practice many adhere to for the majority of their meditation work. It will serve you well as you go forward developing your Ancestor Awareness.

The Healing Road

Let's be clear about a few things that still avoid full explanation by science. We don't know why we have consciousness. We don't know why we dream. We don't know what happens after bodily death. We don't know why the placebo effect is so strong, or why people suddenly heal from terminal illness. We do know there is mounting evidence that consciousness plays a big part in the Universe. We do know that we can hijack our dreams and go lucid. We do know that near death experience studies support the idea of survival of consciousness after bodily death. We know that hypnosis and meditation heal the mind and body, and open doors to entire worlds.

Now you also know that your ancestors have influenced your life, mindset, and wellbeing. You can improve the relationship with your ancestors through offerings. You can communicate with your ancestors in dreams and meditation. You can uncover their influence on you physically and change it.

You must shift your awareness towards healing and change as if it were a dial on a stereo. Trancework will allow you to make solution-focused change quickly, and embody those changes to create a permanent shift. Here's a brief exercise to guide you into an altered state for healing. You may either commit it to memory or record yourself to play back as a guide.

Take a deep breath...Take another deep breath and feel your muscles relaxing...Allow all the muscles in your body to let go of the tension...Imagine the stress and concerns of your day melting into the Earth...

Feel a warmth and comforting sensation return to your body from the depths of the Earth and know that you're supported by your ancestors and the mighty dead...

Focus now on that feeling that needs to heal...This can be your stress, anger, sadness, loneliness...whatever emotion you choose that is attached to you from your ancestry and your own upbringing...zero in on that feeling now...notice where it appears in your body...bring your attention to that spot...allow your awareness to go through that spot as a gateway to the first time your subconscious remembers that feeling in your life...notice what you're doing...whether you're alone or with someone...inside or outside...and allow yourself to be there in that first moment...

Now see your younger self in that moment, standing or sitting in front of you...imagine you can speak to this young version of you...tell that little person that it's not their fault...that you've decided to let go of that feeling...you know that it's come through the generations to you and you wish to lay it down...forgive yourself for carrying the burden...allow yourself to feel that burden lift from your shoulders...and your soul ...let the younger version of you know that you're now free...

Now imagine yourself standing in front of a mirror...the reflection looking back at you is your own yet again, only this time one year older than you are now...this older version of you has experienced one year of life without that feeling...free from that negative emotional influence...what gratitude does this older you wish to express for the decision you've made today...allow yourself to feel that love and support for your decision...know that your intention has shifted the flow of wyrd *in your life...you're now reshaping what you pass on to your descendants in your line, in your community, and those who will take up this spiritual path in the future...you've healed the wound by shifting your awareness towards healing and growth...allow yourself to feel that pride and joy of new life...new direction...and allow it to sink deeper into your heart and mind...every fiber of your being...and when you're ready...gently allow your awareness to return to your body...notice the support of the Earth beneath you...the pride of your ancestors for your work...for your courage...and open your eyes...when you're ready.*

This exercise is built on trance, regression, progression, forgiveness, ancestor connection, awareness training, and healing. Repeat this exercise until you feel you've accomplished a shift in the emotion you wished to change.

You're transforming the influence of the past into more useful states that you choose for yourself. The present is where we live out our lives. You should be in control of your reactions to emotional changes.

I'm challenging you to embrace your power to shape destiny and change the cycle that's been passed down to you. You've inherited a set of skills, and a set of influences on your overall well-being. Some of those will be out of your control. I'm tall with thinning hair. That's just how it is. I'm not controlled by anger, depression, or fear. I made the decision to fight them on my own terms. I'm asking you to do the same.

You now have the building blocks of practices that will help you to honor your ancestors; to communicate with them; to discern influences from outside your mind from your own emotions and thoughts; to meditate; and to use a trance-guided journey to heal emotional states.

Your work with Ancestor Awareness will build healthier bridges to the past while handing a better world to the next generation.

Hel's Home, MichaELFallson

What is Ancestor Worship?
Heimlich A. Laguz

The illusion of separateness is fatal. The illusion that I am the sole author of my nature, my beliefs, my emotions, my desires, my destiny. Certainly my will and decisions matter in that they have consequences. But they did not emerge from a vacuum, and nor do their consequences.

The illusion of separateness, this belief in the vacuum, is silently invoked by the spirit of vacuum, of reductive technocracy, of oppressive hierarchy, of the mentality that will justify any amount of destruction for the sake of convenience, of selfishness so extreme it impairs the individual's self-interest.

The vacuum emerges through distorted ways of choosing to represent the nature of consciousness. We are discouraged from reflecting on the most immediate experience of being a human being with thoughts, feelings, and choices. Of being a being at once embodied and conceptual, at once practical and imaginative. We pass over the experience of our own being, seduced by the ever changing carousel of life unfolding.

This carousel seems to become ever more gaudy, distracting, and compelling, as technology makes the world go exponentially *faster*. Is speed the best thing for us? We do not know. But we can say that it encourages us to forget ourselves, our past, and the possible futures that our actions conjure. It absorbs us in a kind of non-space, a zone of eternal urgency without significance, a rootless tension and Brownian motion.

The carousel of this forgetfulness, this losing ourselves in the thingly doings and disconnected thoughts of the world around, is not new. It has always been a part of human nature. We are stretched between two poles: the all-dissolving world at one extreme, the all-condensing self at the other. Yet these two poles are themselves illusions; all that really exists is the tension of a continuum. Somewhere on that continuum we can plot our human consciousness or presence, and somewhere we can plot the world into which we are born and engulfed and suffused. Sometimes it is the same point. The image of Jormangand, of the Ouroborus, is relevant here.

For some reason, however, it is easier for us to focus on the worldly end of the continuum than to focus on our own inner awareness and experience – even when only a little distance separates the two poles! This is might be because *we are physically looking out into the world*. We do not have eyes that reach within. Despite the confusion of Descartes' "I think therefore I am," the truth of living experience is that we tend to infer our inner existence from the fact of the whirling experience of a world around us. A better formulation than Descartes' could read: "the world *worlds*, I find myself *being*."

We are lost in the world, our world. Each of us has a unique experience, yet that uniqueness is itself only possible on the condition of the shared, muddied, and overlapping vales of presence and absence that make up the theater and audience of existence. Lost in the world, we cannot see things in terms of their causes or consequences. Any one person, animal, tree, meal, story, memory, action is blurred into relative interchangeability with any other. Mass production completes the lie that any one thing can be equivalent to any other.

Yet this is not the case. Every single being has its own non-repeatable and absolutely unique trajectory through causality. Even two mass-produced objects which seem to the vague and lost perceiver to be identical...are not truly identical, no matter how similar they may be. Each is, after all, composed of different molecules, and each of those molecules has its own characteristic and unique history, a uniqueness which is covered over, concealed, forgotten in the seeming uniformity of the final product.

We fall into the same kind of deceptive perception of uniformity with human beings. We label this person a 'conservative,' that person a 'radical.' We divide popular culture into endless, ever more particularized segments. We think we have grasped an individual's nature when we read off a grab bag of these tags of identity – their religion, their race, their occupation, their age, their gender. Our generalizations simplify life for us to manageable levels – which to some extent is necessary because of the ever strengthening power of *faster* – but they come with a terrible price. The more crude our thumbnail sketches of reality become, the more we abandon our curiosity, empathy, and complexity. The result of this process is the world we live in, one of myriad social injustices, environmental catastrophes, and completely preventable horrors.

Though we may be tempted (or forced) to progressively simplify our maps of reality, this does not do anything to reduce the complexity of the terrain itself.

Indeed, we have come to a point where, because our maps tell us we are walking in a straight line, we completely fail to notice the endless digressions and meanderings of our actual path. We look through and past our lived experience to lean on the crutch of our expectations.

The spirit of *faster*, which blinds us in a welter of ever more simplified reality maps, would have us think that questioning the dominant models offered by our contemporary cultural milieu is little more than obscurantism. It is weak-headed romanticism or vapid idealism. The opposite could not be more true, for what is realistic about seeing one's existence in terms of abstract caricatures rather than in its own unique and perplexing forms?

In recent times 'critical thinking' is endlessly evoked in academic institutions, yet this often amounts to little more than circular self-reference within hermetically sealed disciplines. 'Critical thinking' needs to be something more than this. It needs to get out of the endless avoidance of the self, the endless lostness in the flurry of constant streaming experience and the distorted, rootless impressions of both individual perspective and mass representation.

We fear pausing. We fear letting ourselves withdraw from total dissolution in the everyday. We fear slowing down to focus on just one moment, aspect, or thing within the endless stream of worldly experience. We have these fears because we are in a comfortable rut. We have these fears because slowing down entails paying attention and if we were to do that we might find that we are not as happy, wise, honest, moral, or whole as we thought. We are experiencing Stockholm Syndrome, and repetitious habit is the kidnapper.

We fear to embrace *fateful pausing* because it is not the *done thing* (that is to say, fateful pausing is not a mere thing that is mechanically done). We weigh the values of those around us so highly, and chances are those values are also aligned with the lostness that comes when we adopt only the most simplistic maps of reality or experience. We fear becoming isolated, expelled to the other end of the continuum, a state in which we are not only *not* absorbed in the everyday doings of our experience, we are no longer able to find the reflection of our spirit in the world around us at all. Ironically, we are even more alienated when we are ignorantly reacting to our daily, worldly experience without any insight or perspective into our own internal nature.

Yet when we slow down and attend to just one thing – perhaps a tree on a silent morning, the dew gathered on its leaves like jewels, bark rough as it parts the earth, roots clutching the soil – we discover that the continuum between self and world is part of a vast lattice of similar continuums. This truth is available everywhere – in the breath, in observing the sensations of the body, in artistic processes, in lively conversation; any place and any time.

The poles of reality do not simply comprise of 'me' and 'everything else.' Every particular being or entity has its own unique continuum, its own degree of being isolated or enmeshed. When we are lost in our shallow maps, we lose our ability to recognize that all existence is a *weave* of such continuums; we come to chauvinistically think that all reality is just a movie screen in which to dissolve ourselves.

Thus there is no fundamental difference between going *inward* and going *outward*, the latter achieved simply by selecting one being or thing that we encounter and pausing to really take it in, to experience it through our senses, through reading all we can about it, through talking about it, through turning ourselves toward it by whatever means we can contrive.

One needs to choose to dwell, to allow something to unfold itself rather than seeing it merely as a shallow *seeming*, a way-point on a two-dimensional map of this infinitely dimensional universe. In a way, this amounts to allowing for my relationship to the object of my attention to come into being and then to bloom.

What do we discover when we choose to tarry in this way, to become curious about that of which we have previously been vague? When we resolve to pierce the deceptively smooth surface of our everyday, surface haze? When we hold ourselves out for seeing the familiar as if for the first time?

We think that because we are *familiar* with our experience that we *know* it. Yet, the moment we pause to dwell...we discover that our very closeness to our experience renders that experience obscure. Or does so, at least, unless we choose to incorporate moments in which we can honor that experience through reflection, curiosity, even reverence. And of course, even such moments can become dissolved into the haze of vague everydayness if we let them become habitual, stale, rote motions; we must take care against the endless seduction of complacency.

When we pause to appreciate the character, the being, of an object, or person, or plant, or animal, or moment, or idea, or memory, or our own personality – we are confronted with the uniqueness of that entity. No matter how uniform or generic it might seem, we discover that it has some particularity all of its own – even if we can only speculate as to the full story of that particularity.

As we begin to explore that particularity, we begin, as I have intimated, to adopt a reverential attitude. We appreciate the hue of an heirloom rose bush, its particular and distinctive scent. The regularities and irregularities of its leaf patterns. The way its petals hold themselves in cool air. The way the earth at its base is churned by its roots. We are invited to recognize that this is a non-repeatable, unique, singular plant. It carries its own particular story through the stretching-forth present.

That story might be a story of xylem and phloem and photosynthesis. It might be a story of soil and climate. It might be a story of resistance to genetically modified seeds, which is to say, a political story. It might be a love story between a person and their favorite type of flower. It might be a story of the lineage of that particular type of rose, now carefully preserved in a time of monocropping. It might be a story about how human beings have changed and been changed by the plants that we have cultivated throughout the centuries. It might be a story about bees hovering, feet smothered in pollen, carrying one flower's sexual effusions to the next.

In fact, this entire multiplicity of stories is true. And each invites a further multiplicity of stories. Each story invokes new continuums between specific beings and the world in which they are engulfed. We come to see that *this rose* in its absolute particularity leads us to the *infinite tapestry* of all existence. But in tarrying with the rose in this way we are now allowing the world to speak to us. We are listening, curious, without cynical anticipation. We have put aside, to a greater or lesser extent, our maps of existence. We have come to recognize that reality is a vast lattice of stories, that what presents to us now is the precipitate of memory.

So while I describe this tarrying and dwelling as reverence, I do not mean to use the word in any particular received sense, such as a formally religious one. To revere is to take the time to appreciate something in its own uniqueness; and in turn to appreciate just how vastly, beautifully intricate all of the world is. To revere is to honor that fact that the present is nothing more or less than a *living memory* of all the infinite layers and threads that have made possible its coming into being.

Trace the shape of the living memory that is the present and we cannot help but follow the tangled threads that spiral into the mysterious horizon of the past and the unknown territories of possible futures. We cannot help but contemplate the heritage, the ancestry, of that to which we address our reverence. It draws us into the world in a wholly different way; we become utterly distilled into uniqueness, and utterly attuned to universality, *without contradiction*.

It is this which I define as ancestor worship. It is an attitude of present, open, empathic curiosity, grounded in gratitude and generosity of spirit. It is much more than just a mechanical list of 'begats,' and if followed to its conclusion it precludes the prejudiced mentalities that claim to be rooted in ancestor worship but that, ironically, are symptoms of amnesia and irreverence.

Ancestor worship is the bridge of part to whole, of particular to universal, of the nodes of the web of life to the web itself. As such, ancestor worship is an invitation to embrace love.

Dance of Sleipnir (the Smashing of the Fascia), MichaELFallson

Chaos Heathenry: Incompleteness & Elegance

Heimlich A. Laguz

Is the world simple or complicated? Well naturally, that is a reductive, over-simplifying question, but no less interesting for all that. *If* the world is simple, then it follows that a simple life philosophy will do. And if it is complicated? Well, we are not necessarily obliged to have a complicated life philosophy, but we need at least two things: acceptance of incompleteness, and elegance.

Chaos Heathenry is Heathenry that accepts incompleteness and thereby achieves elegance. These two qualities are valuable and rare. Before I explore their significance, I would like to explain why they are so rare.

When we accept incompleteness, we accept our mortality, and we accept the inherently mysterious nature of existence. I mean mortality in a double sense: that we are of finite power (we are not gods, and even they have their limits), and that we are destined to die, no matter how much we try to cover this over.

The ancient Heathens left traces in their myths that suggest they accepted incompleteness, or at least some of them did. Most notably, Odin confronts his own mortality by hanging on the World Tree. The product of this confrontation – this gift of self to self – is winning the runes. Rune means mystery. So Odin embraces his mortality in order to know Mystery.

This action is an action of reverence. By facing our mortality and not fleeing our finitude and our inevitable death, we show reverence for mystery and she embraces us. Naturally, this is a very elegant arrangement. Some of the original Heathens, it follows, could be described anachronistically as Chaos Heathens. From this stream within the old Heathenry we modern Chaos Heathens drink.

I consider this elegant, mystery-loving, honest-about-mortality current with Heathenry to be similar to the *Tariqat*, the hidden teachings of Muhammad from which Sufism traces its inspiration. Hidden right in the open of Islam as a revealed religion are mystery teachings. Heathenry is similar.[1]

Similar both in that there is a mystery tradition and that there is a great mass of adherents to an impersonal, supposedly revealed truth (the same could be said of any religion). People who want to hunker down within a narrow self-conception. Such a form of Heathenry is horribly anachronistic, being fettered by all sorts of modern ideas about cookie-cutter identity. 'Don't cross the streams!' is the motto of these Heathens, forgetting that the Ghostbusters could only save the day by doing just that.

Chaos Heathens cross the streams. Not out of any kind of premeditation, but because it is the truth of what courses through us. True to the ancestral spirit, we seek to honestly face death, and we honor mystery. And in the elegance of this attitude to life, we not only cross the streams, we weave them like threads into a cloth that is simultaneously whole and yet incomplete and ever growing.

Anathema, you cry! Heathenry must remain 'pure!' Aside from the ever mounting historical evidence of cultural syncretism among the ancient Heathens (the runes for example owe a huge debt to the Etruscan Rhaetic cult of northern Italy), the simple fact is that we would be false to ourselves, we would be denying mystery, if we amputated everything that makes us wild, inspired, creative, and reverent, for the sake of assuming a 'Heathen' identity that cuts us off from death and mystery. Chaos Heathens would rather emulate Odin and embrace death and mystery in a spirit of elegance.

Why? Why is denial of death so prevalent? Why do so many Heathens use their religion as a tool to continue their denial of mystery? Religion can be either a door into the unknown or a barrier to entering into the unknown; ironically it is often the most uncanny aspects of a religion that are recruited to the service of close-mindedness. Consider, for example, the maddening mystery of the three-in-one Catholic godhead – what should have been a paradox opening doors to the unknown was instead made into a vicious and leaden dogma.

Yes, it is true that Christianity denies death, and we are still living in Christian times. The resurrection of Christ is a message to the faithful that they no longer have to personally face their own mortality, their incompleteness, for Christ

---

[1] These comments are made in part to underscore what I regard as the perverse absurdity of Heathens holding Islamophobic opinions.

has already faced these threats to ego and animal instinct on their behalf. Brittle, forceful, yet ultimately shallow religiosity all-too-easily ensues (although to be fair, Christianity too has a beautiful *Tariqat*, sometimes itself the remnant of imported Pagan and Heathen traditions).

Jung recognized that death and the unconscious are linked. The unconscious is the underworld, the place from which and to which all life flows. If we fear death then we fear the contents of our own unconscious, and ultimately the collective unconscious too.

In *Psychological Types* Jung launches a devastating critique of Christianity (for all that he is ultimately sympathetic to Christianity). He asserts that Christianity tries to impose the contents of the personal unconscious of one person – Jesus Christ – over the contents of the personal unconscious of each individual Christian. The result is that each Christian's actual personal unconscious is suppressed, denied, pushed aside, and ultimately – demonized.

Thus we have the unconscious of Christ, a man who does not know mortality or incompleteness, being forced by his followers onto a species that can only be spiritually whole when grounded in its inescapable mortality and incompleteness. This is utterly tragic. It explains the horrors of colonial imperialism, patriarchy, racism, crusades, pogroms, inquisitions, witch hunts, and the legacy of child abuse within the Catholic church. All too often, Christians are obliged by their religion to project the demonized content of their personal unconscious psyches onto the *other*.

And modern Heathens often share this habit of mind. They want to be a facile projection of a non-existent, prototypical Heathenry; to exclude whatever does not fit that narrow, shallow identity. In flights of superficial delight they exult in quoting the Nine Noble Virtues (themselves a modern invention of course), or project all sorts of Jehovah-like qualities onto Odin, the very god who seeks above all else to test the limits of his own mortality!

So are these people Heathen, or just unwitting Christians functioning at that religion's worst echelon? They haven't escaped a psychology that is obsessed with *belief*. Yet the original Heathens had little time for orthodoxy. For them, *right action* – orthopraxy – was what mattered. So long as Heathens cannot let themselves breathe into the eye of mortality, the whirling vortex of incompleteness (mystery!) they will really be Christian in that religion's worst possible aspect. So why bother be Heathen at all?

Chaos Heathens embrace irreverence. We embrace curiosity. We embrace play. We refuse to be boxed in. We explore wherever the inspiration of life requires us to explore. We are not less 'strict' in our Heathenry than other Heathens; no, what distinguishes us is that we are honest about our complexity and multifacetedness. By owning our hybridity instead of denying it, we experience a tremendous release of psychic energy, a release which propels us into the seas of mystery, be they within us or without.

Does this make us antinomian? Possibly. The shortcoming of the antinomian philosophy, however, is the inevitability of *enantiodromia* – the fact that extremes tend to turn into their opposites. This great psychological and spiritual truth regularly makes mockery of zealots and absolutists. Thus rebels become establishment, and individualist 'Left Hand Path' magical orders are frighteningly vulnerable to unquestioning group-think obedience. We might consciously reject Christianity, yet it remains lodged within us unless we are willing to do the work to recognize it, own it, and let it go. In other words, the thing we deny becomes ever more insidiously buried within our hearts.

As such, Chaos Heathens are not 'joiners,' yet we are not 'loners' either. We recognize that the meaning of action is far more complex than surface appearances, and we always seek (though rarely with full success) to cut into to the marrow of life's meanings. This is our reverence for mystery. It excludes a rigid commitment to isolation or to communality, for in truth we need both of these and in a healthy, intermixed equilibrium.

What, then, do we believe? What do we teach? What do we espouse? Everything and nothing. We do not insist on any kind of agreement among ourselves. We recognize instinctively one another's marks of mortality, vulnerability, reverence, and play. We make our spiritual home in the hall of Heathenry because it is intuitively right for us to do so; but we readily voyage out from that hall on the back of strong steeds into all kinds of strange other lands. We are neither home nor away; we are the stretching forth of the journey between known and unknown.

We do not insist that everyone be like us. When we can, we try to use our particular perspective to serve our community. Always we try to leave invitations with those we encounter to seek the mystery, to face death with honesty and compassion and humility. Swinging on the gallows is the only sure path to spiritual transformation, a statement which is less one of belief than one of experience. (When asked if he believed in God, Jung replied that he did not need to believe because he *knew* God. This triggered a predictable furor among the many dogmatists who had never faced their mortality).

In our more lucid moments, we do not judge those who cannot or will not own their own mortality or hybridity, who will not or cannot face the enigmas of their own psyches, let alone those of history. We recognize that arrogance causes a closed mind; we try to avoid letting our embrace of mystery become an enantiodromatic tool for the ego to quench our psychic fires. We strive to recall that sometimes our compassion can even be the key that unlocks the doors of perception for the Other (and thus ourselves).

There is a further reason why we try to be conscious of the dangers of arrogance. Although Chaos Heathens cannot help but sense the ironies, hypocrisies, and shallowness of much of 'mainstream' Heathenry (and other things too, of course), this does not make us immune to slipping into the same bad habits. Constant vigilance, humility, and a sense of humor are needed to ensure we do not become the worst hypocrites of all, namely, hypocrites who complain about other hypocrites.

Actually, it is probably impossible to be entirely free of hypocrisy, a further good reason for cultivating healthy senses of irony, humor, and humility. Humility does not have to mean self-abnegation; it just means keeping one's feet on the ground. Chaos Heathens strongly appreciate the earth-based religious aspects of Heathenry, and attempt to apply that grounded worldview psychologically as well as physically and materially.

Given that we consider ourselves rebels against structure, why do we bother with Heathenism at all? Why not just be Chaos Magicians? Chaos Magic made the signature insight that what 'works' in magical practice is true regardless of the belief system involved. Chaos Magicians have successfully shown that made-up spirits and gods can be quite as efficacious and palpable as 'real' ones. So why not cobble together our own idiosyncratic spiritual Frankenstein?

Very simply, we observe that Chaos Magicians almost always end up becoming something else – whether Buddhists, Heathens, or Tantrikas. For whatever reason, we humans need some kind of grounding in a historical structure and –

albeit in a very rickety and contentious way – Heathenry offers that. Furthermore, the forms of religion – myths, rituals, etc. – are useful because they provide a framework for processing the meaning of our experiences, our voyages into the horizon of mystery. Heathenry offers some rich mythic forms to help us navigate our way into mystery's arms as elegantly as we may.

Thus our experience tells us that the parochial modern Heathen illusion of cultural isolation/separation is neither historically sound nor psychologically healthy. We are conscious of the interconnections between different spiritual and cultural milieus. Jung famously traced recurring mythic patterns across many different cultures, and we find the signature images and forces of alchemy to be just as present in Old Norse myths as in ancient Taoist traditions and hoary Egyptian lore. In a sense, Chaos Magic tries to dial direct to this perennial Eros – the KIA! Yet ultimately there is no reliable and reasonably priced hotline to the Great Unknown.

As a Heathen, I am fascinated by alchemy as a spiritual path. Why? It was not always so. I began to have spontaneous experiences that closely paralleled accounts from alchemical texts. Alchemy – which I had always dismissed as charlatanry – suddenly showed itself to be written in my psyche. Then I read Jung's volumes on the subject and realized that I could not ignore alchemy for the sake of being a Heathen. This is Chaos Heathenry in action; we do not deny the numinous simply because it comes to us in an unexpected package.

Yet note that I do not now somehow claim that Heathenry is 'really' alchemy, or vice versa. This is getting away from the *numina* of my personal journey and getting entangled in trying to concoct rules, dogmatic beliefs about mortality and incompleteness. We do our best to avoid this.

In this sense, Chaos Heathenry is entirely *phenomenological* – we take things as themselves and we do not waste time speculating on the irrelevant niceties of dogma. Are the gods real or just figments of our imagination? May as well ask whether *we* are real or just figments of the gods' imaginations! What matters is that they act as though they like to be treated with respect (just like we do). And so that is the phenomenological level at which Chaos Heathens function.

Jung's brilliant colleague, Marie-Louise von Franz, wrote eloquently about why the study of alchemy offers richer psychological insight than even the study of mythology. Her ideas bear quoting at length:

> *Symbolism handed on by [religious] tradition is to a certain extent rationalized and purged of the scurrilities of the unconscious, the funny little details which the unconscious tags on, sometimes contradictions and dirt. That on a small scale, happens even within ourselves...*
>
> *...Whenever a religion seems to be too codified a compensatory sect is usually formed to revivify individual experiences, and this accounts for the many splits [in religious history]...*
>
> *...[In most spiritual traditions that attempt to] approach...the unconscious, conscious direction and a prescribed way, or path, must be conformed to, and certain thoughts which come up ignored. For this reason the symbolism which appears in such forms is not quite of the same kind as that in dreams and active imagination, for we tell people simply to observe what comes up, which naturally produces slightly different material...*
>
> *...The alchemists were in a completely different situation. They believed that they were studying the unknown phenomenon of matter – the details I will give later on – and they just observed what came up and interpreted that somehow, but without any specific plan. There would be a lump of some strange matter, but as they did not know what it was they conjectured something or other, which of course would be unconscious projection, but there was no definite intention or tradition. Therefore one could say that in alchemy, projections were made most naively and unprogrammatically, and completely uncorrected...*

We can see how all of this invites the orientation of Chaos Heathenism. The alchemical tradition allows aberration, deviation, infinite variety and idiosyncrasy. No, it doesn't allow these things. It is these things. There is a definite tradition of rigor (as anyone who has studied the subject can attest), but it is woven from a tradition of dipping into the unknown and embracing whatever it furnishes. This is a posture of profound trust in mystery; and after all, if we are not totally giving ourselves to the unknown then we are not really trusting, we are covertly sliding back into the crutches of dogma and *doxa*.

For Jung, heretical Christian formulations of alchemy were the solution to the problem of the tyrannical imposition of Christ's personal unconscious upon the faithful. For Jung, alchemy could restore the individual expression of the collective unconscious coming through each particular practitioner, reinstating the primacy of the *simultaneous oneness and difference of all things*.

That alchemical formulations of Christ were heretical was not accidental. These idiosyncratic manifestations, so profoundly healing and transformative, were a threat to the supremacy of Christianity as an oppressive socio-political institution. We Chaos Heathens want to make for ourselves a prophylactic against similar forces of spiritual constipation within the Heathen community.

The phenomenological orientation is the antidote to stifling orthodoxy, the insistence on stripping spiritual forms of their numinosity. If we truly accept what our spiritual experiences (and what experiences are not spiritual?) present to us, then we cannot suppress and edit their expression, not without violating our inner sense of right.

As such, Chaos Heathenism adopts the radical position of accepting the mystery that animates even that which seems mundane and familiar. Can we dare to be truly attentive to our experiences, our senses, our relationships? Chaos Heathenism requires us to unlearn so that we can relearn. We cannot be satisfied with the naïve adoption of any kind of spiritual tradition, be it Heathen or any other. No, we are compelled to interrogate that tradition, to let it be a map into strange new worlds, both within and without.

Phenomenology means worshipping the confounding question mark of the everyday. We so easily become habituated to our experience, even to traditions, myths, and deities that we revere. We have to adopt an alchemical approach to our Heathenry in the hopes that we can somehow prevent ourselves from sliding into the unconsidered contempt that mars almost every great spiritual tradition.

For if we are seeking to embrace the open harbor of the question mark, we are doing so to escape the ampersand, the closed coiling loop of *this* and then *that* and then *this* and then *that*. We want to embrace the question mark to pull us out from habituated, complacent routine. The question mark of mystery can save us from the contempt that familiarity breeds for our very life and existence. Yet no mere routine of questioning (no, not even the sciences) can assure us of the question mark, since any routine inevitably slips back into habituation. We have to constantly improvise and create and stumble, and even then there will be long stretches of tranquilized forgetfulness, the illusion that we know who we are and what is going on.

Given the foregoing, we can now return to our initial question: is the world simple or complicated? We are forced to answer that it is *simply mysterious*. And since we are a part of the world, we recognize our own mystery. The divine enigma, the unsayable *Tao*, is just as much within our own constitutions as it is without. For in truth, who may really say where I end and the Other begins?

The collective unconscious objectively exists; in fact, it comprises all of being. We only consider it unconscious, or indeed 'merely psychological,' because we ourselves are lifted up on stilts of ego consciousness; perhaps there is no unconsciousness, just gradations of awareness. Chaos Heathens use the trappings of belief – which so readily disable awareness – as tools to expand both their own perception and the perception of others. How? Through a simple, regular practice of praying every day to be granted with a sense of irony and humor. Or whatever other ideas might come to us when we ask mystery – *Runa* – to give us ideas.

Try it right now! Just say, with all the sincerity you can manage: "*Runa*, please grant me expanding senses of irony and humor." Over time your consistency and patience with this mantra will be rewarded. Feel free to invent your own practices in this vein, since, to borrow an attitude from Jan Fries, it is certain that you can think of better ideas for courting mystery than I can.

In Norse myth, the giant Ymir is slain and dismembered by Odin and his brothers, and the world is made from his corpse. So the whole of this existence is woven from death. And drawn from that one flesh, made many. Why side with either a unitary worldview or a pluralistic one? Chaos Heathens would rather explore the possibilities of liberation regardless of dogmatic formulations.

We have had much to say about incompleteness – in its entwined guises of death and mystery. What about elegance? We consider it an elegant goal to avoid entangling ourselves in dogma. An elegant goal to reject formalization of belief, even though we recognize its inevitability and even its usefulness. We aim for maximum playfulness and we consider play to be far more elegant than dogmatism, arrogance, close-mindedness, or rigidity. We trace ourselves to the spirit of oral literature that animated the original Heathen culture, and therefore we prefer to build new songs on old motifs rather than slavishly and inelegantly memorize the fragmented, ossified remains of our spiritual forebears. This efficiency and creativity is the very essence of elegance.

Chaos Heathenry is an elegant Heathenry that places veneration of mystery at its heart.

Before we move on, one point needs to be addressed. "*Reyn til Runa*," says the Rune Gild; "Seek the Mystery." We applaud this sentiment, yet we do not consider that Edred Thorsson's emphasis on self-deification and isolate intelligence reflects the injunction to seek mystery. Rather, this ego magic orientation is thoroughly suffused with the Christian attempt to suppress the spontaneity of the unconscious. When he received the word *Runa*, Thorsson was given a mandate to honor mystery. That he did not understand that mandate is readily seen in his garbled philosophy of ego masturbation.

In our experience, *we are already divine.* So there is no reason to try to become a god. We emulate Odin because in hanging from the world tree and winning the runes he embraces the limits of his *mortality* in a reverent love affair with mystery; the notion that obsessive power hunger should have a priority in the Odinnic path is absurd. We are aware that for some Rune Gilders, the concept of giving self to self refers to handing the ego over to, or at least tempering it with, the higher self (*id est mysterium*). We applaud this more renegade strain of Rune Gild thought. For if we read the *Rúnatáls þáttr Óðins* poem closely we realize that emulating Odin means seeking to become more *mortal*, and hence sensitive to the mystery of all things. It is this which is the doorway to spiritual and/or magical empowerment and discovery.

More must be said on the shallowness, the lack of ambition, evident in the goal of self-deification. Being as we are foam on *wyrd's* crashing wave, we are already immortal and undying. Only the particular configuration of this ego at this time is lost at death, and who would want to be stuck with just one ego experience for all time? The ego changes radically from moment to moment anyway. So the question is not 'immortality or bust;' it is a question of whether we love mystery enough to embrace variety. We applaud the Gilders who have the deeper, more genuinely mysterious conception of giving self to self, ego to transpersonal light and darkness. For the rest, we hope they will develop the courage to aim a little higher.

Courage and Truth

Truth, like love and sleep, resents
Approaches that are too intense.
– W. H. Auden

So far this essay has consisted of pretty words. To live them is immensely frightening, let us not pretend otherwise! Fear is our companion, for we are compelled to rock the boat, not from malice, but just because we *have* to be ourselves. When we try to pass without trace we risk beginning to go crazy. It is a difficult balance to move between outspokenness and silence.

Perhaps Chaos Heathenry is a matter of temperament. We are driven to search for more depth, more richness, more magic – or more likely, we are less able to ignore the call of mystery that equally plies every human ear, yet which is so often ignored. When we confront the walls of consensus reality – even the idiosyncratic consensus reality of Heathens or occultists – we face difficult dilemmas and often feel out of place. Sometimes we find more spiritual connection with members of other outsider traditions, such as Sufis, than we do with more mainstream Heathens. We are saddened when we see Heathens who are lost in denial of mortality and mystery, Heathenry's very wellsprings.

We need the courage to recognize our own uncertainties, misgivings, and promptings. We realize that often the guidance we receive is at odds with our conscious notions of how things 'should' proceed. It is critical to learn to let go of what we think should be. Chaos Heathens who cling to fixity are not demonstrating the ideal of Chaos Heathenism. Naturally, Chaos Heathens who cling to volatility as a rigid rule are also missing the point. Our touchstone is the *spontaneous heart*, not arbitrary rules. Our challenge is that the heart is not something we have ever been taught how to access or trust.

As such, self-doubt is an almost inevitable part of being a Chaos Heathen. When we find oases of understanding we drink deeply. We prize the elusive deep friendships and connections. In a sense, we are like a hidden gossamer strung through the *wyrd* of modern Western occultism and Heathenism. When we find one another it is a cause of rejoicing.

There is another aspect to the courage that Chaos Heathenry requires, and it is rooted in the call to revere mystery. To explain this idea it is necessary to consider some aspects of the philosophy of Martin Heidegger, specifically his distinction between factuality (*veritas*) and truth (*aletheia*).

At the risk of oversimplifying, for Heidegger the pre-Socratic Ancient Greek conception of truth was remarkably different to what it became in Roman hands and minds, and unfortunately we have inherited the Roman model of truth almost to the complete exclusion of the Greek. Actually, I would argue that the pre-Socratic Greek experience of truth is probably common to many other traditional cultures, including the Heathen cultures.

The Ancient Greek word for truth is *aletheia*, which can be literally rendered as *unconcealing* (*Aletheia* is also a goddess). It expresses truth as a process of unfolding relationships and context between beings. Contrast this with the Roman term for truth, *veritas*, which refers to what we could consider matters of fact; it ignores the crucial questions of context and relationship and tends to be rather epistemologically claustrophobic.

Where *veritas* sees truth as a matter of accurate statements about properties possessed by contextless, disembodied entities (themselves buried in obscurity by the flurry of fact-statements to which they are attached), *aletheia* looks always to context, connections, horizons of uncertainty. It grounds itself in the question mark of an open heart and mind, where *veritas* readily loses itself in the ampersand's endless regress.

As such, *veritas*-truth is based on objectification, and in this it loses its way. There is no such thing as an object; *Being is a verb*, as indeed all nouns truly are. *Aletheia*-truth is animistic, recognizing the sacredness of all and each, whereas *veritas* is always looking for the reduction, the parsing, the impossible equivalence of any two entities. It functions in an 'as if' mentality where the precious, irreducible, nonrepeatable, and fleeting nature of every moment and every place is ruthlessly suppressed.

Technocracy – the instrumentalization of science in the name power-grubbing – is the materially and spiritually destructive offspring of *veritas* when it lacks *aletheia's* balancing touch. Unbalanced *veritas*, so antithetical to Heathenry, is the root of the reductive identity categories used to divide and control, e.g. discrimination along lines of race, (trans-)gender, class, sexuality, religion, etc.

So when do we experience *aletheia*? It is always with us, but covered over by our fact-besotted vision. The matters-of-fact mentality cannot grasp the profound experience we have when exposed to, say, particular music or artwork or words, or a beautiful natural place, or a lively conversation, or a mind-altering fuck, or a mouth-watering meal. It can at best analyze the causal processes of our experience, but the truth of our experiencing relationship remains untouched.

Worse, the *veritas* matter-of-fact mentality cannot touch the causal processes for which we do not already have an intuition; it is this blindness to the so-called 'unknown unknowns' that has lead to disasters like DDT and Glyphosate proliferation, factory-farming, nuclear weapons and meltdowns, human-caused climate change, and a medical community that lags helplessly behind traditional modalities in the treatment of auto-immune and other chronic illnesses. The *veritas* mind is wonderful at producing a result, sometimes a very sophisticated and remarkable result (the dividends of technological modernity). Yet without *aletheian* tempering, we risk destroying ourselves and our planet with these remarkable productions because we cannot intuit/sense/think/feel through their implications and meanings and possibilities on the horizon of mystery.

If this truth of experience is intangible, then it becomes open when we hold space open for it. Thus, says Heidegger, the god cannot be present until we erect the temple in his honor. Only when the *en-closure* is created can an opening exist within it to shelter the becoming of the divine, to *dis-close* its magic to us. In this light, it is worth considering that for the ancient Heathens, semi-cultivated groves and other such locations were considered the most sacred of all settings. Such spaces might be located within the wilds, but by introducing some element of humanity, the closed formation of the world in motion is held open for truth to happen; for us to experience, almost as though for the first time, our sense of connection and meaning with ourselves, with others, and with all things.

The art of Andy Goldsworthy beautifully illustrates the happening of truth; by introducing traces of human intervention into natural environments, Goldsworthy's art resensitizes us to the mysteries of natural beauty that were under our noses all along. Nothing is changed but our awareness of relationships, yet that is everything. *Truth happens*. It unfolds. Like Being, Truth is not a noun. It is the master verb that describes all movements, this whole moving cosmos. If truth, *aletheia*, is literally *unconcealing,* then the necessary condition of its happening is *mystery*, is *RUNA*.

The sacred opening of *aletheia* can thus be found in ritual practice, or a concert hall, or in an alchemist's vessel, or in a psychotherapist's rooms, or in our lover's arms, or in the reverent recitation of the old rune poems. We know that we are close to *aletheia* when we feel a special silence, as though the world were holding its breath in anticipation for whatever might come next. Again, *veritas* thinking might be able to explain the causal processes that enframe and enable the possibility of these moments – but it falls away at the critical moment, and indeed reveals itself as dependent upon such moments of unconcealing for its own generation. To complete the circle, we must wind into *veritas* and then wend our way back to *aletheia's* revelation once more.

This revelation flows from the act of standing out into mystery. This is what Odin is doing when he hangs himself from the world tree. We might suggest that he 'gave truth to Truth,' handed in the tree-besotted, reductive *veritas* vision in exchange for a forest-encompassing, sacralizing *aletheia* moment. To hold open the door of *aletheia* is thus profoundly magical and sacred. It is also very difficult to do because we live in a world that has been powerfully determined by centuries of '*veritas* or bust' thinking and doing.

Mortality, reverence for mystery, elegance – they find their apogee in these moments of clearing and illuminating, these moments when unconcealing emerges from the crowded panoply of the 'ten thousand things.' *This* is what Chaos Heathenry seeks to invoke. It is the sacred opening, and it goes beyond religion or indeed humanity at all. It is literally the moment of truth.

Yet over the centuries – and especially thanks to a *veritas*-based Christian influence on world history – it has become harder and harder to speak of the irruption of *aletheia* without sounding like a sentimental fool. The more self-evident the status quo becomes, the more total and obscuring its stance of denial becomes. Only the experience of opening into mystery can rescue us. Without that experience, religious forms become merely another shackle, another psychic straightjacket cutting us from ourselves and from the worlds of possible experience.

Trying to talk about *aletheia* in this *veritas*-soaked world is very difficult. It is an inherently slippery concept at the best of times; we might say the goddess of truth is shy and retiring to a fault. Worse, modern Western culture makes, in general, only the most vestigial gestures to assuring openings for *aletheia*. Even art and religion have been broadly recruited to the service of avarice and ideology and often offer little capacity for helping us to experience mysterious unconcealings into truth.

As such, it takes tremendous courage to hold out for something so evanescent, so intangible – even though once it comes, its power is undeniable and can totally reshape one's world. Chaos Heathens are irreverent towards the formalisms of consensus belief (be it Heathen, Christian, or anything else) because they are guided by an intuition for a deeper reverence – for mystery.

It hurts us to see the way that mythology in particular is used to bury the experience of *aletheia*. This burying is rarely done intentionally – it comes from ignorance, an ignorance cemented by so many centuries of the abandonment of *aletheia*. Consider Marie-Lousie von Franz's comments quoted above to the effect that mythology often leads us to ignore or edit our spiritual expression in order to make it fit a received template. Because the invocation of *aletheia* requires vulnerability, Chaos Heathens are constantly forced to expose themselves if they wish to do battle with the sway of *veritas* over their fellow humanity – and within themselves.

In a sense, then, Chaos Heathens are profoundly opposed to instrumentalism – even as they embrace the instrumental philosophy of Chaos Magic (*enantiodromia* again). The point of Chaos Magic is to show that it is practice, not belief, that matters; that opening into the mystery of truthful experience is more important than dogma or articles of magical faith. Chaos Magic uses the weapons of instrumentalism against instrumentalism. Chaos Heathenism takes that value over into a profoundly anti-technocratic direction. It upholds reverence before cynicism and wonder before calculativeness.

And this is courage. It is courage to question. It is courage to ask those who fear mystery to embrace it – especially because that fear is born from a secret, inchoate longing that sings mournfully into the long dark night of repressed unconscious contents. Chaos Heathens like to hope that modern Heathenry, as a nascent tradition, does not get unwittingly built on the same *veritas*-soaked foundations upon which both Christianity and technocratic modernity rest. We do what we can to contribute positively in that direction.

Most of all, we need courage to root out these foundations within *ourselves*. Always the work and play has to be done *within*. Otherwise we slip into the demonization of a constructed Other, and again we are entangled in the historical and psychological wreckage of dualistic Christianity. Whatever else it is, Chaos Heathenry is a process of inner alchemy. Not with the goal of immortality or power or any other such foolish illusions. With the goal of making ourselves fitting vessels for mystery, allowing ourselves the vulnerability of openness.

Such vulnerability is attacked at every turn in most settings. Human beings deeply fear vulnerability, even as they crave it. As such, even traditions such as Chaos Magic can potentially lapse into dogma and *doxa*. We especially need to be careful not to slip into lazy hatred for dualistic monotheism, antithetical as it mostly seems to our perspective. It takes tremendous courage to not lose our tenuous grip on *aletheia*, receding constantly as she does. Chaos Heathenry is not an easy calling, but those that feel its call cannot do other than pay heed, even if we fumble and fail at least as often as we succeed.

Perhaps a beautiful demonstration of Chaos Heathenish courage to hold out into the mystery of *aletheia* may be discovered in the *Poetic Edda*, specifically in the lay called *Vafthrudnismal*.

Vafthrudnismal and the Well

In the Old Norse poem *Vafthrudnismal* Odin seeks out the wise giant Vafthrudnir to find out whether "if in wisdom my like the all-wise etin [giant] be." To appreciate Odin's motivation, it is worth reflecting on the complex relationship that seems to hold between the gods and the giants in Norse mythology. At a surface glance, this relationship is one of simple, unremitting enmity; Thor in particular is the bane of the giants, and many of the myths feature his conflicts with them.

Yet the relationship is more complex than this simple good/evil, us/them picture (a picture that we are set up to uncritically adopt as denizens of a post-Christian, technocratic world). When we examine the genealogies of the gods we discover that many of them have giant ancestors, from Odin on down. Indeed, Thor, that implacable giant-slayer, is himself of giant stock, having Odin as his father and the giantess Jord (Earth) as his mother!

So it seems that gods and giants do not differ along genealogical or biological lines. Nonetheless, there is a clear qualitative difference between these estranged families. *Vafthrudnismal* offers an evocative demonstration of where this difference lies.

Vafthrudnir is renowned for his wisdom and knowledge. Odin, in disguise, visits Vafthrudnir in his hall to challenge him to a battle of knowledge. First, Vafthrudnir tests Odin's worthiness with a battery of questions about Norse cosmology. Once satisfied that his foe is a strong challenger, Vafthrudnir consents to the battle of wits, with decapitation as the price of defeat.

Thus does Odin pose his questions, testing Vafthrudnir's knowledge of the universe's creation, denizens, geography, history, and predicted demise. To every question Vafthrudnir has the answer; his wisdom is the wisdom of things, people, places, events, unfolding events on *wyrd's* stage. His knowledge is encyclopedic.

Nonetheless, there is one question Odin can ask to which Vafthrudnir cannot know the answer. The question is: what did Odin whisper into his dead son Baldr's ear as the latter lay on his funeral bier? Mythology does not tell us what Odin's words were, and Vafthrudnir does not know them either. In a flash he realizes both that his knowledge has been overmatched, and that he has been unwittingly battling Odin the whole time. We can presume that Vafthrudnir loses his head shortly thereafter.

At one level we could say that Odin's victory lies merely in underhand tactics, but there is so much more to it than this. Odin's wisdom lies ultimately in a sensitivity to context, boundaries, and meaning, whereas Vafthrudnir's lies in raw volume of factual information. Where Vafthrudnir is a master of *veritas* thinking, Odin's power lies in a sensitivity to the ebb and flow of *aletheia*. As such, he never becomes lost in the rhythmic exchange of their word battle, nor loses sight of the bigger context in which it unfolds.

Odin is able to remain aware of the implicit interpersonal contracts that contain and articulate his exchange with Vafthrudnir. This in turn attunes him to a different kind of knowledge than Vafthrudnir's. For the latter is knowledgeable of things that anyone could know, knowledge that is in essence public, even if some of it is obscure. Whereas Odin has a sense of the meaning of subjective knowing, of relational knowing, and thus is able to deploy a question that cannot be publically known for the simple reason that only he and Baldr share it. It is conditioned by a relationship; it is not a property that inheres in an object.

In a sense, Vafthrudnir has become habituated to a certain way of experiencing the world and a certain theory of knowledge, namely that of attributed fact, of *veritas*. Whereas Odin remains sensitive to truth as an unfolding relationship or process, and thus is able to step out of the implicitly agreed domain of attributed fact to pose a question that is *qualitatively* beyond Vafthrudnir's body of factual knowledge. Out of his depth, Vafthudnir has no *aletheian* skill of empathy with which to intuit the shape of Odin's grief at his son's passing.

Where Vafthrudnir has built his castle of belief upon dogmatic metaphysical assumptions that have obscured his sight of how these might warp his worldview, Odin remains able to disassemble and reassemble his truth-relationship as need dictates, thus remaining open to multiple/new perspectives and the possibilities of the unknown.

One way of reading the actions of the giants, both in Norse myth and more generally in Indo-European mythologies, is that they close down possibilities. They are greedy; they want to capture, control, suffocate the forces of spontaneity, eroticism, magic, inspiration. Thus several Norse myths revolve around giantish attempts to kidnap the goddess Freyja, that peerless font of inspired, erotic, magical spontaneity. Thus the mead of inspiration is stolen by the giant Suttung, who secretes it away in his mountain dwelling, withholding its power from the world. Odin is obliged to use magic and trickery to liberate it (see the chapter "Chaos Heathen Results Magic" for more on this).

We might suggest, therefore, that where the gods are driven by a liberatory spirit, a passion for life, discovery, and the unknown, the giants wish to assert autocratic control over anything unpredictable, chaotic, inspired, or impassioned. They cannot see a way to use such powers, but they will do all they can to bury them, to petrify them. In this reading, the giants have a similar role to that of modern technocracy, the attempt to reduce nature and human beings to units of calculable and hierarchical utility for the convenience of a tiny power elite. The giants, in the thrall of truth as *veritas*, are obsessed with objectification; hence Vafthrudnir's (ultimately useless) encyclopedic knowledge of matters of fact.

The more that the giants attempt to build their arrogant edifices of fact on foundations of suppressed life-spontaneity, the less they are able to appreciate the value of that spontaneous, erotic magic. In contrast, Odin is constantly engaged in a process of disassembling, letting go, dismantling, shedding. Belief becomes a straightjacket; familiarity with the everyday trappings of our living breeds contempt for the kernels of magic that shine in all things. Odin's obsession with death magic is an obsession with tearing away the constantly accreting armor of complacency, the constant temptation to deny the supremacy of mystery (*Runa!*) in favor of constructing elaborate but brittle social constructions of control.

Herein lies the essence of Chaos Heathenry: we seek the ever-elusive spirit of spontaneity, of inspired life. We strive ever to resist the natural and inevitable hardening of belief and expectation that the giants so thoroughly exemplify. There is nothing inherently wrong with the giantish *veritas*-based approach to life, and it certainly has a necessary role and value. However, like the giants it can easily become a greedy usurper, one that ironically destroys its erotic *aletheian* cousin in its attempts to colonize, conquer, and claim. Thus the gods must ever strive to unpick the threads of *wyrd* that their giantish kin sew. The nine worlds are suspended constantly in this tenuous balance, and Midgard not the least.

Spiritual traditions are born from the spark of creative spontaneity, what we might call divine inspiration, yet they all too readily prohibit their followers from tracing that spark in their own individual experience. Consider for example the early Christian suppression of Gnosticism, or the antipathy that fundamentalist Islam tends to hold towards Sufism. These magical currents are the wellspring of formal religious and cultural formations, yet they also threaten those formations with promises of change and new revelation, and these threats are hypocritically suppressed.

Chaos Magic correctly intuited this problem, and thus sought to do away with the content of belief, preserving only the structure and process of belief and insisting that this is sufficient. Yet this calculated rejection of *veritas* in favor of something approaching *aletheia* seems to falter and fail in the long run. It remains lop-sided; *veritas* may constantly try to suppress its *aletheian* origin, yet its forms and narratives also provide both raw material for *alethian* expression and structure for the spiritual explorer.

Thus Chaos Heathenism comes forth as the logical union of obsession with living magic and appreciation for traditional form. We try to cultivate a life in which magic is found in all that we encounter; we immanentize the occult into the everyday. We strive to remain forever open-eyed, innocent, awed by what others dismiss as trivial, self-evident, routine, banal. The cynical, grey-minded attitude is that of the giants, hardening into the stone of their mountain homes. When this cynicism becomes overly ascendant, the individual becomes enslaved to faith in the illusion of temporal power, internalizing narcissistic ambition and/or self-contempt. Their true life-force becomes buried, dormant, suppressed, denied, choked. This environment in turn enables the possibility of the rise of the 'staunch Heathen' who has all the spiritual depth of a shopping cart or a corporate billboard or a self-righteous, jingoistic slogan.

This is the dilemma of many millions of modern humans; technocratic modernity has, more than in any other epoch, waged a systematic war against the well-spring of *aletheian* truth that makes life worth living by remaking the old as new. Chaos Heathens acknowledge that we are just as vulnerable to this complacency, this reductive, stodgy, miserly contempt for life, as anyone else. What distinguishes us is that we are aware of the problem and strive to forge balance between the extremes so that our spirits are not crushed, but rather are sheltered and nurtured even by those commitments to *veritas* that we cannot abandon.

Robert Johnson (the Jungian psychologist, not the blues maestro) relates in his lovely book, *Owning Your Own Shadow*, a story that he in turn received from Jung. This story bears repeating here because it so elegantly expresses the foregoing notions:

> *The water of life, wishing to make itself known on the face of the earth, bubbled up in an artesian well and flowed without effort or limit. People came to drink of the magic water and were nourished by it, since it was so clean and pure and invigorating.*
>
> *But humankind was not content to leave things in this pristine state. Gradually they began to fence the well, charge admission, claim ownership of the property around it, make elaborate laws as to who could come to the well, put locks on the gates. Soon the well was the property of the powerful and the elite.*

The water was angry and offended; it stopped flowing and began to bubble up in another place. The people who owned the property around the first well were so engrossed in their power systems and ownership that they did not notice that the water had vanished. They continued selling the nonexistent water, and few people noticed that the true power was gone.

But some dissatisfied people searched with great courage and found the new artesian well. Soon the well was under the control of the property owners, and the same fate overtook it. The spring took itself to yet another place – and this has been going on throughout recorded history.

Modern Heathenry is very vulnerable to replicating this tragic story, even though its mythology is clearly (on the Chaos Heathen reading presented here at least) a parable warning us against enslaving ourselves to forgetful, contemptuous *veritas* thinking, untempered by its *aletheian* sibling. The root of Heathen cosmology is the Well of *Wyrd*, the repository of time, the dynamic vessel of all possibilities. Yet, buried so deeply in the post-Christian technocratic/modern worldview into which we have been flung, we modern Heathens are at terrible risk of blundering right past the invocation of life-spirit that is the heart of the old Heathen traditions.

Thus we Chaos Heathens tend to be wary of those who want to set hard rules about what Heathenry must be. The rigid, brittle impositions of reconstructionism (trying to base modern Heathenism on historical data) and folkism (the view that Heathenism should be ethnically exclusive in one form or another) concern us because these approaches are so quick to impose absolute (and often, ironically, anachronistic) rules onto complex and ambiguous realities.

This does not mean we do not respect reconstructionism when used to furnish new surprises, discoveries, and wonders (as opposed to being used as an excuse to bully and suppress inspiration). Indeed, we regard it as an essential source of inspiration. This does not mean that we deny the power of ancestral connectedness, however we understand (and appreciate!) that our ancestors had a much more open-ended, cloudy sense of ethnicity than this cynical post-colonial modernity with its insistence on arbitrary barriers and hierarchies of oppression; like the ancestors, we feel no compulsion to conflate ancestry with biology; we recognize the (ironically) historical and political contingency of appeals to essentialism.

It does mean that we stand in opposition to all forms of righteousness, pomposity, arrogance, and above all the desire to assert possessive control over the forms of Heathen tradition. We stand against these first and foremost in ourselves, because we are willing to accept Johnson's challenge to own our own shadows. We constantly make mistakes, and we discover in this process that our shadows often hide vast and exquisite hoards of gold.

Yet we also stand against these forces in others because we recognize these forces as noxious imports from Christianity and from technocratic modernity, that is, the very same forces that crushed the original Heathenry. Our irreverence for human opinion flows from the wellspring of our reverence for the spirit – the flowing water – that moves in all things, that *is* all there is.

We can imagine that when Odin decapitates Vafthrudnir, the torrents of blood spark new life wherever they fall. Long dormant dreams, forbidden thoughts and feelings, radical revisionings, lateral insights, exuberant passions all burst forth, roaring with ecstasy. Everywhere the blood falls, flowers spontaneously bloom, new species are born, dead things resurrect. It is no accident, perhaps, that one of the mythic accounts of the creation of the mead of inspiration is that it is brewed from the blood of dwarves (another mythic species that seem to love to suppress *aletheia* within thick walls of *veritas*, though heroes such as Sigurd seem able to liberate these buried treasures). It is also no accident that in Norse myth there are multiple, contradictory, accounts for the origin of the mead of inspiration!

Perhaps when Odin consults with the mummified head of the giant Mimir (memory) he is using necromancy precisely as a tool to release the flow of life force. It is evident that the old Heathens appreciated the reciprocal, cyclical relationship of death and life, of mystery and certainty, of unknown and known. They were masters of *enantiodromia*, and the remnants of their mythology are no less than doors into their psychological and spiritual wisdom. Only so long as we are dismantling the seductions of *veritas* as an *exclusive* basis for life – only so long as we understand irreverence as the fitting servant of reverence – can we truly be nourished by the flowing waters of Heathenry. Thus we are compelled to call ourselves Chaos Heathens.

Elhaz Ablaze

Chaos Heathenism first emerged from the writings of a group who call themselves the Elhaz Fellowship and who for some years now have run a website called *Elhaz Ablaze*. Said website continues to be a storehouse of ideas, experiments, experiences, and questions. The phrase *Elhaz Ablaze* is thus integral to Chaos Heathenism, and the image it conjures is worth elucidating.

The "Anglo-Saxon Rune Poem" stanza for ᛉ Elhaz (Eohls) alludes to blades of tough grass growing up at the edges of marshland, which can cut the unwary if they try to push through ("sedges have edges" – Nikki Wyrd). Marshlands were sacred to the old Heathens, who regularly left significant offerings in bogs and swamps. We can surmise that these regions, being neither land nor sea, were regarded as liminal, magical places where the tragicomedy of *enantiodromia* could come into dynamic equilibrium.

Such places therefore represent openings into vulnerability, wonder, discovery. They are dangerous to oppressive cultural formations because they facilitate individuals' direct revelatory experience of mystery. Chaos Heathens are dedicated to seeking out, preserving, opening, protecting, invoking these kinds of liminal places, times, modes of consciousness. Not only for ourselves but for our communities, indeed for all that lives (and all things live).

Yet we recognize that these liminal ᛉ Elhaz openings are a risk to pursue. They can be abused and destroyed, like wells around which despotic edifices might be built. When we hold open space for liminality we may be attacked by those who, like some giants, are enthralled by *veritas*, by its avarice for magic that it cannot appreciate (and which it ultimately fears, resents, and repels).

Thus, we must also invoke the elk-sedge, the protective grasses that deter intruders from entering the sacred wetlands. We must cultivate an understanding of the history, assumptions, and machinations of reductive contemporary thinking, its roots in Christian dualism, Roman cynicism, and objectifying technocracy. We need to find ways of letting our connection to the liminal wetlands, the places where the spring of life wells up, inform our words and deeds without showing our spiritual hands and ruining our ability to gamble at the table of existence. We need to cultivate appreciation for the traditions and histories of Heathenry so that we have adequate way-houses on our journeys into mystery.

If we cannot achieve this balance of both protection and openness then we risk falling into dissociation, that arch-fiend of modernity. If we cannot connect our spiritual intuition to our actions and decisions then we become hypocrites, and worse, run the risk of being torn to pieces or of having our inner beings reduced to vacuums. *Aletheia's* liminal charms cannot be imposed like the battering ram of revealed truth or linear ideology; rather we must become adept at leaving trails of hints, at offering invitations to something more, and we must learn to accept even the inevitable times when those around us (and indeed, we ourselves) cannot or will not respond to the promise of a spiritual perspective both alien and deeply familiar.

We set the ᛉ Elhaz rune ablaze to mark our consciousness of death, of the inevitable passing of all things. We strive to accept our fear of death where others' denial plunges them into the arms of untempered *veritas*-mind. Elhaz is symbolic of death as well as of life, and so we know that the burning of the old clears the way for new life to emerge. Thus *Elhaz Ablaze* is an elegant, if incomplete, expression of our reverence for the fleeting, poignant, ironic, tragic, and comedic mystery that each of us finds ourselves inexplicably navigating.

Odin says (more or less) that, in the wake of his inspired passion:

> *One word led to another word;*
> *One poem led to another poem.*

Rilke advises us to "be patient toward all that is unsolved in your heart and try to love the questions themselves, like locked rooms and like books that are now written in a very foreign tongue. Do not now seek the answers, which cannot be given to you because you would not be able to live them. And the point is, to live everything. Live the questions now. Perhaps you will then gradually, without noticing it, live along some distant day into the answer." Thus he declared himself the ampersand's foe and the question mark's friend.

Chaos Heathenry humbly entreats the same. Gods and Mortals, World and Earth ("For I love you, Oh *Quarternity*," Nietzsche redeemed by Jung, fading undertones of Heidegger and an exciting horizon of Alan Watts) let us find our place in the elusive center, the shifting heart. The Heart. The Essence, which is Mystery. We invoke:

Chaos Heathenry: Incompleteness & Elegance ~ Heimlich A. Laguz

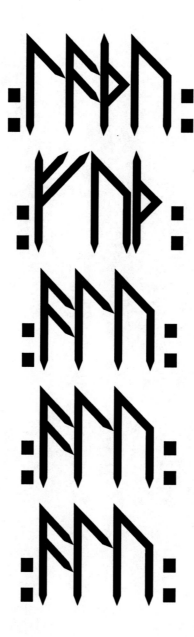

ForestFaceFallson, MichaELFallson

Kalos Sthenos
Klintr O'DubhGhaill

There is an ancient, Indo-European tradition of physical culture that goes back to before the beginning of written history. Yoga is a surviving example of this tradition, as is Olympic Gymnastics. Weightlifting, Kettlebell Lifting, and most of the Track & Field sports are also descended from the same original athletic program. Strongman competitions and events like the Highland Games are, perhaps, even more primal examples of the tradition. The Western Martial Arts – Boxing, Wrestling, and Fencing – all have ancient Indo-European roots.

Of course, most of these activities are not exclusively Indo-European. Many cultures have developed independent traditions of Boxing and almost all have some kind of Wrestling and Fencing. Most populations have developed their own forms of Dance and Gymnastics but the Indo-Europeans have always had a special love of sport and their Physical Culture has distinctive features which are noticeably different from Chinese or African traditions. In this essay, though, I'm going to focus on painting a picture of what Indo-European Physical Culture is, rather than worrying too much about what it isn't or how it differs from other traditions.

The ancient core of Indo-European Physical Culture is bodyweight strength training. At first glance, Hindu Yoga and Olympic Gymnastics seem to be worlds apart, but if you compare the basic postures and beginning exercises, the connection soon becomes more obvious. Yoga is relatively slow, static, and meditative. Gymnastics is fast, dynamic, and competitive. Look at still photos of Gymnasts and Yoga practitioners working out, though, and you'll see that the same positions appear again and again.

Calisthenics, pure bodyweight strength training, is the ideal compromise between Yoga and Gymnastics. Neither purely meditative nor necessarily competitive, Calisthenics can be both...or either. Calisthenics can be a home workout program, a sport, or a key part of daily religious practice.

With a simple course in basic Calisthenics it is possible to develop a very solid foundation of all around fitness, including strength, endurance, coordination, and flexibility. Note that the term Calisthenics actually comes to us from the

Ancient Greek *Kalos Sthenos*, meaning "Beautiful Strength." This is a highly appropriate name for the discipline, since bodyweight-based strength training tends to produce bodies that are lean, hard, and aesthetically pleasing; with not much fat and just the right amount of muscle.

In Persia and India, as in Greece, we find ample evidence for ancient bodyweight training systems. When Westerners think of Hindu exercise programs, they usually just think of Hatha Yoga. What they don't know is that many Persians and Indians continue to practice a very ancient and traditional strength training program. This system, usually associated with Wrestlers, is based primarily around two basic Calisthenic exercises; the dive-bomber push-up and bodyweight squat. The full program also includes club swinging, weight-lifting, rope-climbing, running, and (of course) Wrestling – but the push-ups and squats are the foundation of everything.

Quite possibly, this Eastern tradition provides us with the most direct insight into what the primal Proto-Indo-European Physical Culture might have looked like. The Western branch of this tradition tends to put more emphasis on pull-ups, push-ups, and running (rather than dive-bombers and squats) but it's easy to see that the core principles have always been the same. As we look back in time, throughout history and across Indo-Europa, we see many variations of pull-ups, push-ups, running, and bodyweight squats. Those are the basic exercises that most likely made up the core of Ancient Indo-European Calisthenics.

Walking and Running are the most primal and most natural exercises available to humans. Both are excellent for developing endurance in the legs, the heart, and the lungs. Taken alone, however, a pure program of walking or running is not a complete solution for physical fitness. Too much endurance work, repeated through a limited range of motion, can make the muscles tight and immobile. The heart and lungs are strengthened but the arms and shoulders receive almost no stimulation at all. Running alone, especially for distance, builds bodies that are lean and wiry but weak and fragile. Running combined with the basic Calisthenics exercises, however, provides for an almost perfect foundation of all-around strength and endurance. Pull-ups and push-ups develop the arms, chest, shoulders, and back. Squatting develops leg strength and flexibility, while running emphasizes endurance. Pull-ups, push-ups, running, and squats – when taken in combination – build a body that is lean and muscular, strong, and enduring. This combination also happens to be just about perfect for anyone entering military service or seeking to learn a martial art.

Once the basic foundation has been laid, a little more individual specialization becomes possible. Some people prefer to train for more endurance, others like more strength, and a small minority will always prefer to focus on coordination or flexibility. All of these choices are totally valid but most modern experts will tell you that increasing strength is the quickest way to improve all other aspects of fitness. The Western tradition (at least since the age of the ancient Greeks) has always emphasized strength.

Besides Calisthenics, the most ancient forms of strength training currently available to us are Olympic Weightlifting and Russian Kettlebell Lifting. Both of these traditions are basically concerned with the same thing; picking heavy things up off the ground and lifting them overhead to full arm extension. Olympic Weightlifting is focused on maximum weight for single repetitions, though multiple reps and sets are used in training. Kettlebell Lifting tends to emphasize more moderate weights, done for many repetitions, using a variety of one handed and two handed lifts. Kettlebell Lifting is also actually the older of the two forms, with variants having been practiced all the way from Gaul to the Middle Kingdom. Going deeper into history, however, we find evidence for even more primal forms of strength training.

The Greeks, in addition to their love of Calisthenics, used to practice lifting heavy stones overhead. As primitive as this method seems, some of them appear to have become unbelievably strong doing so. At Olympia, for example, a 143.5kg lifting stone has been found that dates back to the 6th Century BCE. This stone has a handgrip carved into one side and an inscription that reads "Bybon, son of Phola, lifted me overhead with one hand."

Modern Hindu wrestlers continue to lift carved stone weights that they sometimes use like kettlebells and sometimes more like barbells or dumbbells. Regardless of whether you choose to lift barbells, dumbbells, kettlebells, sandbags, barrels, big rocks, or any combination of the above, a program built around the concept of picking up heavy things and lifting them overhead, when combined with basic Calisthenics or Gymnastics, will deliver an unbeatable combination of real-world strength, conditioning, agility, and explosive power. The ancient Indo-Europeans, it appears, working without access modern equipment, had already invented Functional Training several thousand years before CrossFit became a fitness industry buzzword.

The Hindu Wrestlers also practice swinging massive, oversized clubs as an integral part of their strength training. The Roman Legions used to train their troops with double-weighted wooden swords, so that their real weapons would feel light on the day of battle. This idea is certainly not exclusive to the Indo-Europeans (for example, both Japanese and Filipino martial artists do something similar) but it is an extremely effective way of developing grip strength, shoulder mobility, and explosive, full body power.

Fencing and Stick Fighting have been paired since antiquity, with Stick Fighting serving double duty as a preparation for Fencing and as a martial art in its own right. Alexander the Great preferred that his troops learn Stick Fighting, rather than the unarmed combat sports. Much later the English became famous for their skill with Quarter Staff, as were the Irish for their Cudgels. Fencing and Stick Fighting were also often combined with Boxing (Fencing with the Fists) and Wrestling (which sometimes included striking). Many Medieval and Renaissance 'Schools of Defence' taught a complete program, including both unarmed combat and the use of a variety of weapons.

Boxing, Wrestling, and *Pankration* were among the events at the original Greek Olympic Games, though the Greeks also practiced a specialized form of battlefield unarmed combat (known as *Pammachon*) in addition to the combat sports. The Romans learned *Pankration* and *Pammachon* from the Greeks. Their Legions taught these arts to German mercenaries in the North, who eventually mixed them with their native styles of Wrestling to form the medieval martial art called *Kampfringen* (Combat Wrestling). Centuries later, scholars would discover Dark Age unarmed combat manuals and wonder "Who taught *Jujutsu* to the Medieval Germans?"

Rope climbing, like club swinging, is an ancient form of grip training and an explosive, full-body power exercise. Rope climbing used to be an event in Olympic Gymnastics but is now virtually forgotten as an exercise except among the Military, Mixed Martial Artists, and elite level Wrestlers. Sprinting and Dancing in armour were two more events at the early Greek Olympic Games. Leaping, vaulting, jumping, flipping, hand balancing, and a variety of other Calisthenics/Gymnastic exercises – practiced both with and without armour – were included in the training of knights throughout the European medieval period.

Lifting and throwing heavy stones was also a part of both Classical and Medieval physical training systems. The shot put, discus, hammer throw, and javelin are all ancient Indo-European martial sports that develop full body explosive power with practical martial applications. Axe throwing and knife throwing still have a small, dedicated cult following. The game of Darts, such an innocuous pub sport, is actually the ancient Indo-European equivalent of *Shuriken-Jutsu*.

Archery, like its linear descendant Shooting, is generally not thought of as requiring much physical fitness. Prior to the invention of the compound bow, however, archery required significant physical strength. The usage of modern firearms in actual combat applications, likewise, is a much more physically demanding skill than most people realize. Military PT is so arduous, in part, because of the high levels of strength, agility, and anaerobic endurance required to move effectively in a gunfight.

Of course, there are also plenty of physical games and sports that have no immediately obvious military application. Most of the really old sports, however, seem to be focused on testing and developing physical toughness, courage, self-discipline, and teamwork...all essential martial virtues. Indo-European Physical Culture developed and evolved during a much harsher period of human history. The primary goals were always physical dominance and survival, hence the emphasis on competition and struggle rather than long-term health or pure aesthetic development.

For a modern Pagan wanting to become more in-touch with their own body, the ancient well of Indo-European Physical Culture holds deep resources. Begin with a course in basic Calisthenics, knowing that every push-up you perform is a prayer to your ancestors. There are millions who have come before you and performed these movements. Every pull-up, every push-up, and every squat is a prayer, a sacrifice, and a ritual unto itself. When you run a mile, you are following in the footsteps of your ancestors. When you press a weight overhead, you are demonstrating strength in the ancient way. When you Box or Wrestle, swing a stick or loose an arrow, you are participating in some the oldest Martial Arts known. If you choose to test yourself through competition, know that you are taking part in an ancient ritual. The competitor makes themselves stronger, helps their opponents become stronger and, hopefully, encourages the tribe as a whole to grow stronger as well.

Happy Hound, MichaELFallson

Beyond Belief: Toward a Dogma-Free, Rational Heathenism

Sweyn Plowright

I slept with faith and found a corpse in my arms on awakening; I drank and danced all night with doubt and found her a virgin in the morning.
– Aleister Crowley

In setting off on the Heathen journey, most of us started with some ideas and books pointing us in the direction of some kind of Norse-flavoured Wicca. Soon we met some real Asatruar, who exposed the fantasy concoctions and introduced us to more 'authentic,' fully Nordic systems based on Germanic Mythology and literature.

After a while we became familiar with the sources and methods of the reconstruction of Heathenism, and realised that even the oldest literature was largely secondhand hearsay. Very little of the actual Heathen religion was recorded anywhere, and those fragments come from specific times and places within a period of centuries, and spanning an area of thousands of square kilometres. One thing is certain: folk religion is extremely diverse and variable from town to town, and generation to generation. Worse than this, we discover that many groups idolise the 19th-century nationalist romanticism, in which the mythology was moulded to political ends. The reconstructionist effort had invented or borrowed elements to fill in the gaps. Some groups set out to formalise their newly invented systems to create 'churches' that would be recognised by governments.

Despite all this, we can go to the early sources and see the reflection of a rich and glorious Heathen past. Thanks to Tacitus, ibn Fadlān, Sturlusson, and some Christian scribes, as well as modern archaeology, we have a good sampling of tales and information from our Heathen heritage. These form enough of a common foundation to provide a mythical language with which to commune with our ancestors, build our own Practical Heathenism, and come together with others on the path.

Throughout this journey so far, we would have been hearing about 'religion,' 'tradition,' and 'belief system' as terms used fairly interchangeably. How we approach this will be a very individual thing. Most of us have absorbed a concept of religion as something that includes an authority, rituals, and central dogmas or beliefs. We define tradition as something that has been happening for a very long time. 'Belief system' is a catch-all commonly applied to any form of spiritual path.

Very seldom is the role of belief examined. If we are surrounded by Abrahamic religions we may assume, as they do, that belief is the defining and essential component of religion. If we have looked more widely, we will see that this assumption is not universally held, and was not by our Heathen ancestors.

> *The general picture of religious observance throughout the year, and of individual cults of the gods, is one that holds together reasonably well. Moreover, the evidence from Germanic and that from Celtic sources has a good deal in common. It was hardly a demanding faith with stern requirements from those who practised it, in either statements of belief or the faithful following of ritual. We are not likely to hear of converts to this kind of religion; rather, the ritual was there for those who desired to take part in it, and there was no inbuilt hostility towards other forms of belief and practice. It may be seen as providing a framework holding the community together, by regular feasts.*

– H. R. E. Davidson, *The Lost Beliefs of Northern Europe*

As unimportant as belief was then, it is even less important now. If modern educated humans were to believe literally in fairy tales...well actually, we only have to look at religious fundamentalism in recent years, and the lunacy of fanatics, to see that the experiment has already yielded irrefutable results.

> *I don't believe anyone believes in a one-eyed man who is riding about on a horse with eight feet...we see the stories as poetic metaphors and a manifestation of the forces of nature and human psychology.*

– Hilmar Örn Hilmarsson, high priest of *Ásatrúarfélagið* Iceland

Belief, far from being an essential component of religion, is in fact its most deadly poison. To understand this, we must first consider what we mean by 'belief.'

The common usage is that beliefs are convictions that are held without regard to evidence. They are usually synonymous with 'faith,' as things beyond the reach of logic. They are usually taken as assertions meant to be accepted without foundation.

However, in some areas of philosophy, particularly logic, a reasonable belief is defined as the conclusion of a valid argument, with true premises, or at least supported by evidence. Without some training, it is not easy for many people to evaluate the validity of arguments, or the truth of premises, so for them beliefs are things they choose for other reasons.

Different people have different ways of approaching the world. In some quarters, those with a naturally more logical mind are disparagingly dismissed as 'rationalists' and presumed forever barred from the spiritual experience. This not only smacks of bigotry, it is demonstrably untrue. We need only look at various schools of Buddhism that are both highly rational and spiritual.

Now, having the benefit of education, and the knowledge that ancient Heathenism never placed belief as a pre-requisite, modern Heathenism looks like an excellent platform for a belief-free religion. More than that, it can be argued that such an expression of Heathenism is a natural progression of our ancient heritage. The question many will now be asking is: how we can reconcile Heathenism with the modern world? Is it possible to have 'Rational Heathenism?'

There has been much discussion in recent years of the negative aspects of the modern world. The very word 'modernity' has acquired an almost derogatory connotation in some quarters. But what do we mean by 'modern?' There are many variations, but essentially we understand it to mean the cultural current revolving around the technological progress following the 'Age of Reason' or 'the Enlightenment,' usually described as beginning roughly around three centuries ago.

There are also many variations in the way we define 'Germanic Heathenism,' but we can broadly agree that it involves seeking spiritual fulfilment in the traditions and literature of our Germanic ancestors. The question now is whether these two forces are compatible. At the risk of sounding heretical to some, I would argue that they are not only compatible, but that modernity is in fact the most successful lineage of our ancestral culture.

Certainly, there are many things we can criticize in the modern world, but by rejecting it wholesale, we not only risk throwing the baby out with the bathwater, we also neglect our opportunity and responsibility to influence this world. We need to separate the positive key features of the Enlightenment plan from the commercialism, greed, and acculturation that has become a common, but not a necessary, concomitant of modern life.

The important elemental seeds of modernity can be found in the migration of Angles and Saxons to Britain. They brought with them their Heathen Common Law. This treasure of Germanic culture encapsulated the Heathen respect for custom, fairness, and the rights of individuals. Common Law was based on precedent, the accumulated wisdom of previous rulings, which could take local custom into account, while allowing judgments to evolve over time as customs and values changed.

If we look at Roman Civil Law, we find that its focus is on protecting the State and the privileges of its citizens. It is set by legislation, and is relatively rigid. Any examples of fairness were really expedience aimed at keeping order. Citizenship was only granted to those who might be useful to the State, and this gave privileges, not rights. Many non-English speaking countries have legal systems modelled along these lines.

In much of Middle-Eastern history, laws were mostly based on religious strictures and superstitions. Harsh penalties were often inflicted for apparently victimless crimes, particularly for blasphemy. These laws were aimed at enforcing religious authority, and survive today in the Muslim *Sharia* law. A State practicing such laws will necessarily disadvantage individuals who do not practise the State religion.

By contrast, Germanic law had more focus on victim impact and compensation, redressing the balance or *wyrd*. English law even developed safeguards to protect individuals from the law, in the form of due process and the presumption of innocence. With the onus on the prosecution to prove guilt, there was a focus on evidence-based inquiry.

It is no accident that the person often considered the founding figure of modernity was an English lawyer. Around 1600CE Sir Francis Bacon was considering the question of the laws of nature. Academics had always approached this from a philosophical perspective. They thought that they could deduce the laws of nature by philosophical ruminations alone. Bacon could see the futility of this approach.

Bacon was also aware of the work of alchemists. They were trying another method to discover the workings of nature. However, their experiments were fairly random; with no plan or framework to form and test ideas, they tended to collect unrelated facts by chance, without really understanding what they saw. They were another reason that academics rejected and looked down upon, the idea of experimentation.

Armed with the pragmatic common sense and experience of the Common Law, Bacon realized that only by combining reason and experiment could the secrets of nature be discovered. He likened the investigation to the questioning of a witness in court. The questions could be framed in terms of experiments, with reason employed to lead to further questions, creating a more consistent and complete picture. He saw this as the most effective way to free people from being completely at the mercy of nature. Ignorance was the cause of most suffering, and as he put it "knowledge is power." He was specifically talking about the power to use the knowledge of the laws of nature to improve our situation. This was the beginning of the systematic development of technology based on directed research.

The word 'law' comes from the same Germanic root as 'to lay,' something that is laid down, or layered. There was a concept of a primal or fundamental layer, *'orlog,'* which consists of those laws that, by definition, cannot be broken. Some may think of this as a mystical concept. However, there was no such division between the physical and the mystical for our ancestors, including Bacon. That artificial divide was a product of Judeo-Christian Gnosticism, which saw the physical world as unclean. Bacon saw natural law as an expression of the divine, much as most Heathens do. He is sometimes portrayed as advocating domination over nature, but if you read his works more fully, this is manifestly untrue. He clearly proposes that understanding and working with the laws of nature will allow us to live more comfortably and capably in this world.

If our ancestors lived a relatively tough life, it was not because they did not value material culture and its advantages. They were obviously proud of the skill of their smiths and shipbuilders. They made the effort to create fine homes and clothing if they could afford it, and traded or raided to create the wealth to do so. We can see this also in their description of the Native Americans as poor, because they did not possess steel weapons or wear cloth. Germanic people generally have always been early adopters of technology, and their transition to creators of technology was very natural.

Another aspect of the Common Law and its culture was its sense of fairness and tendency to value the individual. This was kept alive in the stereotypical English expression that 'it's just not cricket' if someone takes unfair advantage. We know that an almost fanatical love of fairness is an ancient part of the culture. At the battle of Maldon, the English Earl would not slaughter the Viking army as it crossed a ford. Instead, he waited until they were in a fair position on the field, even though he knew that the odds were against him. He died with all of his men, but became a shining example of English fair play in the epic poem. The idea has not diminished over the centuries. In a recent poll to determine the elements that define the Australian culture, the most popular item by far was the expression 'a fair go.'

This concept of fairness is the true origin of the idea of individual rights, and the Western democratic idea of freedom. Because these are so deeply rooted in our culture, we tend to take them as self-evident and universal values, but some non-Western countries have argued that human rights are not self-evident, and that they are an example of Anglo-Saxon cultural imperialism. This argument is particularly heard from those countries under scrutiny for their mistreatment of ethnic minorities, or other groups with views different from those of the political authorities.

It seems that the Heathen notions of freedom extended to religion. Heathens did not recruit members, and they do not seem to have disadvantaged those of other beliefs. When Christianity came along, Heathens lived quite comfortably along side Christian neighbours, and even spouses. It was not until the Church gained the support of the ruling powers, and revealed its fundamental intolerance for other faiths, that Heathen resistance was aroused (alas too late).

Christianity suppressed alternative ideas wherever it could. It was not until the emergence of English Enlightenment thinkers like Locke, and his greatest Continental fan, Voltaire, that it was possible to argue that persons should only be prosecuted for their actions, not for their beliefs. These concepts of religious tolerance were held in high regard by the creators of the American Constitution. The independence of the State from religious interference required the institution of secular government. It is this that gives Heathens the legal right to practise without persecution or disadvantage.

Thomas Jefferson saw the importance of this separation of Church and State, including the role of English Common Law as one of the few surviving ancient systems independent of Christianity. When Christians tried to claim a moral victory by stating that the legal system was based on Christian rules, he refuted this by pointing out its Heathen origins:

> *For we know that the common law is that system of law which was introduced by the Saxons on their settlement in England...This settlement took place about the middle of the fifth century. But Christianity was not introduced till the seventh century; the conversion of the first Christian king of the Heptarchy having taken place about the year 598, and that of the last about 686. Here, then, was a space of two hundred years, during which the common law was in existence, and Christianity no part of it.*

In many ways, the values developed by the Enlightenment thinkers can be seen as a real renaissance of the Heathen Germanic culture of freedom, law, pragmatic reasonableness, and individual rights. The success of this culture is obvious in the way it has become the basis of the values of the free world. The English language spread along with it, and has become the language of international trade, science, and politics to a large degree.

So, while it is worthwhile connecting with nature and our ancestors, camping out and dressing in Viking gear at feasts, it is not necessary or productive to make that the major focus of one's life. In the larger modern world, a world of our own making, we need to be participants. We need to be there to safeguard and carry forward the legacy and values of our Heathen ancestors as they have come down to us in the form of modern democratic freedoms. Something our ancestors were always prepared to fight for.

I have served in the military as a Combat Engineer in counter-terrorist roles. I have also worked in various civilian security positions, and for the last couple of decades in large corporate and government IT environments working in network security and digital forensics. As such, I have come to appreciate that there are real enemies that seek to threaten our way of life, either for ideological reasons, commercial advantage, state-sponsored sabotage, or in revenge for actions taken by our governments overseas. The potential for disruption to critical infrastructure, and economies, poses a real threat to the daily activities, and sometimes the lives, of millions of citizens.

We all know that governments have their own agendas, but they have a primary duty to protect their citizens. If the very measures they take to combat this threat should lead to a restriction of our liberties, it is up to us all to make such measures less necessary. Our own complacency and lack of involvement gives governments too little choice and too much justification for the measures they adopt. The people demand security, but need to understand that they may trade some freedoms and privacy to achieve that.

It is important to recognize the crucial role of governments in helping, or hindering, our freedom to practise our Rational Heathenism, and also their role in promoting the education and environments in which we will exist. We need secular democratic governments that encourage a rational and informed public. Governments will make mistakes, and we should criticize them, and vote them out. However, the recent popularity of relentless anti-government rhetoric, often accompanied by conspiracy theory or justification for violence, is extremely counter-productive. We don't need to trust them, but we do need to work with them. Alienating ourselves from them only leaves us with less power to change things.

Education is the key, both at home and abroad. Our way of life is often described by dictators and religious fanatics as decadent, and is itself used to incite hatred beyond the justifiable objections to the sometimes unfortunate foreign policies and actions of our governments. We can only mitigate these hostilities by taking some leadership, and reaching out to promote understanding and education on all sides. Extremists may be a minority, but they thrive in places that do not provide the education and freedoms that we take for granted. This is not just something that happens in 'some other country.'

Governments and corporations do have much to answer for in the spread of mistrust and ignorance amongst their citizens. The UK played down the BSE threat. China did the same with SARS. The US and Australia for a long time largely ignored the evidence for global warming. The tobacco industry covered up the glaring evidence of a lung cancer link for years. This not only shakes public confidence in any kind of 'authority;' a far more serious consequence is that it creates distrust and misunderstanding about evidence-based knowledge itself. This encourages scientific illiteracy, and leaves people vulnerable to the various cults of unreason, pseudoscience, New Age-ism, and fundamentalism.

It is a damning indictment that in the most powerful nation of the free world, nearly half the population does not accept the idea of evolution. After a century and a half of intense debate and observation, evolution, much as Darwin described it, is perhaps the most solid, tried, tested, and easily understood process we can witness in nature. Yet ironically, most of these Christian Creationists are quick to label Muslim fundamentalists as backward for their unenlightened views.

The rise of these and other forms of irrationalism pose a real threat, not only to our Enlightenment heritage, but ultimately to our freedom to practise the older parts of our heritage. The plain fact is that we cannot separate our Heathen heritage from its Enlightenment descendant. Our Enlightenment heritage is our connection with our ancestral culture, and provides the frame of modernity in which most of us must practise our Heathenry.

There is a line of thought that we must somehow erase the experience of the last few centuries, and regress to an idealized vision of tribal society. That we may somehow shut out the real world and form 'Asatru Amish' type communities. As nice as it may be for the privileged few to use log fires for heating and cooking, this would not be ecologically responsible or sustainable on a larger scale, adding to deforestation and pollution. But apart from the practicalities, such isolationism is more likely to lead to an out-of-touch and cultish form of Asatru, against which our next generation is bound to rebel. This may be the right path for a minority of Heathens, but it is not one that is likely to be productive for most.

In reality, we can never escape the influence of the wider world. We just have to adapt to it, do our bit to change its less wholesome aspects, and lead by example in keeping to our own standards and traditions. The Enlightenment framework is one that can accommodate most cultures. Only those that actively discourage democratic freedoms will have trouble adapting. In this respect, there is no reason that we cannot continue to value cultural diversity and tradition, within the overarching framework of modern democracy, our own Enlightenment heritage. This is particularly true for Heathens, who share the same Germanic cultural roots as the Enlightenment.

Having a science background, and working in a high tech industry, I used to have some trouble reconciling this life with that of the heroic ancestors I admire. However, in their pioneering spirit, and forward-looking enthusiasm, I can now see a deeper resonance. In the founding of England, Iceland, and America, we can see distinct parallels in the aspirations of exploration, freedom, fairness, and a better future. While I treasure my own mail coat and axe as fully functional reminders of my ancestors, I am happy to offer my inherited attributes of tactical cunning, and implacable ruthless determination, using modern weapons to help neutralize the threats to the freedom of my descendants.

Most of us have used the Internet to make Heathen ideas more widely available. Few of us have ridden a horse to gatherings. Technology and secular government have allowed Germanic Heathenry to flourish, and we have our Enlightenment ancestors to thank.

In the end, there are many ways we can be true to our Heathen heritage, but for those of us like me, who happen to be Heathen technocrats, I say be proud in the knowledge that you are fulfilling an important part of our cultural lineage.

Now that we can see the links between ancient and modern Heathenism, and have seen through the dogma that there has to be dogma, many may still be confused about how to dispose of the need for belief. It has been ingrained in us that we have to either believe or disbelieve, and that we have to choose. This really amounts to accepting a crutch, a false sense of security. It sets up a fallacious and fragile certainty that for some has to be protected at all costs. This is why many religious people are so emotional, and even violent, if their beliefs are questioned.

I was lucky enough to meet some of the creators of Chaos Magick in 1993 while living in a group house in London. Fellow tenant Ian Read was kind enough to introduce me to Pete Carroll and Phil Hine. The view of Chaos Magick is that belief can be used as a tool. One can temporarily adopt a belief system to make a whole new range of ideas and effects possible. It is based on the concept of "paradigm shift," coined by Thomas Kuhn. For myself, and some Chaos Magicians, it seems this could be taken further. Perhaps the real power of changing beliefs at will is in the necessary dropping of previous conflicting beliefs. How much more powerful if we drop all beliefs?

What I am suggesting is not some weak agnosticism, or fence-sitting exercise. It is a position of courage, a leap into an abyss in order to fly. It involves the method of science; rather than seeking certainty, we accept the ideas that best fit the evidence, until further evidence refines those ideas. The power of the scientific approach is that it is not invested in one model of reality, but continually updates models as new data comes in. Non-belief is not the same as disbelief, just as scepticism is not the same as denial. It is merely the realisation that belief is irrelevant, and baggage to be disposed of.

Religionists will accuse science of being unable to settle on the truth. On the other hand, post-modern relativists will claim that there is no truth. Rational Heathens and scientists can dismiss both arguments.

As all representation of truth is symbolic, we need to understand the symbol system to be able to start communicating and modelling truths of the appropriate domain. This is where many become confused, by applying the wrong symbol system to a domain. Creationists apply biblical symbolism to understand the physical world, while some post-modernists have tried to apply quantum theory to business management practices, both equally absurd examples of domain-symbolism mismatch.

If we want to look at an example of an extremely good fit, we can observe mathematics in the domain of the physical sciences. Natural language is a good fit for most common domains. The measure of fitness of the symbol-domain match is its ability to communicate, describe, explain, predict, and successfully innovate. By this measure, it becomes obvious that there are many areas of endeavour that have evolved their own language, jargon, or symbolism, and work very well, for instance in sports, medicine, social sciences, etc. There are also many examples where the symbol system only serves to obscure a lack of substance, charlatanry, and pseudoscience. The measure of fitness already mentioned will easily expose the difference.

For Heathens, the chosen symbol system is Nordic Mythology and imagery from ancestral literature. The domain is spirituality, seen as a relationship between the individual and community, ancestors, and nature. The content of the domain consists mainly of experiences and perceptions resulting from thoughts and actions designed to establish a connection and awareness beyond the limited mundane self we assume is 'normal.' We can commune with the transpersonal domain through the deities and mythical entities in a deep and immediate way without ever having to complicate the issue with belief.

We need to see belief for what it is, namely preconception: the projection of our expectations and imagination onto a closed door. We can only pass through the door by removing the surface upon which we have been projecting, destroying the image in the process. We cannot see beyond without abandoning belief.

Another common problem, related to belief, is the tendency to confuse the symbols with the content of the domain. This may also explain the difficulty some religionists have in discussing their systems rationally, and why the absurd anachronism of the blasphemy law still exists in some places. The reason such laws exist is because the language of their scripture does not permit a rational defence of the content of their system, and so their ideas and dogmas can only be upheld by force, with the symbols and domain treated as the same thing.

Such a situation should be completely alien to a Rational Heathen. Being secure in our relationship with our symbol system, and its relationship to the spiritual/transpersonal domain, we see no need to enforce adherence to dogmas, or to become offended under questioning or even ridicule. We can certainly respect and revere our heritage, but without the rabid and childish jealousy of the religionists that stems from their basic insecurity.

From such a position of strength we will tend to be naturally tolerant. However, we should be wary of tolerating inherently intolerant ideologies. There is always a danger of such systems becoming viral. This is true of most extremes of political or religious fundamentalism. Again, it must be pointed out that belief is the factor that makes these memes so destructive. It is in our best interest to actively criticise and even ridicule dogma where we find it. The first step in cult brainwashing is to get a person to believe one absurdity; this is then the key that will open them to handing over complete control of their actions. As Voltaire said, "Those who believe absurdities will commit atrocities." It is the cognitive dissonance, the crack between belief and reality, that leaves the victim unable to apply their normal moral revulsion to the demands of the cult.

Looking within Heathenism, we can see the divisions caused by beliefs, and the manipulation of language and symbolism. From this perspective we can see both bigotry and political correctness as two sides of the same coin. Both manipulate the language to make reasoned discussion impossible. Rational Heathenism makes most of the existing divisions irrelevant.

If we make use of the scientific method, we will find that much of the work has already been done for us. Issues like the institutionalised racism in some branches of Asatru can be analysed. Stephen McNallen's use of 'metagenetics' and the notion of 'morphic fields' to justify racism can be recognised as pseudo-scientific nonsense. Racism can be seen for what it is, simply the mistaken idea that there are such things as 'races.' Human individuals are just too diverse to fit into the arbitrary categories of a 19th-century science that became obsolete with the discovery of DNA, and a better understanding of the history and movement of people. Some groups try to compensate with a politically correct reverse racism that is equally absurd.

The moment we look into the science, the whole destructive issue of 'race' dissolves, as we realise that the concept itself is invalid. We each have a multitude of ancestors. Each generation you go back, you find double the ancestors. It soon becomes obvious that everyone is certain to have ancestors from other ethnic groups. No human population has been completely isolated for long enough to become another species. The superficial differences we see are local adaptations to the environments that the majority of our ancestors lived in. The assumption that races began as separate entities, and that they later mixed in places, just does not stand up to genetic or historical analysis.

So how does a Rational Heathen deal with the sensitive issues of ancestry and 'cultural appropriation' that drive both the folkish and the PC sides of the current apartheid policies? How do we balance the need for the integrity of our mythology against the New Age tendency to mix everything into an unrecognisable melting pot? First, I would say 'get over yourselves.' The turf wars and preciousness of the whole argument stem from a mistaken idea that there is some kind of 'purity,' either cultural or ancestral, in the first place.

Cultures and genes have been mixing freely for thousands of years. No amount of complaining will stop this process. Even if it could be frozen as it is, we only save what was previously mixed. It just makes no sense. Most of the hostility surrounding these issues is the result of an artificially inflated sense of difference, which has been exacerbated by the twin forces of apartheid thinking: bigotry and political correctness. Both serve in the end to maintain barriers to understanding between groups.

While bigotry is usually obvious in its blinkered ignorance, political correctness is more insidious. It appears on the surface to be a benign redressing of balance. However, in its neurotic fear of causing offense to anyone, it manipulates the language to make everything bland to the point that important issues can no longer be raised without causing accusing fingers to falsely point out straight talk as bigotry. This is often done as a form of point scoring, trying to appear the most correct, or as a holier-than-thou salve for their own guilty conscience. The end result is to make rational discussion impossible, and letting real issues fester.

As Heathens, we can certainly be proud and even protective of our heritage, but complaining about Norse Wicca, or runic Tarot, is completely pointless. Feel free to ridicule what looks silly, but also be prepared to be ridiculed if we become pompous or precious about spiritual tourists borrowing our gods. By the same token, be aware that we could not do much with our surviving heritage without borrowing some forms and techniques from other sources. The best we can do is to be educated in the sources we use, and practise consciously. This will be what differentiates us from the superficiality of the New Age spiritual supermarket.

Rational Heathenism allows us to maintain a detached focus. Unencumbered by the stress of shoring up beliefs against reality, we can explore our spiritual heritage without fear or guilt. Even magic can be practised within our mythic framework, without resort to superstitious or pseudo-scientific explanations and, as Crowley put it, "without lust of result."

To succeed with Rational Heathenism, we will need to study three things: logic, meditation, and the sources.

Firstly logic, either basic or more advanced according to one's abilities. Learn the main kinds of arguments and fallacies. Know what constitutes a valid argument, and how to evaluate the truth of a premise. Look into formal symbolic logic, and see how most arguments can be represented in a form that clarifies their structure, making their validity more easily verified. Fortify this with a basic knowledge of the world, particularly some scientific literacy, as this will make it much easier to evaluate the truth of claims.

Formal logic is an excellent mind training method in itself. It has similar benefits to mathematics, to which it is really a complementary discipline. Indeed, acquiring mental discipline is the key to exploring the spiritual without becoming lost in fantasy and self-delusion.

Secondly, meditation is the key to mental clarity. It allows us to see the illusory nature of belief. Most will begin the journey not being able to help having beliefs. We may not even be aware that we have beliefs. It will take time and regular practice to achieve the insights and emotional detachment necessary to walk without the crutches of belief. The only reason we cling to beliefs is the emotional attachment to the illusion of certainty that they offer, and our fear of losing that. Meditation will expose these fears as shadows.

By meditation, I mean the state, rather than the many techniques. There is much confusion in New Age, Pagan, and Heathen circles when people mention meditation. They usually mean contemplation, visualisation, path-working, or some other use of the imagination. I am using the term in the original sense used by most schools of Buddhism, as awareness without thought, leading to transcendence of duality. Unfortunately, the words may be concise, but until the state is experienced, they will not make any sense to the reader.

We spend most of our time in a state of mental chatter. We constantly describe to ourselves what we think we are experiencing. This leads to a kind of secondhand experience of the world, heavily infused with our preconceptions and beliefs. In meditation, we focus on the origin of thoughts.

The most common techniques involve starting with something to focus on, like the breath, or a meaningless word or image. The word or mantra seems to be easiest for most to control. It needs to be something that does not provoke a path of analysis or chain of thoughts, which is why it needs to be un-associated with meanings. The word is repeated mentally, silently, until other thoughts die down. The word is then observed as an imagined sound that you are mentally repeating. You then look for the thought that begins each repetition, then the origin of that thought, and so on recursively. After a while you will realise that you have been observing silence with no thought arising. That realisation will bring back a flood of thoughts about that, and you will need to start again.

After a few months of daily practice, at least 20 minutes before breakfast and before the evening meal, you will start to achieve the silence more often, and will start to gain insights into it. The first few months are the trickiest, as most people will get into a phase of thinking about absence of thought rather than experiencing it, and be unaware that they are still actually thinking. Some will be sidetracked by seemingly profound visions or realisations, which are really just another train of thought and distraction.

After another few months of regularly achieving the genuine silence, you will gain enough insight into it to be able to switch thoughts off briefly at other times, and experience an intense egoless unity with your environment. This can be brought into many areas of endeavour in order to experience a very direct connection with what you are doing. This is what is meant by the term 'transcending duality.'

Unfortunately, in this age of instant gratification, many have trouble sticking to the routine. However, after a couple of years of this work the insights are life changing. Beliefs, fears, and other thoughts will start to become clear, along with their true lack of substance. Illuminated by the experience of meditation, these thoughts and beliefs appear as faded daydreams, and you will wonder how they ever held so much influence over you. This will bring a great sense of freedom, and have practical benefits in clear thinking, creativity, and even in physical pursuits such as martial arts and sports. There is a feeling of relief, lightness, and effortlessness, but also of being intensely present and focused.

Now the third part of our practice: the sources. Many good translations can be found of the *Havamal*, the Sagas, the Rune Poems, and other literature. There are now a few well-researched books for Heathens that discuss these sources in detail. This collection of literature is the foundation of the symbolic language of Heathenism.

To get the most out of the literature, it is a good idea to study the historical and cultural context as far as it can be known. Find more than one translation, and if possible a copy in the original language. Many Heathens will have already immersed themselves in academic books and historical novels that cover the culture of our Heathen ancestors. We need to be a little discerning however, as it is easy to be drawn into less academic and more fanciful inventions. These range from the 19th-century romanticism of Rydberg, to the early 20th-century 'rune yogas,' and the later plethora of Nordic and runic fantasy magical systems of the 1980s and 1990s.

In warning about the recently invented systems, my intent is not to say it is necessary to judge them as bad or even ineffective, but merely to emphasise the value of starting from a foundation that can be agreed on by all. It is also to dispel the claims of many of these systems to 'authenticity' or tradition. If we want to revive Heathenism, we should at least start from the sources closest to the Heathen ancestors. This gives us the most consistent symbolic language. The recent inventions each have their fans, but introduce too many variations, contradictions, rivalries, and agendas to be workable in a wider context. They also take us further from the spirit of the ancestors we admire.

This is not to stifle innovation, but we should at least let the innovation be the creativity of the individual or group, practised consciously, rather than the fevered imaginings of the would-be gurus and cult leaders, followed slavishly.

At this point, we can start to think about the forms and practices we might consider. As long as we are well grounded in the sources, we have a multitude of techniques to choose from. Various groups have developed systems of practice, some of which will resonate with us individually, or with the group we form for a particular occasion. Some folk will be horrified at the thought that we do not follow one of the established brands of modern Heathenism, and that we may even draw from practices used by different religions at times. Some will accuse us of being eclectic with our mix-and-match, even comparing us to the dreaded New Age spiritual dilettantes. However, what will distinguish us from the anything-goes occult fans will be our deeper understanding and familiarity with the sources. This will give us the consistent foundation that provides authenticity to the moment, rather than seeking somebody else's authorised version of ritual and dogma that was only put together within living memory anyway.

This is where I see Chaos Heathenry forming a nexus between various freeform Heathenisms. Rational Heathens will be able to practise effectively with Shamanic Heathens, Mystical Heathens, or any number of other possible kinds of Heathenism that folk can come up with to reflect the diversity of people who are drawn to the Northern Traditions. The idea of a one-size-fits-all church, with a central authority and dogma, is just not a model that fits the individualism and diversity of real Heathens either now or in the past. This authoritarian mindset has been the source of division and bitter rivalry since the Heathen reconstruction effort started. If we want to bring Heathens together, we need to focus on the Feast days and gatherings that emphasise fellowship, dispensing with the pompous claims of whose version of tradition is more authentic.

Beyond Heathenism, I see the same need for Rational Paganism more generally. The world needs to grow out of belief-based religions. Fundamentalism has become increasingly destructive, particularly with the power of the Internet as a medium for propaganda and recruitment. Fundamentalists are becoming ever more extreme as they desperately fight against a world in which education exposes their cherished beliefs as ridiculous. This extremism drives many educated people away from religion in disgust. The world is becoming ever more polarised: non-religious against stupidly religious. Perhaps Rational Paganism could offer a middle ground, as well as a way for cultures to reconnect with their older traditions.

It is my hope that this book will provide some alternative perspectives, and the prospect of possibilities for those who have been dissuaded or disillusioned from their interest in Heathenism by less than favourable impressions. All it will take is some openness to the diversity that Heathenism was and can be once again.

Recommended Reading:

Waking Up, Sam Harris

Believing Bullshit, Stephen Law

Knowledge is Power, John Henry

Learning Logic: Critical Thinking with Intuitive Notation, S. Plowright

Chance, Cause, Reason, Arthur W. Burks

Gods and Myths of Northern Europe, H.R. Ellis Davidson

The Rune Primer, S. Plowright

Any of the books and documents listed in the appendix on academic sources.

Untitled, Mark Morte

"Everything Fornicates All the Time:"[1]
An Ancient Pattern that Journeys Far
Matthew Hern

If I cast my eyes before me, what an infinite space, in which I do not exist; and if I look behind me, what a terrible procession of years, in which I do not exist; and how little space I occupy in this vast abyss of time.
– Blaise Pascal, *Pensées*

All beings are Buddhas...there is no being that is not enlightened, if it but knows it's true nature.
– *Hevajra* Tantra

I have been waiting beyond the years
Now over the skyline I see you're travelling
Brothers from all time gathering here
Come let us build the ship of the future
In an ancient pattern that journeys far
Come let us set sail for the 'always' island
Through seas of leaving to the summer stars

Seasons they change but with gaze unchanging
O deep-eyed sisters is it you I see?
Seeds of beauty ye bear within you
Of unborn children glad and free
Within your fingers the fates are spinning

---

1 This quote from Austin Osman Spare reformulates the ancient Hindu Tantric idea of Shiva-Shakti (or Yub-Yum in Tibetan Vajrayana Tantra), namely that the male and female principles – Consciousness and Energy – unite ('fornicate') and thus create the universe. He might also imply other ideas according to his "New Sexuality" doctrine. Spare was one of the first occultists to adopt psychoanalytic ideas into his magical model of 'suppressing' desires in sigil form, so that the desire could be fulfilled. By that he thought to invert the mechanism of neurosis, which according to Freudian psychoanalysis was the result of suppressed sexual desires. By *intentionally* suppressing desires in sigil form, Spare believed that not neurosis but the actual fulfillment of the desire would be the result. This method seems to work quite well, especially for beginners in magic.

The sacred binding of the yellow grain
Scattered we were when the long night was breaking
But in the bright morning converse again.

– The Incredible String Band, "The Circle is Unbroken"

The Way to Enlightenment

According to Crowley, who boiled the Eastern teachings down to their essence after having travelled to India and other places in Asia,[2] the way to enlightenment is very simple: "Sit down, shut up, stop thinking, and Get Out!" Simple, but not easy. Even the Tantric scholar, Hugh B. Urban,[3] admits that Crowley had a fairly well-grounded understanding of Yoga, as his book *Eight Lectures on Yoga* (a book still worth reading) proves. Let's look closer at what Crowley meant by this formula.

---

[2] There seemed to exist a certain form of 'positive Orientalism' among occultists of the 19th century that projected the East as the fountain of wisdom religion. This attitude was the opposite of the ignorant contempt that dominated mainstream Western perceptions of Asian cultures in colonialist times, as Edward Said analyzed in his book *Orientalism* (1979). Meanwhile, I question whether Crowley grasped the 'essence' of Eastern teachings and I am well aware of his racism, misogyny, and megalomania. Nobody is without 'sin,' one might think; after all, like every artist or philosopher he was a product of his time. Rather than summarizing Patanjali he was reinterpreting Yogic teachings through many lenses and thus reinvented them; like Blavatsky and others, he took the Eastern teachings and filtered them through the perception patterns of Western occultism, adapting them to his worldview or system of 'magick.' Nevertheless, I would argue that Crowley's meditative methods were of great use to his Western contemporaries, who otherwise would have had no access to them. His Golden Dawn teacher, Allen Bennett, later became a Buddhist and was one of the first Englishmen to bring *Hinayana* Buddhism to England. Crowley is a dwarf among giants in the *philosophia perennis* tradition, yet he contributed a fresh and creative view on magic as a means to experience the Divine in an age of scientific materialism; his apotheosis of man is simply the hubris of modernity. Crowley's 'scientific' and results-orientated approach to magic has since been stressed even more by many Chaos Magicians. On a psychological note, Crowley was a prisoner of his childhood trauma and never overcame his painful experiences with Christianity (his parents were fundamentalists), which created his pathological '666-prophet' obsession.

[3] See Urban 2006: *Magia Sexualis.*

Sit down: This refers to *asana*, a term in Yogic literature for posture. It needs to be solid, but also comfortable. After all, you are supposed to sit in this posture for half an hour or more. The point is not to move, to scratch, to yawn, or to do any other thing. Sit still, don't move, do nothing. The body is brought under control and is supposed to cease being a source of distraction. In our age of constant distractions this can be rather hard. But "persistence is all," as Perdurabo maintained.[4]

Shut up: Once we have sat we have to invite silence into our heads. This can be achieved, among other techniques, with *pranayama*; ultimately it leads to the state of *prathyahara*, the 'withdrawal of the senses,' a stage in which the mind is fully turned inward and in control of the senses. This is basically achieved through the mastery of our vital energy, the *prana*, as this is what drives our senses. The whole point of this practice is to stop the scattering of our energy, of our *prana*. We need to seek control over it and harmonize our body-mind with it. This is done through various practices such as bringing the entire focus of one's attention to a single point in the body or to the breath. In having achieved this focus we reach the final stage: *mano pratyahara* – the "withdrawal of mind." We consciously withdraw our attention from any distracting force outside of us and all concentration is directed inwards. The rune ᛁ Isa is a perfect representation of this kind of state of consciousness.

Stop Thinking: This is impossible, you say? I hear you, fellow seeker. But do we not quest for magic, myth, and mystery because we strive for that which is miraculous and fills our hearts with Joy and Awe? Isn't magic "the science of the extremes"[5] and the impossible? The violation of probabilities?[6] They told you that sigil magic doesn't work, that it cannot happen – yet when you tried it, it did work! In the same way we must push our boundaries of Achievable Reality with every – *pranayama* – breath we take. We learn slowly. Magic cannot be solely learned at a retreat or weekend workshop. We learn by

---

4 "Perdurabo" is Latin and was one of Crowley's magical mottos. It means "I will endure." The phrase "persistence is all" was used by John Balance of the band Coil in reference to Crowley. Anyone who desires to become a magician should internalize the wisdom of that phrase, as nothing is deadlier than boredom and laziness – the two enemies of everyone who ever tried to work through a magical curriculum.

5 Phil Hine: *Condensed Chaos.*

6 See Ray Sherwin: *The Theatre of Magick.*

applying our insights in daily life. This is an endless process. On the way we must accept our imperfections, stop worrying, stop wishing, yes, stop thinking! We must learn to watch our thought patterns and thus become aware of the origination of thoughts. We must not strive for anything, we must not force our minds to do anything, but just watch. 'Breathe in, breathe out...thoughts... breathe in, breathe out...' and so forth. Finally, we will establish mental silence, or to be more accurate, it establishes itself. And even a few seconds of this mental silence are like a short glimpse at eternity, a foretaste of the Goddess's kisses. So here we go: having actualized the *pratyahara* stage – the consciousness of the seeker is internalized in order to shut out the sensations from the senses and the outer world (which we perceive through our senses) – we take the next step and achieve real concentration: *dharana*.

Get Out: This leads to profound stages of gnosis. It doesn't make really sense to talk about it, because language is not created to express the eternity that a meditator has experienced in silence, although we humans need words to get an idea of the higher states of Consciousness; they act as bridges and catalysts for entering the Void. The idea of 'getting out' ultimately points to the experience of illumination, which is known in Sanskrit as *dhyana* (meditation) and *samadhi* (mystical absorption), being the aim of all Yogic practice. *Dhyana* and *samadhi* are the last stages of that process and they represent stages of illuminated Consciousness.

Thus with the formula *"Sit down, shut up, stop thinking, and Get Out,"* Crowley manages to summarize the essence of the Eight stages[7] of Patanjali's *Ashtanga*

---

7 Out of these eight stages I have left out two: *Yama* and *Niyama*. While *Yama* stands for a series of ethical rules of "right living" (the "negative duties" of non-harming other living beings, non-falsehood, non-stealing, non-cheating on one's partner, and non-possessiveness), *Niyama* represents "postive duties", i.e. recommended activities and habits for healthy living and spiritual enlightenment, like persistence, charity, vegetarianism, modesty, the acceptance of one's past, etc. These are thought of as helpful requirements for a Yogic discipline. Crowley, like most Yoga practitioners of his time, was profoundly influenced by Vivekananda's *Raja Yoga* and took from him central ideas. Vivekananda was influenced by the Brahmo Samaj Hindu reformation movement, and especially its founder K. C. Sen (1838-1884), who incorporated ideas from the Christian Unitarian movement (a radical liberal Protestant denomination) and Emerson's American transcendentalism into his philosophy that promoted religious experimentation and valued personal experiential revelation over mediated, dogmatic religious truths. This influence is echoed in Crowley's system of magick and his Western approach to Yoga. Hence Crowley gave a far more pragmatic and anti-dogmatic interpretation of *Yama* and *Niyama* in his *Book 4* as well as his *Eight Lectures on Yoga*.

Yoga, as mentioned in the classical work, *Yoga Sutras* of Patanjali (composed in the 2nd century BCE). This yogic practice corresponds with the six-branch yoga (*ṣaḍaṅgayoga*) of the Buddhist *Kālacakra* tantra, which refers to the withdrawal of the five senses from external objects so they may be replaced by the mentally created senses of an enlightened deity. For Patanjali, this process bridges the *bahiranga* (external) aspects of yoga namely, *yama, niyama, asana, pranayama,* and the *antaranga* (internal) yoga,[8] namely *pratyahara, dharana, dhyana,* and *samadhi*. Having actualized the *pratyahara* stage (= "Shut up"), the magician is able to effectively engage into the practice of *samyama*, a Sanskrit word for 'holding together, tying up, binding;' the 'holding together' of the senses and the concentration of all mental focus on the object of meditation, so that 'mystical absorption' (*samadhi*) can be achieved.

This practice is part one of Crowley's magnum opus *Book 4: Magick*. The second part describes the various magical weapons necessary for Ceremonial Magic. Part three describes his system of magick, the various technologies, and explains the occult terminology of his system. The fourth part of that book is considered to be *The Book of the Law (Liber AL vel Legis)* itself, Crowley's "revelation" that he supposedly received from a "higher being" in Cairo in 1904. This fourth part is seen by his followers as some kind of bible and they turned Crowley's work into a religion. To the Chaos Heathen much of Crowley's work will remain of little interest, but as we have seen there is much in it that can illuminate certain philosophical and practical aspects of magical work. Maybe his work would be more interesting for us Chaos Heathens if he had turned to the Northern Gods instead of following the fad of 19th-century occultism and gone for the Egyptian Gods. Regardless, the main question remains: what is illumination? Well, the short answer is: I don't know. But we can look closer to what has been said about how magic and illuminated states of consciousness are connected.

Correspondences and the *Unus Mundus*

Besides Yoga, another fundament of Crowley's teachings is the modern version of Qabalah/Kabbalah. Though I respect Qabalah as a mystical current in Judaism I think that too many 'occult masters' turned Qabalah into an intellectual exercise of little real spiritual value. This is unfortunate because

---

8 See https://en.wikipedia.org/wiki/Pratyahara.

the study of correspondences, which lies at the heart of Qabalah, is an ancient art that belongs to the great "Arts of Imagination,"[9] which were practiced back in the days when Imagination was not just dismissed as fantasy. One of the most influential humanist philosophers of the early Italian Renaissance and a reviver of Neoplatonism, Marsilio Ficino (1433-1499), rediscovered this ancient art during a time when Florence was the place to hang out for hip artists and 'avant-garde' intellectuals, an important center in the last days of the Mediæval Age. In Florence, cultural innovations and developments arose that led to an end of the dominance of the Church. New ideas began to spread that resulted in intellectual transformations of a grand scale.

The Renaissance is viewed today as a bridge between the Middle Ages and the Modern era. It saw revolutions in many intellectual pursuits, as well as social and political upheaval, but what I find most fascinating is that it was inspired by the past, the classical age: Ancient Greece. So it does not come as a surprise that it also featured a revival of Magic.[10] Humanists asserted "the genius of man...the unique and extraordinary ability of the human mind." In that special intellectual environment Ficino taught what he considered to be 'Natural Magic,' and so laid the foundation for what is now called 'Ceremonial Magic,' known to us through magical authors like McGregor Mathers, Dion Fortune, Aleister Crowley, and Israel Regardie. This form of magic is still practiced in occult orders all over the world.

> *Ficino's magic was grafted on to an existing tradition of medieval magic, which in turn had derived from Arabic sources such as the notorious manual of spirit evocation called* Picatrix. *The fundamental idea was the doctrine of correspondences, which teaches that everything in the universe corresponds to other things on higher or lower levels of being.*[11]

The idea of correspondences, then, is really old. It seems it never disappeared completely. Yet with the rise of modern science in the 17th century, Johannes

---

9 See Godwin 2007: *The Golden Thread.*

10 Of course, magic has always existed. The point is that in the Renaissance magic blossomed in its highest form: as philosophy and the art of the ascent of the Soul to the Godhead.

11 Godwin 2007: *The Golden Thread*, p. 99.

Kepler (1571–1630) and Isaac Newton (1643–1727),[12] though themselves both deeply into the occult, cut through the bond of psyche and nature, humanity and world, subjective and objective, that was born with the rise of human consciousness, and which was known to the ancients as the 'World-Soul' or *Anima Mundi*.[13] For the ancients the world-soul was the *vinculum amoris*, 'the band of love,' that connected the inner world with the outer world, psyche and nature. In severing this connection, the Newtonian revolution has had profound ramifications for the history of consciousness. It would take three centuries before we would be able to *re*-imagine this sacred bond between humanity and nature. We needed quantum physics and a Swiss psychologist to *re*-member: Carl Gustav Jung's ideas of the archetypes and the collective unconscious made magic possible again. He wrote in 1916, after a spiritual crisis:

> *Man is a gateway, through which one enters from the outer world of the gods, demons, souls, into the inner world, from the greater world into the smaller world.*[14]

What Jung meant was that we can enter deeper, hidden realities by finding pathways of communication with our unconscious, which Jan Fries calls the "Deep Mind."[15] When we open up to these possibilities we begin to interact magically with our environment, and a sacred psychogeography is thus created:

---

12 "Significantly, even in his monumental Newton biography of 1980, this great scholar still felt he needed to defend himself for doing his job as a historian: 'I am not an alchemist, nor do I believe in its premises…Nevertheless, I have undertaken to write a biography of Newton, and my personal preferences cannot make more than a million words he wrote in the study of alchemy disappear'." (Westfall 1980, cited from Hanegraaff 2012: 325, Fn. 261.) Also see Westfall 1980: *Never at Rest: A Biography of Isaac Newton*, Cambridge University Press, Cambridge.

13 Actually, both Kepler and Newton saw the harmonious order of the divine creation in the physical laws they discovered, a kind of clockwork universe (*instar horologii*) and 'world machine' (*machina mundi*). However their physical laws made the idea of a divinely ensouled universe (*instar divini animali*) obsolete.

14 Jung 1916: "Sermones ad Mortuos," in: Jung 1963: *Memories, Dreams, Reflections*, p. 380.

15 See Fries 1993: *Visual Magick*.

> *It is through the human unconscious that one passes from the 'greater world' to the 'smaller world' of the interior universe. The God of the 'exterior' universe is the sun; and the interior world is, accordingly, illuminated by the sun of man's personal inner divinity.*[16]

Hence the archetypes of the collective unconscious are simultaneously part of the macrocosmos (the outer world) and the microcosmos (the inner world), which leads to the fascinating, magical conclusion that the world of the psyche and the world of 'outer' reality are ultimately only reflections of a higher reality, the *unus mundus*, the mystical oneness of the world. Or to put it differently: *the world and the psyche are each mirroring the one reality.* This means that Jung assumed a monistic meta-level behind or beyond the subjective (psychical) and objective (physical) reality – the *unus mundus*, the concept of an underlying unified reality from which everything emerges and to which everything returns (and which Jung himself borrowed from the alchemist Gerardus Dorneus [1530–1584]).

To me this conception is the fundament of magic. Being a modern practitioner – educated in a school system based on the Enlightenment tradition of rationality – I often imagined the magical path in scientific terms. My thoughts ran along these lines: If there was a Big Bang then everything in the physical universe has the same origin. And when we look to quantum physics, it tells us that two particles from the same origin can somehow behave as if they were still connected, even when they are separated by a huge distance. This means that if one of the two particles gets affected by certain events, the other is affected in the same way despite being physically somewhere else.[17] Now, if this action at a distance is true, and yet if all things come from the one point of origin, then in principle any two entities could influence each other sympathetically. One would have to be blind if one did not see a connection between these new discoveries and the old conceptions of correspondences, even if we cannot conclude from this that modern science is now approaching some of the conclusions magicians reached millennia ago.[18]

---

16 Hanegraaff 1996: *New Age Religion and Western Culture*, p. 503.

17 See Robert Anton Wilson: *The New Inquisition*.

18 This is the old occultistic dream. I refer here to William Burroughs' remarks on the back cover of Phil Hine's *Condensed Chaos* book.

Or can we? Wolfgang Pauli (1900-1958), an Austrian theoretical physicist and one of the pioneers of quantum physics – in fact a recipient of the Nobel Prize in Physics – examined the synchronicity principle[19] with Jung, and he argued that there must be a psychophysically unified reality that connects the psyche and the world. He thought of it as an invisible, potentially existing reality that could only be unlocked by studying its effects on the visible world. He sought a 'new language' that could describe that reality. I think he found it in Jung's theories. We have found it in magical systems and occult terminology. It is no mere accident that Jung became so popular in magical circles for there is a sublime truth in his psychology: the aforementioned underlying unified reality, the *unus mundus*.

It is also not a coincidence that when scientists like Metzner, Leary, Grof, etc. took LSD, Mescalin, and other chemognostic sacraments, they entered weird inner landscapes where the 'laws' of the *unus mundus* reigned. Certain drugs can lead you to the experiences of unitary consciousness. Yet the experience of that underlying unified reality is not always bliss and joy. It happens sometimes that when an unprepared person takes LSD – has a 'wrong set,' as Leary said (a wrong attitude, for example feels bad or is depressive or anxious) or is in an inappropriate environment (like a disco, a 'wrong setting') – then such a person gets a 'bad trip,' which mainly means paranoia: everything in the universe, strangely connected in weird ways, is a conspiracy against you.

There is, however, a way of perception that inverts this process and it is an effective method to communicate with the Universe and experience a 'communion.' This way is to can conceptualize the Universe, like the Tantrics did, as the body of the Goddess – known to me as Eternity, or Nuit. This is a form of gnosis that Satanists and Setians will never know: it's called *pronoia*.

I came across this term in Humphries' and Vayne's fascinating grimoire, *Now That's What I Call Chaos Magick*.[20] Pronoia is a state of consciousness that is intimately connected to the Holy Guardian Angel concept. Here the seeker

---

[19] The synchronicity principle, Richard Tarnas argued, is the discovery which makes the paradigm of scientific materialism collapse. Tarnas claims that its implications can only lead to a new mystical, holistic paradigm that includes the possibility of magic, as Cosmos and Psyche are interconnected and reflect each other. See Richard Tarnas: *Cosmos and Psyche*.

[20] Humpries & Vayne 2005: *Now That's What I Call Chaos Magick*.

discovers that the Universe is actually alive and that it cares for you and tries to help you in any way possible to get closer to your Self that – on a profound, meaningful, and transcendent level invisible to the eye – is One with the Universe. The realization of this Oneness implies a particular attitude on the part of the adept toward cosmos, for example in Ficino's Natural Magic or in Hindu-Tantra, whereby the adept feels integrated within an all-embracing system of micro-macrocosmic correlations. The Universe here is not just a thing 'out there,' but *Her*: She, the Mysterious Universe, the Goddess Herself. Every attempt to conceptualize Her/Him/It leads to an anthropomorphization of Her, leading to the Goddess in Her various forms: Nuit, Freyja, Kali, Babalon – the Holy Whore.

The Goddess and the Two-Handed Path

> *All our ancient ways are wrought with love of Her, lifting up Her skirts and showing off Her irresistible flesh, our flesh, all flesh...For only a real fool, the worst drudge, would ever refuse Her come-on. Even those with little wisdom know in their hearts that She has but one aim: to bring you ecstasy, to destroy the illusion of separateness...*[21]

I do not know why, but for a long time I felt very attracted to the perception of the Goddess (on one level of reference) as Nuit. Probably it is because she was the first Goddess I encountered on my Path when I discovered *The Book of the Law*. Nuit has been described by Crowley in various ways. First of all he equated this Egyptian Goddess of the Night Sky with the Qabalistic concept of *Ain Soph Aur* (אור סוף אין), the Limitless Light; the Godhead, prior to Its Self-Manifestation, before It emanates into manifestation on various levels of existence and thus creates the world(s). This idea probably derived from Ibn Gabirol (1021–1058), an Andalucian Hebrew poet and Jewish philosopher, who coined the term "the Endless One" (*she-en lo tiklah*). *Ain Soph* may be translated as "no end," "unending," "there is no end," or "the Infinite." Hence a term like *Ain Soph Aur* means "Endless Light." *Ain Soph* is the divine origin of all created existence, which emanates out of infinite no-thing-ness (*Ain*).

---

21 Dave Lee 2006 [1997]: *Choatopia!*, p. 203.

Another way to approach the Mystery of Nuit[22] is to understand it as a certain state of being that the Buddhists called *Nibbāna* (Pali), or *Nirvāna* (Sanskrit: निर्वाण). This is a state of being free from suffering (*dukkha*). In Hindu philosophy, it is the union with the Supreme Being (=God) through *Moksha* (Sanskrit: मोक्ष) or *Mukti* (Sanskrit: मुक्ति), which literally means "release" in the sense of "letting go." The concept of *Nirvāna* is often mistakenly associated in Western minds with the impression of a nihilistic, life-denying stance, because it means 'blowing out.' However in truth things are more complicated. *Nirvāna* basically refers to the blowing out of the fires of greed, hatred, and delusion. Over centuries this concept was transformed in Tantric Buddhism to the idea that *Nirvāna* is a purified, non-dualistic 'superior mind,' unclouded by any dualistic perceptions. Again we find the *unus mundus* at play.

Unfortunately, in Western occultism we now have the confused, dualistic impression that the ideas of 'Self' and 'No Self'[23] are somehow contrary, and certain so-called 'Left Hand Path' adepts assume that the Right Hand Path traditions lead to 'self-annihilation' and that the Left Hand Path traditions lead to a 'preservation of the self.' Don Webb, an initiate of the Temple of Set, writes:

> *Crowley believed that when one left the Adept Grade, one could either give up one's ego or become a Babe of the Abyss, being at one with Nuit OR one could shut himself away from the universe and become a Black Brother, a follower of the Left Hand Path. These unfortunate SOBs were eventually destroyed by the universal tides acting upon them, much like stones being worn down by sea waves. We in the Left Hand Path (LHP) see this matter differently. If we didn't we would scarcely have an interest in the First.[24] Crowley believed that the Master of the Temple obtained a true Union with the objective universe and by so doing*

---

22 At least in Crowley's sense; I'm not concerned with Old Egyptian religious conceptions here.

23 For a full investigation of these concepts of 'fullness' and 'emptiness,' c.f. Bäumer and Dupuche 2005: *Void and Fullness*.

24 The 'Second Beast' being Aquino for Setians, the founder of the Temple of Set. They believe that Aquino is Crowley's 'Magical Son,', as prophesized in *Liber AL* by Crowley. All of this is, of course, occult speculation and of no real interest to Chaos Heathens.

> *could interpret any event in that universe as a communication from its meaningful and purposeful side. Ultimately one would realize the unity of spirit and matter, and the folly of believing one's thoughts to be separate from the Cosmos. Crowley saw himself as a teacher of the Right Hand Path.*[25]

This is just a terribly confused position. It results from the Setian idea of 'Isolate Intelligence,' which is based on the *cogito ergo sum* proposition[26] of the Christian philosopher Descartes. It is not without irony that the basic concept of Satanists (or Setians) and their 'proof' for Satan/Set as the 'origin' of consciousness stems from the work of a famous Christian philosopher. Be it as it may, Kepler's and Newton's destruction of the *vinculum amoris* (band of love) and the rise of modernity through the 'autonomous self' made this development possible. That Satanists would turn the modern myth of the 'autonomy of the self,' separated from nature, into a religion and create an apotheosis of this 'self' is rather ridiculous; such a way of thinking has no relation to any deeper or ancient tradition. It is a modern, neo-Satanic myth that somehow developed between the antagonistic positions of Madame Blavatsky and Michael Aquino. Both of these figures got it all wrong, because according to Tantric tradition the Right Hand and Left Hand Paths' goal is the same: the *Unio Mystica*, the sacred marriage of *Atman* and *Brahman*, the higher identity of 'fullness' and *Suñyatā*. All that differs between the two paths are their methodologies.

The same confusion arises when Hindu and Buddhist concepts are compared. Whilst *Advaita Vedanta* (*Advaita* means literally "non-duality"), a monistic school of Hindu philosophy, promotes the idea that the Self (*Atman*) and the Whole/"God" (*Brahman*) are identical, thus presupposing a True Self, Buddhism describes exactly the same phenomenon, but calls this discovery No

---

25 Webb 2005: *Aleister Crowley – The Fire and the Force*, p. 32.

26 "I think, therefore I am." This is certainly a powerful statement that is, so to speak, the beginning of the Western modern conception of the 'autonomous self.' However, it was not only the philosophical foundation of the 'modern self;' it also led to a radicalization of the split and separateness of matter and mind. This separateness has existed in a 'soft' and complementary way since the ancient philosophy of Plato, but Descartes fully broke the 'band of love,' the unitary connection, between humanity and nature and the Cosmos and the Soul.

Self (*Anātman*), and thus presupposes an Emptiness (*Suñyatā*).[27] The truth is that both True Self and Emptiness are descriptions of the same thing, but we less insightful seekers, lacking sufficient meditative experience, get lost in concepts and conceptions. And as so often happens, the truth gets lost in translation, too. We must keep in mind that these things are extremely hard to grasp, and it is even harder to put those experiences into words.

But to come back to Nuit: She, as Goddess of Eternity, embodies these concepts of *Ain Soph Aur* and *Nirvāna* in a beautiful and unique way, beyond words and reason. The Holy Guardian Angel, then, is that kind of entity which tries to reconnect you with Nuit. I assume that from here comes the idea of Angels as intermediary beings, as the 'messengers of God,' the *Pleroma* or *Nous*. We need a very clear and grounded understanding of the Angel's nature if it is to be of any use to a modern individual today. Crowley stated several times that he incorporated the notion of a Holy Guardian Angel into his system of magick because he found it so 'ridiculous' that, he assumed, no one would ever confuse the Holy Guardian Angel with Angels in a literal sense. Rather, he thought his readers and followers would look for the higher and deeper meaning of the necessity of that experience:

> *The Holy Guardian Angel is everything you are not. It is other. It cannot be described, for if it could it would be part of you. The search for it is therefore not the search for a specified goal, but a great search for other. It is the search for some kind of metaphysical experience and unity, bliss and joy. As you grow and your knowledge increases so the Holy Guardian Angel changes, leading you further along the path into the unknown. The magician is aiming to establish a set of ideas and images that correspond with the nature of his genius, and at the same time receive inspiration from that source. It is your purpose in existing. It is what you are here for, it is why you chose to incarnate at this time, in this place. Its goals become your goals, it cares about what you do and wants you to achieve them. To ally your desires with its desires is to enter into a divine communication...*[28]

---

27 Again, for a meaningful discussion from Sanskrit scholars, c.f. Bäumer and Dupuche 2005: *Void and Fullness*.

28 Humphries & Vayne 2004: *Now That's What I Call Chaos Magick*, p. 141.

This idea has totally seeped into my Life and it is connected to my deep drive to reconnect with the Divine: a hidden, deeper reality that lurks behind the outer forms of the visible, measurable world. It was exactly this mystical fire that burned in my heart when I entered the magical path. Only later did I come to know that concepts such as sigils, magical power, and sorcery are part of what is called magick. It is the mystic's passion that pushed me ever forward on my journey towards *Runa*, the eternal mystery. This mystical fire of Consciousness and Transformation I identify as the main purpose of my life, and according to the Indian philosopher Ravi Ravindra, it is identified in Vedic sources with the Vedic god of fire, Agni.[29] But life and magic, at the very core, are the same, "and both can only be about a spiritual journey, a path towards a Re-Union...with God, with the Divine."[30] Even if I do consider the idea of a 'Creator' as an anthropomorphic concept that is unnecessary in my understanding of the Divine, and even if the concept of 'God' sounds heavily Christian or monotheistic, it has always been clear for me why I have entered the magical arena: to reunite with the source of All. Nothing else is serious.

And the source of All is No-Thing or Nuit, 'the Boundless Light,' as modern Qabalists put it. In this sense I consider the modern, neo-Satanic conceptions of the supposed Left Hand Path, with their notion 'preserve the self at all costs! Resist the evil mystics!' as being rather misleading.[31] I do not believe that the mystical process known as *coincidentia oppositorum* (coincidence of opposites) leads to 'self-annihilation' as Aquino and his followers believe. The principle of the uniting of opposites is ancient and constitutes a fundamental element of what Agostino Steuco called the *philosophia perennis*, the "eternal philosophy." The experience of the *coincidentia oppositorum* was used in describing an alchemical process, to be exact, its third or fourth stage, *rubedo* ('reddening'): the unification of humanity with God. In Thelemic mysticism this is the unification of the limited (individual consciousness), or *Hadit*, with the unlimited (cosmic consciousness), or Nuit, 'the Boundless Light.'

---

29 Ravi Ravindra: https://temenos.thelincolncentre.co.uk/20120903/

30 Genesis P-Orridge.

31 It may be useful as a passage, a phase of transition, during the initiatory process, especially for those who have no stable ego-identity and personality. But to confuse the ego with the Self is a profound misconception and error. Again Kelly's remarks on "Ego and Self" in *Apophis* (2009) are indispensable. This book is still very influenced by his Setian background, but it allows for more subtle interpretations of the ego/Self relation whilst still maintaining a heavy Left Hand Path focus.

In this regard the mystical experience can be seen as a revelation of the oneness of things previously believed to be different. Such insight into the unity of things is an experience of a transcendent reality, a meta-level, the *unus mundus*, as described above. This level of being (actually transcending being and non-being) should not be regarded as 'foreign' to magic, but as its fundament – the origin and aim of all magic – that helps us to explore the metaphysics of our practice. The experience of the coincidence of opposites is known in Germanic spirituality (consider the Norse cosmogony of Fire and Ice) and continued in Christianity. It can be found in various descriptions of German mystics, who constituted a religious current known as German or Rhineland mysticism, a late medieval Christian mystical movement that was especially prominent within the Dominican order and in Germany. Although its origins can be traced back to Hildegard von Bingen, it is mostly represented by Meister Eckhart, Johannes Tauler, Henry Suso, Rulman Merswin and Margaretha Ebner, and the Friends of God (*Gottesfreunde*). Actually this "golden thread" (Jocelyn Godwin) can be found in magico-mystical traditions all over the world. The idea occurs also in the traditions of Tantric Hinduism. These mystical features are shared by the esoteric teachings of many religions. They do not seem to be just bizarre or irrelevant products of the fantasies of certain religious enthusiasts, but rather the lived and embodied knowledge of each religion that is central to its thorough understanding.[32]

> *Just as previously our deficient understanding of Christianity has been corrected by considering mysticism and such figures as Meister Eckhart and Saint John of the Cross and our understanding of Judaism has been corrected by the study of the Kabbalah and such figures as Isaac Luria, so our understanding of Hinduism will be revised when Tantrism and its key historical figures are given appropriate scholarly attention. Issues and individuals that were once considered bizarre or irrelevant must now be considered essential; without them our understanding is not merely intellectually impoverished but historically negligent.*[33]

---

[32] See my remarks on *Arfr* in this book in the chapter entitled "The Marriage of Chaos Magic and Heathenry."

[33] Douglas Renfrew Brooks 1990: *The Secret of the Three Cities: An Introduction to Hindu Sakta Tantrism*, p. ix.

In the same way it is true that our understanding of Islam will be transformed when Sufism is taken into account. These essential, dare I say eternal, truths are also known in the various Tantric schools of Mahayana Buddhism, including Zen, and in Daoism. Already in my teenage years I was aware of the significance of the mystical experience on the magical path, even if in an overtly romantic and 'psychedelicized' way. This might be the reason why in the beginning I did not understand the point of Chaos Magic, with its emphasis on 'results,' and why LaVeyan Satanism made me only shake my head in disgust or shrug my shoulders in apathy.[34] Then again, the 'old' systems of Western Magic (the Golden Dawn-style approach developed in the 19th century) seem to lose themselves in tables of correspondences and intellectual exercises for climbing up 'Jacob's Ladder' towards abstract conceptions of the Divine. This is why the Chaos approach popularized by Pete Carroll became necessary and why the chaotes developed such a rigorous, 'technocratic' approach to magic, where results are of main interest, not mystical mumbo-jumbo and cosmic foo-foo (with which the New Age became obsessed in an unhealthy way).

Over the years and decades some Chaos Magicians became drawn towards mystical experiences, despite Carroll's exclusion of mysticism in the Chaos Magic current. This can be explained rather easily from my point of view. It is because magic and mysticism are connected in profound ways. They are two sides of the same coin. If you exclude one from the other you do so at your own peril. It seems that the accumulation of many forms of gnosis, of many altered states of consciousness, leads to a mystical longing in a magician.

> *Repeated experience of higher states of consciousness eventually leads to some experience of the core paradox of individual being. The mind starts asking questions like: Why don't I always feel this ecstatic? Why don't we just get ecstatic when we finished our day's work? What is the origin of individual consciousness? Why does the ego keep twittering on in its tedious internal monologues of past-oriented identity, and what can I do about it? How can I get to an unconditioned mind? The occasional extra bit of money, sex, personal power, and healing no longer satisfy; everything is*

---

[34] Having said that I must say that nowadays I quite appreciate LaVey's Satanism via its influence on the works of Michael Kelly, as a path to unravel the Mysteries of the Flesh. Chaos Magic, of course, became a profound influence later.

> *muddied by the taste of the ego. Transformation and ecstasy become urgent.*[35]

The Genius of the chaos-mystical stance, which Dave Lee has formulated in *Chaotopia*, is that all descriptions of these higher states of consciousness (all these *Nirvānas*, *Ain Soph Aurs*, Nuits, *Pleromas*, *Suñyatās*, Gods, Holy Ghosts, etc.) are regarded as descriptions or 'maps' invented or developed by other psychonauts, who made their journeys to the hidden chambers of the Soul before us (mystics, tantrics, yogis, senseis, magi, gurus, enlightened teachers, etc.). And their 'maps' are not the 'territory' itself. A chaos mystic does not accept any theories about enlightenment, immortality, eternal bliss, or 'Big Daddy up there.' These are all theories. There are then two types of seekers if you like: those "working from a top-down/theoretical perspective (presumably because the reports they read resonate with some deep part of their own experience), and those who need to proceed from bottom up, proving the reality of the stages of higher consciousness to themselves at each stage, without assuming a pre-determined endpoint of enlightenment."[36]

To me this is the true difference between a Left Hand Path and a Right Hand Path initiate, if we still consider these categories to be useful at all. To me the Left Hand Path magician must strive to become the seeker who goes out, personally looks for what is behind the curtain, and afterwards develops a uniquely individual psychocosm, psychogeography, and magico-mystical system. In this sense, I believe that the best definition of the Left Hand Path is that one does not follow anyone or any fixed route to enlightenment, but rather that one follows one's own path. No dogmas, no popes, no generally accepted maps, no fixed roads and no final destinations – just Consciousness, Energy, Mystery, Willpower, Love, and 'the Endless One' – *She-en lo tiklah*. Shalom. Amen. And AUM.

---

[35] Dave Lee 2006 [1997]: *Chaotopia!*, p. 151.

[36] Dave Lee, personal communication.

Pine Ranger, MichaELFallson

Pine Ranger Love Song
MichaELFallson

Do spell Hel with just one L
DarkDark Green Lodge here we dwell
Fire 'pon thee when no-one sees
Gleaming darts from ancient trees
Sow our lives into your deaths
Harvest time your dying breath
Mumb bull ling your lord above
Is the king of light and love
All we hear is fear and war
Is that what you made god for?
You pervert our sacred sign
She will cull you and your kind
She has come to dictate now
Crush your domes 'top sacred sow
Nature grants our dearest wish
Homotheist feed the fish.

Goddess of Summer, MichaELFallson

Chaos Heathen Results Magic
Heimlich A. Laguz

Principles of Practice

One of Chaos Magic's crucial contributions to occult practice is the insight that it is the intensity of one's belief that causes the magical effect, not the content of one's belief. Thus magic can be effective for a vast variety of different practitioners, even for people who hold diametrically opposed beliefs. If I can work myself into a state where my everyday ego-self sloughs off and only the symbol of my intention remains in my consciousness, then my magical action stands a much better chance of working.

This means that really complex, elaborate ritual magic is not necessarily any better than sudden, improvised spell casting. If the complexity of my magical spell is so great that I have nothing left to actually feel the magic sweep me away, then it probably will become nothing more than empty motions. Conversely, if I feel deeply impassioned about something then the most minimal action can suffice as a vehicle for my magical intention to come to fruition.

An important implication of this approach is that *it makes belief a means to an end rather than an end in itself*. Counterintuitive though it may seem, right belief (orthodoxy) becomes a distant second to right action (orthopraxy). To safely and effectively use belief as a tool we have to continually work to shake it out of our systems, like a dog shaking off water. Once we regard belief as a tool we free ourselves from a lot of gratuitous complications, so long as we are fairly consistent in maintaining our sense of good-natured irony.

Unfortunately, many of the so-called magical authorities earned their reputations by foisting unnecessary complication on the rest of us. For example, when I acquired my first rune set I wanted to prepare it for divinatory use in as thorough and 'good' a way as possible. I turned to Edred Thorsson's recommendations, which included a complex ritual, memorization and recitation of extensive poetry, and so on.

None of these are necessarily bad things, but neither are they requisite for doing good magic, nor do they guarantee the quality of the magical act. Unfortunately, such voluminous directives were discouraging to say the least, and I procrastinated for a long time on preparing my runes. The implicit message Thorsson's words conveyed was that unless one is somehow *already* an occult master, one can do nothing.

Then one day I grew fed up with this situation. I let my impatience flood me, my frustration turn white hot. I stormed off, bought a paint brush and some paint (just plain old commercial acrylic paint with no 'occult' properties whatsoever), and reddened my runes in a fit of steaming fury. I recited no 'proper' incantations, wore no ritual garb, made no attempt to magically banish or hallow the space in which I worked. I probably broke every suggestion made in Thorsson's books.

And yet the runes, when done, throbbed with power, and I have used them for over 10 years to good effect. I have loaded them which such intense magical force that I don't need to do any kind of symbolic gesture or complex invocation when I want to do divination with them. I just have a quiet conversation with the querant, *actively listen until we agree that I understand the question*, throw the runes, and then discover all sorts of intriguing stories in their patterns. Sometimes I don't even look at the runes; just the act of throwing them opens my mind and, straight from intuition, I tell the person what they need to move forward.

So if this is all true, why bother with any kind of disciplined structure for practicing magic? I and other Chaos Magicians have been perfectly successful with getting a magical effect by evoking a deity, magic symbol, or other device that was only invented a few minutes before doing the magic! What benefit is there to struggling to understand the complex, vague, contradictory, and downright alien remnants of Heathen belief?

Two reasons:

1) it gets us out of our egos. I find, for example, that the imagery of the old rune poems inspires my magic in myriad ways. Those poems help me find a way of articulating my desire and intentions, creating rich weaves of association and depth of intent. I could make up my own magical alphabet of desire, but for some reason the ancients seemed to be more imaginative or more creative

than we moderns, and their mythological legacy affords better opportunities to blow my mind open.

2) The discipline of a tradition, even a sketchy, half-imagined tradition, helps the magician's psyche to cope with the shock of experiencing the extremes of magical-emotional intensity that dedicated practice can trigger. Jung suggests that religion serves to protect the vulnerable mind from being torn to shreds when it begins to voyage into the numinous unknown. We use Heathen mythology, then, as a harbor and a compass as we explore the wild magical seas. Myth is only a map, not the territory – of magical practice or of life. Nevertheless, it shelters and guides us in unexpectedly helpful ways.

All that said, how do you do results-focused magic, by which I mean, magic intended to produce some kind of more or less specific change in the self or the world? *Here's a basic template for casting a spell:*

1. Decide what you want to achieve. When you are learning to do this, I suggest creating goals that are altruistic or trivial. The more our ego is attached to a goal ('make me rich, beautiful, and loved!') the harder it is likely to be for us to reach a magically charged consciousness.

2. Create a symbolic representation of your intention. The classic Chaos Magic method is to write out your intention, knock out any repeating letters, and then arrange the remaining letters into an abstract symbol, a sigil. A Chaos Heathen would do the same, except that they might write out the intention in runes. Do not limit yourself, however! A sigil can be a song, a smell, the feeling of certain clothes, physical movements, a chant, or just about anything else (let your unconscious guide you!).

3. Achieve a state of focused attention on your sigil. For example, you could work yourself into a fit of emotion while focusing on your sigil; you could chant your sigil until you completely exit normal consciousness; you could visualize your sigil while exercising to a point of profound exhaustion; you could suddenly douse yourself with freezing water while visualizing the sigil; you could inscribe the sigil on eggs and then throw them into a roaring fire, letting the intention literally explode into being. The possibilities are limited only by your imagination, so feel free to say to yourself, "Deep Mind, tell me how best to fire my sigil," and listen carefully to whatever advice you give yourself.

4. Once you've 'peaked' and fired out your intention, let it go. Distract yourself, lose yourself in some other, irrelevant activity. If you find yourself dwelling on the intention or getting lost in thoughts of lust for result, gently turn your mind to the mantra "does not matter, need not be" or perhaps the mantra "that, or something better" (better yet, combine then into one statement). Chances are, you will find it hard to let go of your magical intention. That's fine – perfectionism is a waste of time, a demon well worth dismantling and defying. This is the bit where our efforts to detach from rigid belief pay dividends, which is a roundabout way of saying that the more inner, spiritual work you do, the better you'll get at results magic (albeit the less you'll probably need to use it).

You might like to write down what you did in a diary, but make sure not to look at it again for some time. It can be very fun to go back and review your record of things you enchanted for; many of them will not have come to pass, but a surprising number will have indeed manifested, often in ways that defy any rational expectation you might have harbored.

If you really want to short-circuit the traps of belief, attachment, and lust for result, create a bunch of sigils, set them aside until you've forgotten their purpose, and only then fire them. Or get together with other folks and exchange sigils without explaining what they mean. You can hardly lust for a result that is unknown to you!

Personally I no longer bother to track my results because I trust that the spells that will benefit me will work and the ones that I framed with unhelpful or foolish intent will fail. Our goal is to graduate from entertaining the illusion that we are 'imposing our will' on the world. Really what sigil magic – runic or otherwise – involves is making ourselves into fine-tuned antennae to the radio waves of *wyrd*. We are learning how to ride the tides of causality by making ourselves attractive to outcomes that are in our interests.

This is reverence for mystery in operative terms – by that I mean, this is internalizing a runic (= mysterious) spirit within ourselves...or rather, scraping away the illusion of egoic certainty and connecting with the fabric of mystery that bubbles up through our beings. Setting our spirits on a more profound, if ineffable, footing than anything the mere ego might furnish (though, of course, we still need the ego if we are to remain alive).

In *Visual Magick*, Jan Fries describes a lovely technique for doing sigil magic, one that he says is inspired by archaic magical praxis. Basically, we go for a walk! Along the way, we let ourselves be attracted to random objects in our path – sticks, trash, rocks, whatever. We do not set a hard intention of our destination, although we might have a special location in mind. When we get there, we create a sigil out of whatever we picked up on our journey.

We invent some simple or complex poetic statement to charge up the sigil, and we let ourselves become obsessed with the symbol we have been guided to create. When we are done we leave, perhaps destroying the sigil, but better yet leaving it to decompose naturally, its essence seeping into the web of *wyrd* and guiding it into new directions.

This way of doing results magic does not require a pre-determined intention or outcome, and can be a lovely way of showing reverence for mystery. I use it often, and especially recommend it when in environments of natural beauty.

An example of my own runic sigil results magic practice:

I lived in an apartment on the ground floor. A family moved in upstairs with three very naughty children. There was always fighting, loud noises, and drama radiating through our ceiling. There was a lot of anger in that family and we could hear everything – slamming of kitchen drawers, breaking of plates, kids screaming at each other (the parents seemed helplessly overwhelmed). Then the children started throwing garbage off their balcony into our courtyard. Then, one of them urinated off their balcony into our courtyard.

When this happened, I went into a rage. I grabbed a random piece of paper (I think it was a shopping list) and on the back drew a very crude image of a wolf eating a child. In runes I scrawled "I have you now." Then I screwed the paper up and tore it to pieces. The children immediately became much better behaved, and stopped vandalizing our courtyard. Interestingly, there was more laughter and much less screeching and thumping.

However, it was clear that this family was not happy in their apartment. There were too many of them and they were too boisterous. We found the parents to be very irritating; they turned into supercilious and difficult neighbors. Again, I let my feelings build to boiling point. I made a ᚱ *Raidho* ("Riding") rune out of clay and put it in a cupboard near the ceiling, imagining that its power radiated up into their apartment. It symbolized the message "move on" or "move out!"

A week later, they moved out, breaking their lease to do so. We were utterly stunned at this turn of events. It was most satisfying, and the new tenants were very quiet and polite.

Although I used anger to drive my magic in both cases, I did not have a vindictive intention as such. For example, I truly think it was in this family's interest to move to a more appropriate dwelling. In general, it is effective practice to wish for good things to happen even to those we dislike. Not only because compassion is a powerful and worthy discipline, but because healing someone's misery will prevent them from venting that misery on anyone else.

Note that in these two cases of doing magic, I did not at all forget my intention; albeit at the time I was disciplined in my thinking and gently distracted myself from lusting for a result.

One reason people find themselves needing to employ over-elaborate magical practices is because their egos get too overblown and they cannot let go of themselves enough to let the magic work. The pedantic over-ornamentation of rituals offered in, say, Edred Thorsson's books suggest to me that the author has acquired a bloated opinion of himself and as such struggles to actualize his magical potential. How ironic (and tragic, give his contribution to modern rune magic).

In contrast, both spells I just described were very simple (the second just a single rune!). What made the difference was not elaboration or perfect, ritualized pedantry – it was clarity and openness of emotion and intention.

Learning to be unattached to outcome is so important. It is very hard to get into a deep state of ecstasy, anger, stillness, silliness, or concentration if one is riddled with worries about whether the magic will work. This is one reason why I often do sigil magic without framing an intention; I ask my Deep Mind to invent an intention without telling me and to furnish me with a sigil for that intention. In this way I again am able to practice reverence for mystery. I choose to fully trust that my Deep Mind, my well into the collective unconscious, into *wyrd* itself, will do what is best for me.

Magic wants to be fun, even wants to offer us the opportunity to make fun of ourselves. Like everything else, it benefits from being practiced with a slight spirit of irony.

If you want to get good at results magic, set the goal of casting one spell a week. Let it be as simple and clumsy as you like. It doesn't even need to have a strong emotional drive behind it. Say to yourself, "I want to receive a piece of unexpected good news in the coming week," draw a random symbol or compose a random nonsense chant, and then fire it off by drawing it vigorously, repetitively, and playfully for a few minutes, or chanting and whispering and singing and shouting it until you get bored or feel ridiculous. Record the intention, then forget about it and get on with life.

Doing sigil magic isn't just a means to an end; letting ourselves play with nonsense and whimsy is inherently restorative for our psyches. It is hard to remember to indulge in this luxury, because we live in a world that celebrates boredom, narrowness, and habituated complacency. To quote a magico-anarchist movement I partook of, we need to "color the gray" of consensus reality, with its environmental degradation, racism, greed, imperialism, paranoia, dualistic thinking, arrogance, and shallowness (to name a few).

The architects of our fatuous consensus reality are often not so much evil as pathologically bland (or perhaps, to follow Hannah Arendt, evil just happens to be banal), and they want us to be that way too. That way we'll acquiesce to whatever nightmares they see fit to concoct. If we want to honor the Mystery, the Rune, the deepest origin of our being, we can explore recolonizing our psyches with color and motion and life. Playful, non-attached sigil/results magic is a lovely tool for achieving that goal. Especially when it involves going for long walks, staring at the sea, swimming in a river, dancing, eating good food, attending virtuoso musical performances, having sex, climbing trees or mountains, or doing push-ups until our ego-selves wink out in a hail of endorphins. And don't forget Austin Osman Spare's death posture!

Galdor and Recitation of Poetry

I like to sing and I like to chant, and sometimes (perhaps incorrectly from an historical perspective) such activities are referred to by the archaic term *galdor*. Chanting runes is a wonderful practice. I like to chant the Elder Futhark in order, which to me simply means 'everything in its right place.' When my life is out of control and I don't know what to do, the Elder Futhark can be a wonderful purgative and restorative. I recommend it for just about anything that ails.

But remember: irony! Archaeology tells us that the old Heathens wrote the Elder Futhark order in a couple of variants, as well as over time changing it into the Anglo-Saxon Futhork and the Younger Futhark. Experiment, like the ancestors did, with swapping the order of, say, ᛟ Othala and ᛞ Dagaz. They were irreverently reverent, and reverently irreverent. What fun!

So chant with abandon. Drum, dance, sway, shake, gurgle, tremble, shriek. If you can open up enough to indulge in glossolalia then you're really getting somewhere. Your bodymind has so many wonderful possibilities of expression that you cannot even imagine. Let go and let it come forth. The runes are a door to embodied, exultant mystery.

One of the nice things about using runes as sigils is that each rune is both a drawn character and a spoken name. Furthermore, it names an object or activity. Furthermore, it references the old rune poems, which conjure lovely images that our Deep Minds can ride into magical places.

Memorizing the rune poems, and learning more about the cultural history that gives them sense and meaning, is a wonderful way to attune them for results magic purposes (as well as a wonderful way to cultivate a more primordial, magically-charged, everyday mindset). In fact, I regard this as essential if you want to get good at rune magic, and good at transforming your own consciousness. Plus, being able to recite the rune poems is one heck of a party trick!

Get more ambitious. Memorize mythic poems. Watch Benjamin Bagby's live DVD performance of Beowulf with nothing but a harp and his memory – now *there's* a fucking poet (the extras on the DVD will teach you a lot about galdor and Heathen poetic expression, too)! Better yet, write your own poems. If you don't know how to do this, I suggest reading the myths. In the *Prose Edda*, Snorri gives lots of advice on how to do it. Read Seamus Heaney's translation of *Beowulf*. Read J. R. R. Tolkien. Read Steven T. Abell.

Inspire yourself! If you can, do what the Old Norse did. Find the grave of a famous writer and sit out with it all night, invoking the spirit of the dead genius to educate and inspire you. Or, perform the ritual presented below, which is designed to invoke Odinnic inspiration. In truth, the term galdor probably referred more to reciting poetry than it did to chanting runes.

A good poem is a transformative monument in itself. Consider this one of mine. I wrote it and eight other poems in the course of a few days. At the start of those days I prayed to Odin for inspiration, and I made sure I gave a little time each day to listen for inspiration. I also set myself a deadline, which I found motivating. And I set the intention that the process would trigger inner transformation. Now I wear these poems as badges of inner spiritual growth, medals of psychic valor, as well as portals for future growth.

Redux

My skull shatters
Gives birth to a flower
In halos of blood, bone,
and raw desire

A tender marionette
Hinged limbs and grinding joints
Shedding rust like hail

This discovery, restoration
The sap pours violent
Burns with laughter
Irrepressible resonance

The agony of the ecstasy of desire
Exultant in the fury of flowing,
white-hot honey

Recover my fertility
Erupt from mediocrity
Scythe gripped in one hand
Plowshare in the other

This poem is one I have memorized (in fact I just typed it out off the top of my head!). I record myself reading the poem, then I listen to it on repeat, gradually getting to the point where I can say it along with the recording, until I have it stored in my mind. Once I have it encoded, I make a point to recite it periodically. I have poems that are so ingrained that I can recite them after years of not even thinking about them! Do this while traveling to and from work, school, or whatever. My workplace is a nice 45-minute walk from my home, and this gives me good opportunities for memorizing poems that grow ever more rich with sigilized meaning.

The old Heathens were basically an oral culture. Their poets and law-speakers had to rely on memory alone. Re-enacting this can be a powerful way to take in a magically charged, archaic spirit that can serve us marvelously even in a modern, literate era of forgetfulness.

Runic Inscription Formulae

Mindy Macleod and Bernard Mees are two Australian archaeologists who wrote a marvelous book called *Runic Amulets and Magic Objects*. It's a great summary of runic archaeological finds. Along the way, they analyze common elements in these inscriptions, and in so doing provide a handy instruction manual for anyone wishing to use runes for magical purposes. Read their book! You'll be amazed at how much more creative, inconsistent, silly, ribald, and lush the old Heathens were in their runic magical practices when compared to contemporary esoteric runic authors.

But in case you aren't going to read their book right away, I will here quote the main elements that Macleod and Mees identified in the magical runic inscriptions they studied. Not every runic formula included every one of these elements, but they are so ubiquitous that they seem essential. While we need not make a slavish obsession out of reconstructing historical practice, we will benefit greatly from educating ourselves about the past. Often it proves much deeper and more inspired than anything that we novice moderns can squeak out with our own pitiful attempts at 'unverified personal gnosis.' Maybe in a few centuries we'll catch up with the ancients' creativity and playfulness but right now we're too weighed down by habits of dogma and belief, and we're far too self-conscious of how shallow and awkward our modern Heathenry still is.

Here are the five elements of historic magical runic inscriptions/talismans that Macleod and Mees identify from their exhaustive review of extant runic finds (quoted from page 82 of *Runic Amulets and Magic Objects*):

1. LETTER SEQUENCES: either Futhark sequences or apparently coded assortments of runes.

2. NAMING EXPRESSIONS, often just a single name, but sometimes a more complex construction, typically in the first person: 'I am called NN.'

3. The terms often called formula or CHARM WORDS, including alu and laukaz.

4. SYMBOLS, such as tree-like shapes, tamgas, swastikas, and triskelia.

5. ITEM DESCRIPTIONS, such as 'brooch,' 'pendant,' 'horn,' or the like.

Not every historic inscription includes all five elements, but many might use, say, three of them. A few comments are in order.

Firstly, the **letter sequences** are the sort of thing we generate using, say, the method described above of writing a statement of intent and then scrambling it and reducing it down to nonsense. Many magical inscriptions are difficult or impossible to decode, perhaps to help fool the ego and get the magic flowing.

(In this vein, a clever trick is to take some statements of intent, reduce them to statements that give no hint of their meaning, write the statements in runes, then put them away for six months so you totally forget the intention they represent. That way you are freed of the burden of lust for result and can just have fun as you release your desire-seeds into the world.)

Secondly, **item descriptions**. What seems to be happening here is the use of a runic inscription to awaken or cultivate the spirit of an object. Say I take a small slip of wood and carve runes that express the statement (possible in a coded or scrambled form) "health giver." I then drop this in my shoe and forget about it. Meanwhile, I seem to be just that little more able to shrug off injury and sickness than I used to be. Imagine creating talismans with names like "Lucky," "Joy," "Inner Growth," "Bravery Bringer." "Generous of Heart," and "Mind-Opener" would be good ones too. "Helps-Relinquish-Attachment-to-Belief" seems like a wonderful amulet to create.

In this case the runes are a trigger to give the spirit of the object direction and intention. If all things are alive, then we can instill them with focus for that life. Granting them positive names, carved in runes, in a ritual process of caressing, calling, complimenting, celebrating, and sharing, might be the way to forge this bond. Runes are here used to unlock our relationship to the magic of all things, dispelling the illusion that the universe is composed of inert matter.

Thirdly, **charm words**. The meaning of many of the charm words found on archaeological inscriptions are debated, and I will not here enter into that debate. Suffice to say that they seem to lend additional potency to the incantations. Sort of like how "final notice" makes an unpaid bill seem more important to its recipient, or "USDA organic" gives a certain food product an aura of quality. Use *alu* and *laukaz* freely; the old Heathens seemed to throw them into runic inscriptions indiscriminately. Better yet, read Macleod and Mees' book and get a deeper sense for the logic of this element of rune magic.

Fourthly, **symbols**. Abstract symbols of all sorts can please the eye and the unconscious alike, and it seems that some of the runes may have started out as such symbols themselves (ᛞ Dagaz comes to mind). Again, use them freely. Or draw, say, a big circular serpent biting its tail and draw runes inside its body. Old Heathen inscriptions often combined art and runes. Here's a chance to let your improvising, playful spirit run wild.

Fifthly, **item descriptions**. I have a journal. I write "journal" on it in runes. This is really primitive magic, naming something for what it is, nothing more and nothing less. It is magic that celebrates the fact that this world is always-already loaded with beauty, potency, wonder, mystery. That, even in all its horrors and depravity, it is somehow sublime. Such item descriptions are a kind of runic existential celebration of Being: This is This. Gratitude is a very, very powerful magical attitude to cultivate.

Item descriptions probably help the item to do its job that much better: "computer," "guitar," "car," "sunglasses," just as readily as "knife" or "wand."

So perhaps I carve a small slip of wood with runes that say "this tine is called Lucky – ᛚᚢᚲ ᛚᚢᚲ ᛚᚢᚲ ᚴᛦᛦ," and then carve a small quartered circle. I have just connected myself, in a living, creative, fluid way, to a tradition that goes back several thousand years. I am grounded in a tradition without being stuck in rote, hide-bound tedium. This sort of reconstructionism opens our possibilities for imaginative creation rather than hindering them. I drop this in, say, a drawer of my desk at work. Maybe, just maybe, daily events at my job start to work out just a little better for me than mere chance would suggest I deserve.

A runic results-magic activity I enjoy doing is creating a statement of intent, scrambling it, then turning the runes this generates into a sigil that I paint using an application on my smart phone. I then post this on Facebook, usually with a line or two of off-the-cuff, non sequitur poetry (often humorous or incoherent). Every time someone then 'likes' or comments on the image, the spells gets pushed a little deeper into the well of *wyrd*.

Sometimes I create these without knowing myself what they mean, but trusting that they'll do what they're supposed to do. They certainly seem to work well, particularly when I do them on others' behalf, and even when I don't invest a lot of emotion into them (incidentally, it is excellent, excellent form to do lots of magic for the sake of other people; one trait the ancient Heathens celebrated highly was generosity).

Ritual as a Sigil

Although I've been pooh-poohing the use of elaborate magical rites or practices, they can be very helpful. The trick is they have to come from a spirit of creativity, not just rote action. Look at other peoples' rituals as sources of inspiration for your own. Don't feel obliged to digest them wholesale. Become your own kind of magician; only you can be the best at being you.

I will here offer three examples of my own ritual practices. The third is a full and complete template for ritual practice. It is simple enough that you *could* do it as written, but complex enough that it will stretch you into new territory. So even though I don't generally recommend slavishly following other peoples' ritual ideas, I make an exception for this one since it is set up as a nice learning tool. But really, please, cannibalize it to your heart's content. Don't be a drone!

All of these rituals have had profound effects on the course of my life; partly this is because that was my goal for them. If I am going to do something elaborate, the intended outcome should be proportionate. I like to leave it somewhat open-ended, too, since I've learned that my conscious ideas about what is best for me are often a shadow compared to what the gods can guide me towards.

Also, a strong ritual will start to affect you even weeks before you undertake it. As it comes closer and you get more and more prepared for it, it begins to exert a kind of gravitational force. Meaningful coincidences, sudden psychological breakthroughs, happy culminations begin to gather like clouds to a storm. We are seeking to open ourselves as conduits to the Unknown in a vulnerable, creative, celebratory, honest, playful, passionate, *fully alive* fashion.

Ritual Example one: Reconnecting with Odin

This ritual emerged from a period of spiritual constipation. In my arrogance I sought to curry favor with a god who is not meant for me, and in so doing offended my patron, Odin. I indulged in a series of meditative/visualizing journeys and conversations with Odin, and it became clear that I needed to make amends. As it was, seemingly due to my ill-conceived actions, my health was falling apart, my emotional life was haywire, and everything was misery. I was in a state of desperation and chaos.

For my ritual to set things right, I arranged to have an audience of one other person, because the vulnerability of having an audience helps with ritual as a performance. You are forced to either go there completely or not at all. I prepared offerings of beer, organic butter, organic sea salt, water, fire (from a candle that a close friend and I used on a necromantic adventure), garlic, ginger, and tissues soaked with my blood.

I set the atmosphere by putting on some ambient Odinnic music of my own composition.[1] I opened the ritual by singing the singular rune ᚫ Ansuz, getting progressively louder and more aggressive until I was purely screeching and screaming my guts out.

I also banged a hammer and a magical wooden sword, using these rhythms to build the intensity of the moment.

Then I called Woden in all his dark aspects, as god of bloodshed, war, hate, fear, betrayal, violence, destruction, and all that fun stuff. Then called him as god of poetry, song, sex, wisdom, hospitality, healing, and all of that fun stuff.

---

1 You can find out more at https://einskopudhrgaldra.bandcamp.com/album/ein-skopudhr-galdra-mistsorrow-split-release

I called him by many of his old names...and a few new ones spilled from my lips too, like Elric of Melnibone, and The Raven King, and Saint Nick, and even Satan (who Goethe describes as blue-cloaked, one-eyed, and raven-friendly in *Faust*, after all!). I was a Chaos Heathen at work.

While all this was happening I was involuntarily writhing, staggering, thrashing, shuddering, shaking – *seidhr*, at least as I experience it as a Jan Fries-loving *seidhmadr* (I freely acknowledge the historical limitations of his take on *seidhr* of course). My body was plunging into wild paroxysms of its own, my consciousness going right on with it.

Until I calmed a little. I started calling "Woden" quite softly, over and over. A most tremendous sensation, like lightning bolts, spread through my scalp and from my hands up my arms. It spilled down over my brow like a helm – I wonder if this was one meaning of 'Helm of Awe.' If you can imagine pure awe, transformed into a vast electrical charge, and then run through your body, but with pleasure instead of pain as its effect, then you're getting the general idea.

It's rare for me to get such a dramatic energetic and physiological response from my possession work. Such experiences are so beyond my ego and the domain of its power and they're so reassuring, healing, and humbling. I cried a little with joy that my patron would impose himself on me so strongly that I would feel it right there in my nervous system.

And then I was his.

I cannot say too much about what happened because it's all very vague, but he accepted the gifts and gave my audience a bit of a freak out. My cat didn't recognize me when He was in charge and avoided us. I physically changed in appearance. Things were made good between us. The rift, healed.

He cast some runes for me too – funnily the first rune to come out was ᚨ Ansuz, His rune! And they portended lovely things – healing, positive change, hard work rewarded, blockages destroyed.

And in the next two days all my hitherto intractable health issues resolved without explanation, my emotions became equanimous, and I found a renewed sense of purpose and creativity in my life. I had become frustrated and frightened by Odin's inconsistencies and chaos, but I discovered that without that connection I began to wither away. The ritual healed the breach of my own cowardice.

While possessing me, Odin said something, I vaguely recall, about an irony of my personality. Namely that I give myself an awful hard time for not being perfect (and therefore a better agent for him). Yet my imperfections arise because Woden is himself imperfect, and thus make me closer to him in nature. I love irony, and this ritual taught me how to better appreciate it.

Ritual Example Two: Six-Fold Flame Sequence

The purpose of this series of rituals was to push myself to the 'next level' in healing old traumas, perfecting strengths, and shedding blockages, fears, and so forth. To become a consummate vessel of inspired action. At the time of writing it is a year since I completed the rituals, and I still feel their unfolding impact on my life.

As with the first ritual example, I developed the ideas for this sequence of rituals through visualization and automatic writing. I sit with pen and paper, turn my attention inward, invite Odin to instruct me. Then I write what comes to me and ask questions as we go. Sometimes I work with Odin, sometimes other figures. On this occasion, it was with Odin. You will no doubt discover your own guides if you decide to explore automatic writing.

I was instructed to perform six interlinked rituals, six weeks to elapse between each, with ᚲ Kenaz (the sixth rune) as the runic theme. Each ritual was in honor of my connection to Odin. The goal was to accelerate the burning away of all that is inessential in me, to move significantly closer to becoming a consummate incarnation of the Odinnic river of fire.

The components of the rituals included fasting, sleep deprivation, physical ordeal, and memorization of poetry. Offerings were made, and oaths of renunciation. I found that even the discipline of keeping these rituals happening in the midst of my outrageously busy life became itself a ritual privation.

Fasting was not a great imposition as I was practicing intermittent fasting anyway. Sleep deprivation was easy due to my demanding schedule of work and graduate study. Physical ordeal came from sitting in difficult postures without moving (something that I have come to make a mainstay of my meditation practice, in keeping with the instruction of S. N. Goenka). The poems I memorized and recited are the nine poems described above; for the first ritual I had four poems and for each subsequent ritual I added one more until I have all nine for the final rite. More recently I have turned these poems into the basis for ritual performances.

Offerings included mead, incense, singing/chanting, and wine (described to me as "dinner for wolves;" in the myths it says Freki and Geri eat Odin's breakfast and he consumes only wine, and so by the power of free association and the love of obscure 80s fantasy films...). Each ritual I renounced one poisonous (at least for me) luxury, in order: caffeine, refined sugar, chocolate, corn products, dried fruit, and meals within certain times of the day.

The structure of each ritual was pretty loose, but looks something like this:

1) Stay up all night (not easy with my schedule, and being a self-made morning person!).
2) Chant the Elder Futhark and invoke the hail form of Hagalaz to clear and open the space.
3) Recite the statement of intent given to me: "I purify and prepare myself as an avatar and conduit for the River of Fire. Let the waters rise and flood the banks." Then recite the memorized poems.
4) Offer incense and chant specified runic combinations until exhausted or a feeling of completion makes an appearance.
5) Offer mead and wine, along with more chanting or other madness.
6) Final improvised concluding remarks.

The changes and developments brought about by the rituals have been beautiful. An unexpected gift for which I am most grateful is that Odin used this magic to push me into connection with another deity who has in turn granted me profound love and guidance.

The rites have triggered what has been a strange journey for me into the gradual cultivation and revision of a more extreme yet balanced sense of gender identity and sexuality: libido into the broadest sense of lust for the senses and celebration of life. I am instructed to become both an ascetic and a sensualist. I am learning in subtle ways the spiritual benefits of not only pushing myself beyond, but also pacing, listening, softening.

This sort of results magic is, for all of the elaborate preparations and activity, more subtle because it deals in deeper strata of *wyrd*. The practices I performed – particularly the memorization – have had a strange rewiring effect on my nervous system. In this light, the seemingly bizarre self-destructive practices of Indian *sadhus* now make a new, visceral sense to me.

The discipline of staging these rituals every six weeks, with various preparatory activities before each, helped keep me from slipping into vacant, day-in-day-out complacency. If we do not make space for the magic to open into our lives then we are condemned to a thin existence. Is this still sigil magic? Absolutely. It simply goes far beyond the narrow focus of specific operant spell casting and into territory altogether more wild and strange.

Ritual Example Three: Bolverkr Mead of Inspiration Rite

As noted, this ritual is presented as a template for what you can do. Feel free to try it as written, or better yet adapt it to your personal needs!

Unsubstantiated Personal Gnosis alert: While the ritual is directly inspired by Heathen mythology, the practical side of things is pretty much cobbled together from made up techniques which might or might not approximate historical practice (and which I adapted from various sources of which I have now lost track).

Before undertaking this ritual, you should fully familiarize yourself with the tale from the *Prose Edda* which inspired it (the tale is in the *Skaldskaparmal* section, pages 62-64 of the Everyman edition).

This is a solitary working, although adapting it for group use seems possible.

Because this ritual works with extremes of unconsciousness and hyper-consciousness, you need to be prepared for the possibility that repressed trauma or the like may come forth. Working with powerful images of the collective unconscious is always a calculated risk and this is not something to be undertaken lightly.

Be sure to thoroughly familiarize yourself with all aspects of this ritual, especially remember the props, etc., that you will need. You may like to tape yourself reading the guided visualization, leaving long pauses at points where a lot has to happen. Then you can play it during the working if you prefer to have the actual guide as written during guided meditations. Personally, though, I don't think this will be necessary.

The images of serpent and eagle are easily tied to body energy systems. You might like to experiment with corresponding the appropriate energy centers with the energy extremes this working involves. You might also like to open up these two energy centers after the hallowing so as to heighten the effects of the working.

Finally, regarding the visualization meditation, if you are female you may be uncomfortable taking on Odin's male form. If so, simply imagine Odin as female. Simple! Alternately, you might want to imagine yourself as Freyja (the 'seeker of *Odhr* [inspiration],' or for those of non-binary gender, Loki. If you take one of these latter options, you might want to change the names invoked in the poetry to mention Freyja or Loki as well as Odin/Bolverkr. Be creative.

1) Hagalaz Hallowing

Perform a hammer hallowing, but trace the hail form of Hagalaz instead of the hammer, and call on Hagalaz instead of Thor. Of course, the 'hammer hallowing' has no basis in historical practice, but we'll overlook that for the present purposes. Feel free to substitute something that seems more appropriate. Given the magical focus of this rite, incorporating runes into the opening is appropriate.

2) Guided Visualization

For parts of this visualization you may want to impressionistically glaze over certain sections (Odin doing work all summer, etc.). The point is to activate the images and interactions, not to slavishly imagine every detail in 'real-time.'

Lie down. Make sure you are wearing comfortable clothing. Make sure you are in a posture that is relaxing. Background music such as something by Ein Skopudhr Galdra may be appropriate. Take a few deep breaths and relax.

Now close your eyes, allow yourself to move into a regular and easy breathing pattern. Visualize...but also hear, smell, taste, and feel what you see:

...You are standing at a crossroads. The sky is dark and broods with clouds. The land is verdant and wet. In the distance, the jagged fangs of mountains loom, and dark forests of pine and ash cast mysterious, menacing shadows. It is dusk, and the light is fading.

About you is thrown a deep blue cloak, and from one eye you can see nothing, for it is gone. To the northern road, you see a field of hay, being mown by nine hard-laboring peasants. You walk towards them.

When they see you, you should greet them and offer to sharpen their scythes. Do so. Afterwards, they will be much impressed, and when they ask for the stone, you avoid suggesting a price for it. You toss it in the air, and in their haste to claim it, they slay one another.

You take up the stone, gingerly, for you take no pleasure in your killing, but it is needful for your quest.

Ahead is a great long hall, and you continue towards it...

...Outside the hall sits Baugi, a towering etin of brute features and rough clothes. He seems distraught, and when greeted, he tells you his peasants are dead and his livelihood at stake. You tell him you are Bolverkr and offer your services in exchange for the mead of Suttung, his brother. He accepts, and you work until winter, the land turning grey and white around you ...

...Baugi leads you to the foot of Suttung's mountain, and points to the tunnel he claims to have carved.

But as you move to enter this dark and shadowy hole, he turns, unfurls his bulk and height, and raises his club to block your passage. He ripples with rage and might, and threatens all manner of dreadful suffering to you should you not turn back. You must outwit this slow-wit – in some way earn passage past him. Violence will merely get your defeat, however, for he is too strong.

When Baugi is passed, you fall down to your knees. A dreadful heat and agony fills you, as the solidity and structure of your form, your mind, your sense of self, all dissolve. With a piercing cry, you fall to the ground, a serpent, and slither deep into the mountain...

...Darkness. For how long? Here you are in your deepest unconscious, your personal Well of Wyrd, in the land of Hel where the past sleeps, waiting to be made into the future again. Only you will know what you experience. Let yourself fall into a stillness of mind, visualizing darkness. Allow the hidden content of your deeper self rise to awareness, and feel the powerful will and force that lies slumbering beneath. Then, gradually, let the hidden powers and force of your unconscious rise, rise up, a tide at first gentle then violent. When the intensity is right, you slither from the hole into the darkened cave of Gunnlod...

...And open your eyes, ready for the next part of the rite.

3) Statement of Intent

Face north, standing in the ᛉ Elhaz (arms raised upwards 45 degrees from ground) posture. Speak forth the following:

Odin!

As Bolverkr, Baugi ye fooled
And crept at wisdom's call
As grave-born serpent hard and cold
'Neath Suttung's mountain hall.

Lay thou then with Gunnlod
Though nights of lust three
And drank from three of deepest bowls
Mead of poetic ecstasy!

Soon after swiftly flew thou didst
From Suttung's deadly chase
Eagle wings fast borne on wind
Thy foe you far outraced

I call you now to wrench aside
The walls 'tween Asgard and Hel!
Throw me deep in wisdom freed
As I remake thy spell!

4) Loading

Leap up and take up your horn and fill it with mead. Scream/vibrate/vocalize/sing/chant the following, focusing on unleashing the energies of your words into the mead (visualize too!). Play around the format, using repetitive chanting, drumming, dancing, whatever it takes to get you really pumping.

Bolverkr!

Othroerir!
Bodn!
Son!

Fehu!
Laguz!
Dagaz!

ANSUZ! ANSUZ! ANSUZ!

5) Drinking

Drink down as much of the mead as you can, in three great gulps. Remember to leave some of the drink in the horn for the giving (see below).

Raise the horn above and imagine/feel ecstasy and inspiration burning through your body as the mead spills through. Its fire streaming through your veins, your flesh, your mind. Let the sensations flow through your nervous system, opening your awareness as fully as possible, completely infusing you. It is likely that each individual will experience the effects of the rite differently.

6) Poetics

Speak (perhaps shout?) the following:

Suttung's weight will hold me not!
'Cross the heavens I have shot!
Soaring over worlds so wide
Kvasir's blood burns inside!

I return to poets all!
I return to Asgard's Hall!
Hail Bolverk who shows the path!
Wisdom claimed, I win my task!

7) Sharing

Pour the remaining mead into a bowl. This is Bolverkr's share.

8) Closing

Declare: "By Hel and Asgard, this work has been wrought!"

9) Giving

Take the remaining mead to the foot of a (presumably nearby) tree and pour it there, saying "To Bolverkr, and earth spirits all."

I have only used this working once but I fully intend to do it again. I experienced a number of synchronicities leading up to it, including strange mead-fuelled and inspiring meetings with different folks on the two nights leading up to the ritual. You know you're headed for a powerful ritual experience when you can feel such reverberations radiating from it in advance.

The guided visualization triggered some pretty far out energy flows in my body, and the trick I used to outwit Baugi made me laugh out loud. I won't say what I did, however – this is something that others who try this working might enjoy working out for themselves.

The rite proper made me veritably explode with life. The mead tasted especially potent. As I transferred the mead from drinking vessel to bowl, some of it spilt to the ground! The "poets' share" took care of itself, and you might like to cause this to happen on purpose if you do this ritual.

The ritual certainly produced results; I wrote and recorded some amazing music, which was eventually released as the Ein Skopudhr Galdra/Mistsorrow split CD (see Bandcamp footnote on page 154; yes I use music inspired by one ritual to empower others). It was also an important learning experience – and hence I offer it as such for my reader.

Naturally, this is just a template. Use it as a starting place to create rituals with more drama, humor, playfulness, weirdness, gracefulness, intensity, and sheer delight than anything I could conjure.

Fake it Until You Make it

Fake it 'til you make it is a classic Chaos Magic slogan (and sometimes a valuable thinking tool in the realms of psychotherapy as well). It is a pithy way of recognizing that sometimes the way we achieve personal change is by 'acting as if,' leaning into the curve of our discomfort and anxiety until a new, more preferable, mode of being becomes established.

A similar idea that I find helpful is the realization that the way one gets good at a skill is simply by consistently being bad at it for a while. If you keep showing up and trying, your chances of achieving a change are much higher than if you give up at the first hardship. This is not only magically effective but a powerful vehicle for personal growth, as Crowley suggests in the *Book of Lies*:

> *Practice a thousand times, and it becomes difficult; a thousand thousand, and it becomes easy; a thousand thousand times a thousand thousand, and it is no longer Thou that doeth it, but It that doeth itself through thee. Not until then is that which is done well done.*

In magical contexts, 'fake it 'til you make it' involves identifying a habit, belief, or personal limitation one does not like; establishing what the preferred alternative would be; working out what would look different in that preferred alternative; and then attempting to push oneself into that new role until it begins to stick.

Naturally, the less rigidity and attachment one has in one's personality, the easier it is to drop old aspects of self and cultivate new ones. At the extreme application of these tools, the goal is to become like quicksilver, like Odin or Freyja: a shape-shifting, many-named, wily shaman. If you want to get better at faking and making, cultivating non-attachment is a real asset – for example through regular meditation, which helps us to de-habituate ourselves so that we are less ruled by automated or unconscious responses to the people, places, and things we encounter.

Here I share a couple of examples of how to use this skill. After that I would like to offer a couple of caveats to the practice, the potential pitfalls of which I have blundered into several times.

Becoming Milton (and Carl, too!)

Milton Erickson was the psychiatrist who resuscitated hypnosis as an efficacious psychotherapeutic technique. Anyone interested in magic can benefit from studying him; I like to imagine that he was an avatar of Odin's healer aspect.

Erickson's use of trance is legendary and is documented in hundreds of case studies from his work as a psychotherapist (*My Voice Will Go With You* is an indispensable compilation of his teaching examples). In one of Erickson's cases, he found himself presented with a very challenging client. Recognizing that he was out of his depth, that even his formidable abilities would not be enough, Erickson did not despair. Instead he let himself go into a trance to become the kind of person who *could* succeed with this client.

The trick worked wonderfully and the therapy was brought to a successful conclusion, although Erickson reported having no recollection of what he actually did in the treatment sessions. This sort of trance work, when you get down to it, is simply the application of the 'fake it 'til you make it' dictum. Erickson didn't know if he could succeed, so he used trance to pretend – at a deep level – that he was someone who could succeed. It worked perfectly.

As an admirer of Erickson, I have on occasion 'become' him when I have felt out of my depth. For example, a few years back a close relation needed to have mouth surgery, about which she was anxious because there was the risk of losing teeth. I read the runes for her and they were reassuring, but nonetheless it was (understandably) a stressful situation for her.

She had the surgery on a public holiday when the hospital was running a skeleton staff and had less patients in care than usual. I received a phone call from her several hours after the procedure was completed. She called from her hospital bed, in a state of extreme emotion due to a negative interaction with a hospital staff member, as well as the trauma of the surgery, which had indeed cost her several teeth. It was clear that she needed support, so off I went.

I travelled to the hospital by train, thinking about the situation. Given how she had presented on the phone, I knew my relative was having a very hard time. Then it hit me: I felt truly out of my depth. I just didn't know how I was going to succeed in calming her down or defusing the situation. Then I realized that I didn't have to know: I could just call on someone who would.

That someone was Milton Erickson – I was inspired by his own story of using trance to become someone more capable than he judged himself to be (here we can see, incidentally the value of cultivating non-attachment, particularly to the peccadilloes of egotism). So as I rode the train, I thought about Erickson. About how he spoke, how he thought, his way of moving in the world, his life experiences, his beliefs about human nature, his profound optimism and faith in the innate healing power that all humans possess.

I thought about how Erickson's power to influence others came from his compassion, intuition, empathy, and creativity; from his sense of humor and flair for the dramatic. I thought about his life story, and about the books I had read by and about him. I thought about imaginary conversations we had had, about rituals and prayers I had done in which I had honored him. I was deeply familiar with who Erickson was, and this was critical to the success of the fake-make magic (you can see how all this applies to working fake-make techniques with a deity).

So on the basis of this deep relationship, I let myself become more and more obsessed with Milton Erickson. By the time I reached the hospital, he had become more or less the sole object of my consciousness. I went in, found the right ward, and tracked my relative down.

When I walked into the empty ward, she was clearly very upset. Eyes streaming, voice taut with emotion, she declared that she needed to immediately leave. I/Erickson could see she was in the grip of powerful anxiety and also that she was in no physical state to be going anywhere.

Yet as Erickson, I felt none of the sympathetic emotionality – and perhaps anxious paralysis – that I might otherwise have entertained. Smirking as only Erickson could, I very kindly suggested to her that "I don't think you are panicking enough, perhaps you could try a little more?" Erickson was the master of the paradoxical injunction. She immediately dropped from the plateau of her fear into a much calmer state. I/Erickson told her she wasn't going anywhere, and then kindly listened to her concerns and reassured her.

In a few moments, a person in a state of severe distress turned into a calm, soothed, even cheerful presence. By myself, triggered by this close relative's power to affect my own emotions, I simply do not know what I would have done to help; I certainly would not have had the courage or creativity to suggest that she panic more! But I faked Erickson until the difference between he and I dissolved, and that enabled me to access abilities that normally I cannot reach. It turned a stressful situation into a playful, slightly magical one.

More recently, I have been working as a group therapy facilitator. This can be very rewarding and I have developed quite a taste for the group psychotherapy format, but for a long time I found it very hard not to freeze up, lose track of what was happening, or dissociate. As the facilitator of a therapeutic group, one needs to be able to sit with complex layers of thoughts, feelings, emotions, and relationships – conflict, grief, fear, and anger. I found the intensity most exhausting and checking out was my dysfunctional coping mechanism.

Reflecting on the problem, an answer came to me. I recalled that when Carl Jung worked with a client, he and the client would sit facing one another, so close that their knees almost touched. This image seemed very intense to me; it would have been very hard for Jung, or his client, to be anything other than radically present in the unfolding therapeutic exchange.

So I found a subtle way to fake-make invoke Jung's radical presence. When facilitating, I began to experiment with my posture – leaning forward and opening up when I felt myself sliding away. Soon I found that just altering my posture could move the group through an impasse or give a client permission to enter into vulnerable healing territory. I felt quite liberated and confident. In time I stopped having to intentionally invoke Jung through my posture. The shift to being deeply attentive became permanent almost effortlessly.

Again, it should be emphasized that I have an intimate intellectual and even spiritual relationship with Jung (another Odinnic avatar in my own personal microcosm). So just the act of adjusting my posture triggered cascades of association, years of reading, reflection, magical practice. Faking it until you make it can seem like quick-fix magic, but it works best when built on a solid foundation.

What Would a Chaos Magician Do?

Like most people, I have moments of feeling out of my depth, unable to contain myself in the face of frustration, disappointed expectation, physical or emotional pain, financial stress, or even just overwhelm at the onslaught of suffering and cruelty that floods this world. This tends to dismantle my ability to function effectively.

I am grateful for this flaw, this tendency to feel out of control, unable to cope with daily challenges, making epic drama out of what are in truth mostly very modest problems. Although this tendency has caused me pain, misfortune, lost opportunities, and so forth (and at times made me into a hypocrite), it has also made life into a creative challenge for me. And this leads me onto a path of growth, exploration, dedication to transformation.

It also leads me into curiosity, empathy, and a voracious hunger for inner peace. Nietzsche assures us that "spirit is the life that itself cuts life." I like the idea that spirit is something embodied in the world as this quote proposes, rather than some rarefied and inaccessible obscurity. In order to be more spiritual I desire to be a life which cuts deeply and easily into life: and that means finding ways to rewire my thinking and feeling so that I can experience ease of action and relief from the perpetual motion machine that negative thinking can trigger.

I have used fake-make thinking games for years to help me on this path. A game I play quite often, and which brings me great relief and inspiration, is called "what would a Chaos Magician do?"

I am not exactly sure now how I invented the game of "what would a Chaos Magician do?" – though it probably emerged from morning prayer/meditation sessions (which means I probably shouldn't claim sole credit for it).

It works very simply. When I realize I am stuck, confused, obsessing, negative, or otherwise wasting precious mental resources on the generation of psychic dreck, I stop. I collect myself. I ask "what would a Chaos Magician do?" And then I do that.

A word of clarification is needed here – after all, I clearly have my own particular idea of what I mean by "a Chaos Magician." In my experience not all self-proclaimed Chaos Magicians are created equal. So I have a very definite idea of the kind of being I intend to emulate.

I take it that the goal of Chaos Magic is emancipation from the arbitrary rigidity of personality. The ideal Chaos Magician has tremendous self-knowledge but also tremendous non-attachment. Such a one is entirely able to let belief be a tool and not an end in itself, and as such is free to manipulate themselves towards their own ultimate well-being.

Furthermore, such a being has a tremendously playful, joyous spirit. After all, to live without the usual fetters of identity – yet still be grounded within incarnate form – would have to be wonderful. To never be in conflict with oneself, but rather to be absolutely congruent. To have great insight, but not at the expense of being active, embodied, and emotionally attuned.

So! This is the kind of being I have in mind when I ask my question. Funnily enough, the first answer I get is usually "well, I would certainly stop overthinking, self-criticizing, worrying about what I cannot control, and catastrophizing." In fact, I realize that if I were the archetypal Chaos Magician, I would cut myself and everyone else some slack and let things be as they are.

The result of this thought tends to be a deep psychic (and often literal) breath. And then other possibilities – blocked out by my worry or preconceptions – begin to present themselves. Often they are quite obvious, but simply unavailable because I could not see clearly what was in front of me.

What would a Chaos Magician do? Have fun. Keep it simple. Expect life to be easy and not worry when it is not. Take nothing personally. See the humorous side of things. Give kind words to self and others. Listen to the body and its wisdom. You cannot encourage a plant to grow by berating it or by tugging on its leaves; the Chaos Magician, like the Heathen cosmologist, knows that all life is a tree.

The ultimate goal of fake-make games such as this one is simply to be more present in life, to enjoy it more, to smile more, to be more playful, inspired, creative, and relaxed. Less hung up on being perceived to be right and more willing to *do* right. Which incidentally sounds a lot like what I think Heathenry is (or could be) about, too.

Do people who self-identify as Chaos Magicians relate to this philosophy? I have no idea. But it doesn't matter because Chaos Magic is whatever you want it to be. Nice, huh?

Avoiding the Pitfalls of Fake-Make Magic

As we cultivate the ability to shift our shape, we risk doing ourselves harm. It is wonderful to be able to step into personal qualities that one otherwise lacks, but if it is done from an egoistic desire for domination, manipulation, or control, then we risk a psychic backlash. The egoistic controlling mentality is fundamentally antithetic to the dancing spirit of play (how Nietzschean!) that animates fake-make practice.

For example, during the period of my life when my hypnosis skills were at their highest, I used these skills to fake my way out of facing a series of health, relationship, and spiritual problems. My chronic migraines – a dividend of adrenal fatigue that had been caused by running myself down badly for many years – I just hypnotized away! My professional anxieties, which were trying to tell me important information about choosing the right path in life – I just smoothed over with mind tricks. Through fast-talking fake-make I kept deferring the incongruities and tensions in my own psyche and in my relationship, until my inner fake-make dialogues started to approximate the shape of hollow vessels of self-deception.

Here again the importance of self-knowledge is highlighted. Results magic does not happen in a vacuum, and if we are unwilling to quest after mystery and sacrifice lower self to higher self – "*sjálfr sjálfum mér*" as Odin put it – then our clever results magic strategies are likely to bring us undone. Non-attachment, it follows, does not mean withdrawing from life. It means embracing life in as de-habituated, de-automated, conscious way as possible, so that our results magic becomes at first potent...and then finally unneeded.

A final word regarding fake-make's pitfalls. This sort of magic leverages a certain kind of dishonesty in order to achieve an effect, to divert the flow of the waters of *wyrd* into new channels. Without self-awareness, this can lead to all sorts of trouble. Therefore, Chaos Heathens are well-served if they can develop a robust ethical sense. By that I mean much more than just some infantile list of commandments or virtues. I mean the honesty and sensitivity to be able to recognize that the world is complex and that the implications of a decision or action are rarely clear. We have to learn to be comfortable with our inevitable hypocrisies and failures, while still aiming for some sense of higher ethical calling, and setting ourselves standards worth the keeping.

Conclusion

The foregoing ought to offer plenty of ideas and inspiration for anyone to work with. Ultimately, the goal of sigil magic, rune magic, results magic, rituals, and all the rest is simply to make life more aesthetically pleasing. If we feel more alive and engaged with our daily existence, if we feel less bored, habituated, cynical, or despairing, then our efforts are succeeding, even if not a single spell produces its intended outcome.

I will also say that Jan Fries' book *Visual Magick* is an essential guide to, as he calls it, "freestyle shamanism." The spirit of that book is one of play, experimentation, sincerity, and humor. I hope that its influence is evident in this essay, and that my reader finds enough of a glimmer of adventurous curiosity from these words that they are inspired to *practice* Chaos Heathen result magic and thus enrich their life in delightful, unexpected ways.

If you want to make sense of the runes and build a relationship with them I suggest reading about them, chanting them, meditating on them, doing readings with them, and studying the myths, history, and archaeology. It is ok to have no idea about what you are doing at first; the best way to get good at something is to be bad at it for a while (I cannot emphasize this teaching enough, for it really is a cornerstone of all magic; I learned it from Crowley and have found it thoroughly confirmed in my personal experience and observation). Cultivate a thirst for knowledge and make offerings to Odin (and other runically implicated deities such as Thor, Frey, and Heimdall)[2] regularly.

Keep it simple, keep it complex, keep it flowing, and trust that *wyrd* wants to help you become what you already are, a vortex of spirit and wisdom and discovery and deepening becoming.

---

[2] I mention these in particular because of references to them in connection to rune magic in both the Old Norse mythic poems and in archaeological finds of runic artifacts.

Eternity Three, MichaELFallson

Chaos, *Wyrd*, and the Left Hand Path
Matthew Hern

No-Thing is true. Everything is trance-mitted.
– The Fool of the Sacred Chao

Introduction

Evelyn's question[1] has been driving my whole search, my whole life, my every act of magic: why are we here? The answers we find are never the final destination, but rather shores and islands at which we rest for a while before we set out for the great ocean again, on this mysterious journey we call 'life.' The answers we find can lead to great ecstasy, but then the mantle of newness wears off and we realize that 'our answer' turns into another comfort zone, another mental construct, another habit. All concepts are tools, another rung on the ladder, another step on the staircase, another door, which we must exit to continue on the Path of Mystery. Thus the nature of our Quest is eternal in a mythical sense: every single image is a reflection in the mirror, and ultimately we are the mirror reflecting, not the reflected images.

As such, all our illuminations are but fingers pointing: at the eternal sky, in the sudden moment of awakening, like the snap of your finger, in the moment of relaxation in total presence, suddenly we see: yes, everything is the manifestation of our wisdom-light.[2] And then another yes: just as a mirror is unchanged by the things reflected in it, so too is our nature. And yes again: like a crystal that is pure no matter what light flows through it, so is our nature. It was always here, the great mudra, the perplexing pattern, the self-originating mandala, the infinite Self, the vastness of space, "the great ocean upon which

---

1 See Heimlich A. Laguz's introduction to this book.

2 A term used in Dzogchen Buddhism for the 'nature of mind' or our innate 'Buddha nature.' This term describes our divine essence and points at the inseparable unity of awareness and what Buddhists call *suñyatā* or emptiness. I explore *suñyatā* to some extent in the chapter "Everything Fornicates..." "In the modern world, we do not have a real understanding of the mind. Most people think of the mind as being merely thoughts and emotions, but these are simply the appearance of the mind, not the true nature of the mind itself?" (Sogyal Rinpoche).

the endless waves crash down,"[3] the eternal Yes. All our practice is only for this, this one perfect moment out of time, like a figure 8 lying on its back, like a serpent's perfect movement, like ᛞ Dagaz dawning...

So when I introduce certain concepts, ideas, and systems, they are never the final answer, but rather another step on the runic Path. Chaos Mysticism[4] and the Left Hand Path,[5] Galdor and Chaos Magick, as well as the larger field of esoteric Runology, are the main currents that I have learned to explore and to synthesize under the umbrella of Chaos Heathenism. The aim of magic, as we understand it, is encoded in the myths and stories of Óðinn, this "master of words and of mind and of all inspiration,"[6] which presupposes the desire to fall in love with divine mystery ᛫ᚱᚢᚾᚨ᛫ and to reawaken the ancient wisdom in one's own Soul.

But magic is a slippery guest that changes its appearance like a lizard in danger and you can never tell in what disguise, system, philosophy, or form it will visit you next time. Magic has no form. God has no name. And Spirit-in-Action ever drives you to evolve toward the next developmental stage as you seek the Mystery.

---

3 Current 93 (David Tibet) 1994: "This Shining Shining World," Album: *Of Ruine Or Some Blazing Starre*.

4 A term coined by Dave Lee in *Chaotopia* (1997) as an attempt to widen the perspective of Chaos Magic and to open it up to mystical, higher states of Consciousness that were rather neglected by practitioners of the Chaos Magic Current due to its focus on sorcery or results magic. Certainly the older currents of Ceremonial Magic of the late 19th and early 20th century, with their weird mix of neo-Platonic and monotheistic, Kabbalist mysticism, were a major reason why Chaos Magicians discarded this essential part of magic altogether. Dave Lee's book was an important step towards allowing mysticism to re-enter the field of postmodern magic and is an original masterpiece in that field.

5 I understand the Left Hand Path mostly in Draconian terms as explored and explained in Michael Kelly's works, especially *Apophis* (2009) and even more so in *Draconian Consciousness* (2012). I largely disagree, however, with the Setian superstructure that became associated with it. My own take on the LHP, which is grounded in its original Tantric meaning, is basically summed up in my and Durga Mahavidya's essay "Kali's Daughters," in Michael Kelly (ed.) 2014, *Gods and Monsters*.

6 David J. Jones in the song "Looking for Mr. Wednesday" (performed by Fire + Ice, album: *Fractured Man*).

There was always a strong attraction on my part to the conception of a perennial philosophy,[7] which supposedly appears under different guises independent of epoch or culture, and which embodies the eternal mysteries. One of the maps of special interest to me that represents an expression of that perennial wisdom is the Runic tradition as it manifests in the cosmological and magico-mystical structures of Northern European spirituality. But what separates me from most on the Northern Path, or any path actually, is that I don't hold belief in high regard. My beliefs have always been subject to change on my journeys along the pathways that lead down, around, and up the Ancient Tree, which is the *Axis Mundi*. That's why I believe that beliefs and all dualities are fetters to be loosened (the mystic's aim) or played with (the magician's game), rather than unchangeable dogmas set in stone. This understanding is reflected in two of the major influences that introduced me to the Northern Mysteries: Fire + Ice, the band of Ian Read, and *True Helm*, the famous martial arts book by Sweyn Plowright.

I explore the Runic Mysteries by emulating the divine archetype of the Rune-Master Óðinn, who is seen as a mythical role model for spiritual development.[8] But I look at all philosophical, metaphysical, and magical worldviews not as reality, but "as models or maps, and no one model elevated to the truth."[9] Having gone through all kinds of phases and systems, beliefs and dogmas,[10] 'enlightenments' and delusions, I stopped looking for an occult system that 'explains' everything and thus deludes the seeker that the inexplicable could be presented in a 'step-by-step' system to a final illumination. Finally, I came to

---

7 See Godwin 2007: *The Golden Thread – The Ageless Wisdom of the Western Mystery Tradition.* For a more academic perspective, see Hanegraaff 2012: *Esotericism and the Academy – Rejected Knowledge in Western Culture.*

8 This idea is basically taken from Edred Thorsson's work and he calls it Odianism as opposed to Odinism. The Odinist worships Odin as an external source, outside of himself. But the Odian doesn't worship Odin, he emulates Him, His deeds, His ordeals. By that the seeker transforms his Consciousness according to the archetypal Óðinnic patterns and thus becomes himself a divinely inspired being, very akin to Tantric Buddhism, where you transform yourself into an enlightened being on attaining Buddhahood. Tantric Buddhists don't worship Buddha, they discover their own 'Buddha nature.'

9 Robert Anton Wilson.

10 For many years prior to becoming a Heathen my main focus was Crowley's system of Thelemic Magick.

ponder the chaos-magical saying: "Nothing is True, Everything is Permitted,"[11] but then came to discard this phrase as another manifestation of postmodern relativism, which ultimately leads to the 'anything goes' triviality of New Ageism and "spiritual consumerism."[12]

This is my main criticism of the Chaos Magick Current, though here also we begin to hear diverse voices.[13] However, once I heard clearly *"das Raunen der Runen"* (the whispering of the Runes), I turned my face towards the North. In this regard I take the reconstruction of the Runic Tradition very seriously and definitely do not think that it's just another 'paradigm' for the "paradigmal pirate"[14] to exploit. Such a person will never grasp the profundity of the Runes – especially when one considers that *Runa* can never be fully grasped. In Chaos Heathenism there are no members, there are no gurus, there are no systems, and there are no dogmas. There is only you: you and *Runa* – the eternal and sacred Dance of Consciousness and Mystery.

For the Runic Quest to begin, some essential qualities are required, such as a thirst for knowledge, a longing for something that is hard to define (probably what deRopp called "the Will to Power," "the Will to Meaning," and "the Will to Transcendence"),[15] a strong self (as opposed to what is commonly called ego), courage and, certainly, humor – just to name a few. But the nature of collaboration or participation in Chaos Heathenism, as far as I understand it, is defined by every individual for themselves.

---

[11] However, consider this: If the first sentence – *Nothing is True* – is true, then this sentence is not true either. This insight was given to me by Sven Kreyenfeld-Kuniß.

[12] Chögyam Trungpa.

[13] See Dave Lee's criticism of the use of postmodernity in Chaos Magic, in his Masterwork *Bright From The Well*. See also Vayne & Humphries' statements and approach in *Now That's What I Call Chaos Magick* and also Alan Chapman 2008: *Advanced Magick for Beginners*.

[14] See Wetzel 2006: *The Paradigmal Pirate*.

[15] See Robert deRopp, *The Master Game*.

Chaos

Chaos defined, in many ways, my approach to sorcery, because it appeared more authentic to me, it allowed for individualistic aesthetics, it was result-orientated and compatible with a world that has gone mad, the *Kali Yuga*. However, it must be said that the Chaos approach was not invented by the Chaos Magicians themselves, but came out of the Zos Kia Cultus of the artist and sorcerer Austin Osman Spare. But it was the Illuminates of Thanateros (IOT) who took on the sparks of this flame and made a huge fire of it, a blaze that burnt down most – if not all – assumptions of Western occultism, and thus created a *tour de force* that has changed the underworld of occulture forever.

Chaos for me means that magic has no form, that the origin of the universe is *Ginnungagap*, its essential nature is made of 'void-stuff,' which is identical with the Chaos of the Chaos Magicians and the *Ginnung* of the Germanic Heathens. The Chaos Magic approach gives us the opportunity to look at different systems of magic as arbitrary models, children of their time and culture, rather than fixed and eternal truths that introduce the risk of constricting one's personal approach to sorcery. Chaos Magic encourages the individual sorcerer to explore different perspectives and applications in order to develop one's own system of magic rather than following the worn-out paths of others.

Thus Chaos becomes the major tool to look at various schools of magic and to choose those elements that are appealing to and work for the individual sorcerer. However, to my mind this is also the great weakness of the Chaos approach. In a way, the traditional assumption that everything must be kept in balance is, once again, also true in this case. By concluding that every traditional system of magic uses an arbitrary classification, we blank out the fact that the traditional ways of thinking are ancient and have been in use over dozens or hundreds of generations. They reflect what Carl Gustav Jung has called the Collective Unconscious. Hence, although individualistic approaches to sorcery are useful, an Alphabet of Desire will never achieve what a system like the Elder Futhark embodies.

> *I find that the more I research actual magical traditions the more I realize that the average modern occultist or Heathen has far inferior ideas to those that mythological or occult traditions have left behind. We really need tradition as a source of material for our creative, spiritual, and unconscious aspects to weave into*

reality. The depth and texture of a whole magical ideology cannot possibly be replicated in the half-hearted attempts of individual seekers of whatever sort to invent their own. How can one person compete with centuries of people organically and indirectly collaborating across the ages?[16]

Order

Chaos is not my aim, it is my primal condition. Basically, the human being is a multiplicity of selves, a morass of chaos, "a 'schizophrenic' identifying in one moment with a dominant thought, emotion, or sensation that wears the mantle of self, just to be pushed aside by some other 'I' in an equally mechanical and accidental manner."[17] Thus it must be the first aim of the sorcerer to make his willed order out of this chaotic condition, to create a *Magnetic Center*, to create a 'Soul,' as it were. Though the Chaos approach is very useful, I practice no apotheosis of Chaos. But also, Chaos is not a condition that has to be overcome, but only controlled to an extent that enables the sorcerer to exercise their will upon the multiverse. Chaos is necessary and can never be controlled completely, which is not desirable anyway. Chaos and Order must maintain their inherent moment of tension. A universe which is fully controlled, from which Chaos is abolished, is dead; yet in a universe where order is absent, intentional action is impossible. That's why the intelligent sorcerer looks – as in every area of his life – for a harmonious balance. Chaos and Order are two polarities from which existence, as we know it, emerges.

Left Hand Path

The idea of the Left Hand Path (LHP) has been an important philosophical feature of modern occultism since Mme Blavatsky's days. But this concept has always caused much confusion, because she used it as a pejorative term for 'black magic,' which was uncritically adopted by Crowley to call anybody whom he didn't like a "Left Hand Path adept" (e.g. Austin Osman Spare). Later, in the 1970s, the terms LHP and 'black magic' were redefined by Satanists as something good, and Aquino of the Temple of Set identified Crowley as a LHP

---

16 Heimlich A. Laguz, lost article from *Elhaz Ablaze* website.

17 Robert deRopp: *The Master Game.*

black magic magician who couldn't admit that fact to himself. This history is somewhat weirdly and brilliantly summarized by the Schrecks in *Demons of the Flesh,* and the philosophy of occultism according to the Satanic/Setian definition of the LHP has been quite thoroughly dealt with in Edred Thorsson's (Dr. Flowers') *Lords of the Left Hand Path*. I personally prefer a different approach to this whole topic. Genesis P-Orridge once said something about "the Path of No Distinction," which is a Tantric idea. And Tantra is a good starting point to bring clear light into such a confused darkness, because, at its heart, the concept of the LHP developed in the context of Tantra. We should look there first to find some answers.

Tantra is:

> *[a]n attempt to place* kama, *desire, in every sense of the word, in the service of liberation...not to sacrifice this world for liberation's sake, but to reinstate it, in varying ways, within the perspective of salvation. This use of* kama *and of all aspects of this world to gain both worldly and supernatural enjoyments (*bhukti*) and powers (*siddhis*), and to obtain liberation in this life (*jivanmukti*), implies a particular attitude on the part of the Tantric adept toward cosmos, whereby he feels integrated within an all-embracing system of micro-macrocosmic correlations.*[18]

David White adds:

> *Tantra is an Asian body of beliefs and practices which, working from the principle that the universe we experience is nothing other than the concrete manifestation of the divine energy of the godhead that creates and maintains the universe, seeking to ritually appropriate and channel that energy, within the human microcosmos, in creative and emancipatory ways.*[19]

In India the LHP-Tantrika uses unorthodox, transgressive means to achieve *bhukti, siddhis,* and *jivanmukti.* Such practitioners cut their bindings from

---

[18] Andre Padoux, "Tantrism," in Mircea Eliade (1986), *Encyclopedia of Religion*, Vol. 14, p. 272-276.

[19] David Gordon White: p. 9, in White (ed.) 2000: *Tantra in Practice.*

consensus reality and thus liberate the enlightened nature of their limitless Consciousness. They transcend the limitations of the 'socially constructed reality' of the society and culture in which they live. By this they often work with behaviors, symbols, ideas, and things that appear abominable to their identity and that are taboo in their culture. Thus sex, death, drugs, and madness become methods of transforming mundane consciousness into a state of enlightenment. Because everything is One, part of the same divine source whose nature is limitless consciousness (=Shiva), there is nothing to fear or to be rejected. Thus the Tantrika is freed from the delusion of separateness and embraces all existence, including the body and the material world.

Because in India the left hand is used to do 'unclean' things, this path to liberation has been called the Left Hand Path. Nevertheless, it is presumed by spiritual scholars that both paths, the Right Hand Path (RHP) and the Left Hand Path, lead to enlightenment. Not so in the Western conception of RHP and LHP in modern times. Here the basic idea is that every system of religion, mysticism, and magic(k) that belongs to the RHP ultimately leads to dissolution, the *Unio Mystica* or the absorption of personal consciousness into godhood. Contrary to this popular conception the LHP magician initiates a process that is known as Self-Deification. Rather than dissolving into God by confronting the abyss of existence/non-existence, the LHP magician tries to resist the urge to be absorbed and chooses to separate his psyche from the 'objective' universe and to "create a self-aware, individual, enlightened, immortal, and semi-divine entity" out of his 'subjective' consciousness.[20]

To my mind, this way of defining the spiritual journey is short-sighted and rather an intellectual affair. I think the urge is rather stronger to be not absorbed and to maintain a kind of an ego. The whole discourse of opposition between separation (LHP) and annihilation (RHP) is a neo-Satanic construction, based on a history of Western misunderstandings, false translations, and inaccurate knowledge of the Eastern Yogic and Tantric traditions. It was certainly also a reaction of Aquino to Crowley's unhealthy 'ego-death' fantasies, for the latter had a megalomaniac personality and was haunted by a strong 'death drive' in a psychoanalytic sense.

---

20 Ross G. H. Shott: *The Dark Arts of Immortality.*

Lack of psychological self-knowledge represents a tremendous danger in practical occultism. Western psychological schools like Freud's system teach to strengthen the ego, whilst Eastern psycho-spiritual traditions teach that the ego is an illusion. These different approaches to the human condition aim at different stages, levels, and areas of psychological and spiritual development, which has been masterfully analyzed and categorized by Transpersonal psychologists like Ralph Metzner or Integral Philosophers like Ken Wilber. It is better to rely on Buddha than on LaVey or Aquino, trust me on this one. And Buddha once said something to the effect that what looks like annihilation to the outsider is innermost bliss and illumination to the meditator. *Timendi causa est nescire.*

In any case, the confusion thus arose in modern Western LHP philosophy that the 'self' would be abolished and the adept's Soul would be annihilated if it undertook a 'merging with the universe.' This is a profound misunderstanding of the initiatory process in Eastern teachings. What Western occultists missed was the mystical insight that it is not just an either/or option of preservation or annihilation of self, but about the simultaneity of being self *and* non-self, the irrational moment of the *coincidentia oppositorum*, as Nicholas of Cusa would call it – the paradox of *Oneness*. Fuck Hegel, the last great apologist of Christianity, when he mocked that the *coincidentia oppositorum* is "the night, when all cows are black." Because the mystical, paradoxical experience of the *coincidentia oppositorum* is the profound moment when the otherwise useful tools of logic, rationality, and the intellect collapse. Here language fails or becomes mystical poetry.

So basically, my rejection of these modern LHP conceptions comes from the fact that the attempt to preserve one's ego is born out of fear and "denies thousands of years of meditative experience."[21] Eight seconds spent in *samadhi* and such philosophical constructions would be burned in the inmost flame of uttermost ecstasy! The whole question of this appears so important to me because the way one perceives the Sacred Self (or True Self) determines one's interpretation of what happened to Odin during his Yggdrasil Ordeal, where he sacrificed himself to himSelf – expressed in his enigmatic words: *sjálfr sjálfum mér* (myself to myself).

---

21 Sweyn Plowright, personal communication.

However, one can identify certain threads that can be found in both definitions of the LHP. First of all, there is the rejection of the common values of morality. Left Hand Path sorcerers decondition themselves from the cultural fictions they were brought up with – the cultural memes, as it were. However this does not lead to an inversion of the values of one's own culture, because choosing to be anti-cultural would just mean submitting to another form of control and herd conditioning. The core idea here is to break inner taboos, to confront oneself with inner fears, disgusts, dislikes, repulsions, etc., and to free oneself from self-imposed limitations of one's identity. Thus a more authentic, flexible, fluid, and free state of Self-consciousness can be attained. This procedure has been called antinomianism in the Western LHP tradition. It should lead to a rejection of dogmatism in general, which enables the sorcerer to question the 'truths' of any magical tradition and any route or map that pretends to show the entire path towards perfection.

This leads to the second aspect of a genuine LHP magician from my point of view: the developing of one's own system of sorcery. The sources for this process have been given to occultists by Austin Osman Spare and by Chaos Magick writers. Further, the LHP adept doesn't fall into the trap of denying their own ego, body, and the material world. All of these are tools to power and fulfillment. LHP magicians don't deny this world, they embrace it! LHP sorcerers realize that every individual has to follow their own path, their own unique explorations of what is possible for the body/mind/spirit trinity, without being dependent upon any person or system. Finally it must be added that sorcerers on the LHP are not interested in the 'common good,' 'God,' the 'state,' or any other abstract idea that submits the individual to some 'higher purpose.' In the first place, the LHP sorcerer strives for Self-Empowerment and their own enlightenment.

Wyrd, Magic, and the Pursuit of Power

Ceremonial Magic(k) has been associated for a very long time with so-called 'High Magic,' which suggests that there's some kind of 'Lower Magic.' In the late 19th and early 20th centuries this meant that High Magic strove toward spiritual aims, whilst Lower Magic was orientated toward material results, a sorcery of the rural population – folk magic.[22] The divisions between matter

---

22 See Phil Hine: *Condensed Chaos*.

and spirit are problematic in a pagan context and, though Platonic in origin, reflect a rather monotheistic and dualistic Christian worldview. This is one of the reasons why I came to reject Ceremonial Magic(k) and turned towards chaos, and later, Germanic folk magic.

Magic, as Dave Lee has demonstrated in his brilliant book *Chaotopia*, includes three things:

> *1) Making things happen to consensus reality (sorcery);*
> *2) Making things happen to one's own consciousness according to will (self-transformation), and;*
> *3) Experiencing higher states of consciousness, often leading to unitary consciousness (mysticism).*[23]

In the first case, sorcery, we manifest results in Midgard, in the material world. In the second case, self-transformation, we change the world of our subjective experience, which is the only way we can truly experience reality anyway. Self-Transformation (making things happen to consciousness) often leads to mysticism, as Dave Lee suggests. This process, mystical experience, cannot be easily recognized by others as producing results in Midgard, which is probably why it has been excluded from Chaos Magic – a mistake Dave Lee corrects in *Chaotopia*. In the final analysis, magic is a sublime art, and either the results of a working are 'material' in its plain sense or they remain – for the skeptic – subjective. The reason why I believe that chaos-mystical operations should be included in the concept of magic has wide-ranging philosophical implications that stem from my vision of the world. This vision is holistic, integral, and mystical – suspending the immanence/transcendence divide. Here the idea of *Wyrd*, which I sometimes refer to as the Net of Power, is very useful. This multivalent term is reflected in the Indian mythology of Indra's Web and, most importantly, in Teutonic sorcery, as seen in the idea of *Wyrd* and the myth of the Three Norns.

> *"Wyrd can be translated as 'Coming Into Being.' Wyrd is imagined as a tapestry woven by the three Norns, called Urd, Verdandi, and Skuld, representing an interconnected 'fabric' underlying all events that is manifest in every shape. Urd – still resonating in the*

---

[23] Dave Lee 2004 [1997]: *Chaotopia*.

> *German syllable* Ur *– suggests the primal or ancient and stands for the unseen influences underlying an event. It is the unmanifest potential, wherein all possibilities exist. Skuld means 'should –' that is, what should happen if all progresses without interference."*[24]

Here we can see the wisdom of the Germanic peoples of old: Skuld is not a deterministic future, like the idea of fate in Christian conceptions of time. It can be influenced, is changeable and open to 'chance.' "Verdandi is the process of 'Coming Into Being,' that which is becoming or manifesting, the present moment, which we perceive as the manifest world."[25] The magician gains empowerment by realizing that this vast Net of Power exists. Depending on our mind and our intentions, we can either say that we pull an entire system of symbolic signs and correspondences over this Net of Power, or we can say that this magical system emerges from the Net itself, or both simultaneously. This magical network of symbols, signs, and correspondences creates our magical universe, what Chaos Magicians call a "psychocosm."[26] This enables us to manipulate the Net, or our *Wyrd*, according to our congruent Will. In this way Chaos Heathen magicians empower themselves by establishing a magical "meta-communication"[27] system as a means to influence the universe to make flesh their innermost dreams, desires, visions, and their quest for wisdom. Hence the definition of magic has been often described as the *pursuit of power*. This power is actually a part of our Soul-complex, called *hamingja*.[28] This is an innate power to change one's Consciousness and the world. In Shaivism, the magical philosophy of Hindu Tantra, the world is a product of the unity of Shiva (= Consciousness) and Shakti (= Energy). By tapping into this sacred power we can reclaim our Souls and become who we really are.

The Heathen ancestors used, among many others, the formula ALU (ᚨᛚᚢ) to raise their state of Consciousness. A is ᚨ Ansuz = divinely inspired

---

24 Sweyn Plowright: *True Helm.*

25 Sweyn Plowright: *True Helm.*

26 See Phil Hine: *Prime Chaos.*

27 See Don Webb: *Uncle Setnakt's Essential Guide to the Left-Hand Path.*

28 I explore Germanic Soul-Lore in my "Dagazian Paradox" essay in this book.

Consciousness. L is ᛚ Laguz = Growth ('the Ur-Waters of the Collective Unconscious'). U is ᚢ Uruz = vital energy. So ᛚᚢ could be esoterically interpreted as "Divine Consciousness Growing In Vital Energy." That ᛚᚢ became 'ale' – beer – in common English tells us another story. It is one of a hundred examples of how magical wisdom was forgotten and dishonored by the ignorant. In this case, ᛚᚢ was a sacred formula for a Consciousness raising ritual, which was profaned into a public event of drinking oneself silly with ale. Irony, mystery, and the secret history of a sacred technology: this is how magic hides and survives in culture. So next time you have a beer, remind yourself of the sacred past of this drink, sketch a blessing to the powers, and maybe you'll share the Holy Mead with us, always in dreamtime, and remember again how to change your perception with the songs that were given to teach you to create your own memory:

> *The sacred word ᛚᚢ, which was carved into the tine*
> *Reminded me of a power that was mine*
> *If I called its spirit knowingly and treated it with care*
> *When the Holy Mead was for the aethelings to share.*[29]

---

[29] Ian Read in the song "Holy Mead" (Fire + Ice, album: *Runa*).

Elektrik Vitki, MichaELFallson

Not a War but a Rescue Mission: Heathenry, Gnosis, & Liberation
VI

Not all sick men are utterly wretched:
Some are blessed with sons,
Some with friends,
some with riches,
Some with worthy works.

The halt can manage a horse,
the handless a flock,
The deaf be a doughty fighter,
To be blind is better than to burn on a pyre:
There is nothing the dead can do.

It is always better to be alive,
The living can keep a cow.
Fire, I saw, warming a wealthy man,
With a cold corpse at his door.

A son is a blessing, though born late
To a father no longer alive:
Stones would seldom stand by the highway
If sons did not set them there.

He welcomes the night who has enough provisions
Short are the sails of a ship,
Dangerous the dark in autumn,
The wind may veer within five days,
And many times in a month.

The half wit does not know that gold
Makes apes of many men:
One is rich, one is poor
There is no blame in that.

Cattle die, kindred die,
Every man is mortal:
But the good name never dies
Of one who has done well

Cattle die, kindred die,
Every man is mortal:
But I know one thing that never dies,
The glory of the great dead

Fields and flocks had Fitjung's sons,
Who now carry begging bowls:
Wealth may vanish in the wink of an eye,
Gold is the falsest of friends.

In the fool who acquires cattle and lands,
Or wins a woman's love,
His wisdom wanes with his waxing pride,
He sinks from sense to conceit.

–*Havamal*, Auden & Taylor translation

The *Havamal* is not holy writ. It is not some *Decalogue*, some list of commands. It is a poem, and must be remembered as that which was spoken in the halls of Iceland.

Yet, as a poem, we have to understand: these words were recited to the audience by the skald, as the words of the High One, the wisest god of all. Imagine then, if you will, these words spoken in a room lit by flame, occluded by smoke, filled with the press of bodies. These words are spoken, not in a revelatory context, but rather, in a realm of cultural knowledge.

Even if it never happened that way, even if the details are wrong, recall that these words, these concepts were not spoken in isolation, but as the product of, and part of, a living breathing culture.

Imagine then, the rise and fall of the skald's voice, the poet's rhythm; see the heads nod – the wordless agreement, the murmur of *yes, this is known. This is how it is.* Truths are revealed through the words, the metre of the poetry, the rich trove of kennings and allusions. Deeds are highlighted, connections are recognised, made, and reconfigured.

Laws are spoken in similar ways, in this place of combined Thought and Memory – customs enshrined by being spoken in the holy places of the Thing. Words follow words, becoming deeds which follow after each other. Laid down like threads, woven together. For if memory serves – and it always must, lest so much be forgotten (even Odin fears loss of Muninn) – we find ourselves confronted by the sheer *humanity* of our ancestors.

Have we not all been in that place, experienced a heart's knowing, a gut-certainty which seems to possess, in that moment, so much more potency and depth than an intellectual knowing?

Have we not known something in our bones, felt it in our water, a primal understanding which can be communicated with a glance, with a nod; a knowing which passes between people, between folk who live in each other's world?

Understand that what I am saying to you, though it will be long, is not a thing of intellect. It is a thing of humanity, of shared bone and blood. Of survival and compassion in a world that shows itself not as some heaven, but instead as a forest in which there is much to nourish and strengthen us, but also much that might disrupt our existence and perhaps even make things appear hostile.

Understand then, that when I speak of liberation, I do not speak of freedom in the absolute, but within the context of room-to-move, a territory in which we are allowed to pursue our individual Beingness.

When I speak of sovereignty, I do not speak of the tyrant; instead I speak of the proto-monarch. I speak of the one who has-the-knowing-of-how-to-Be-and-is-constantly-doing-so. The One who recognises and remembers that they are merely First-Amongst-Equals. I speak of the person who knows that a gift demands a gift.

And we all have gifts – the poem says that, does it not? The crippled, the sick, the deaf – are not these mentioned in *Havamal*? Were they not uttered, these words in that old hall, full of smoke and shine and laughter?

Were there not nodding heads? *Yes, it is known. Yes, so it is.*

Known, aye.

Known by virtue of a gift of an eye. Known by a gift of pain, of blood and stolen breath, upon a windy tree. Known by nine nights of hunger and sacrifice upon the gallows. For the old meaning of 'victim' was sacrifice:

> ***Victim** (n.) late 15c., "living creature killed and offered as a sacrifice to a deity or supernatural power," from Latin* victima *"person or animal killed as a sacrifice." Perhaps distantly connected to Old English* wig *"idol," Gothic* weihs *"holy," German* weihen *"consecrate" (compare* Weihnachten *"Christmas") on notion of "a consecrated animal." Sense of "person who is hurt, tortured, or killed by another" is recorded from 1650s; meaning "person oppressed by some power or situation" is from 1718. Weaker sense of "person taken advantage of" is recorded from 1781.*

A holy, embodied creature; a functional participant in the numinous world of the Powers. A necessary bridging of the gap between thought and action. A thing of blood, breath, and bone, of meat and chemicals and electric lightning crackling down nerves.

There is a form of theological engagement within certain streams of Roman Catholicism known as Liberation Theology. In this theology, it is held that the revelation of Christ's sacrifice on the Cross was for the benefit of all; that the suffering of that god was undertaken to liberate all mankind from suffering. For those who follow this theological stream, it follows that to be Christian is to act as that god would, to do all that they can to liberate others from forms of oppression, social injustice, and inequality. Furthermore, it suggests that those who suffer and are oppressed are, in some sense, directly connected to Christ's sacrificial act, that the death of that god was *even more* for those who suffer and are oppressed in everyday life.

A gift demands a gift. This is known.

As Heathens, we are aware of the threads of *wyrd* that bind us together. Yet Ygg, the Terrible One, did not sacrifice himself to another higher power.

Instead, the hanged god sacrificed himself to Himself. There is none higher – he is High, Just as High, and Third, as Gangleri found. He is Fetterer and Loosener.

That sacrifice, that willing participation in the numinous flows of power and experience, even unto death and beyond, revealed the runes to Odin. It gave the master of fury, the roaring shrieker, knowledge of the secrets, the doors of which are found in sound and glyph, in the heart of language and song itself.

And it was not, unlike Christ, a gift for all. Not in the sense of intercession or redemption. The Gallows God hanged himself for himself, not for mankind. He doubled down on his Being, tripled down even – hanged, wounded, and starving.

Thrice on Thrice. for nights all Nine. This is known.

Yet for all that, we benefit from his wisdom. We benefit from the wisdom learnt through that suffering, that most terrible ordeal. We benefit from his blinding, from his wounding, from his starving, from his thirst. We benefit from his pain, from his agony.

For without that wisdom he would not be the Being that he is. Would not be the beloved of Frigg, the student of Freyja, the blood-brother of Loki, the stealer of the mead of poetry, the witch-dancer, the eagle-headed raven-black shaman, the wandering wizard, wrapped in corpse-blue, whispering to his child on the pyre, Baldr protected from the coming storm by Hel's hollow hall.

Would not be the High One who seizes the poet, and stirs the cauldron to bring the intoxication of inspiration so that the words of the High One might be written, that even *these words themselves* might be written nearly nine centuries later.

Would not be the Father of Victory, who sends the spear to claim all sides in the battle as his own. For those words make clear a truth – all that will endure is the memory, the glory of the great dead.

All that will endure is the poetry and song; these mead hall moments, these rites and acts of numinous power which cast us, even now, into the closest proximity with our ancestors; into the heart knowing, the blood-gnosis of our ancestry, our history, our songs.

Word followed word. Deed followed deed, from me. This is known.

A gift demands a gift – the reciprocity is clear, for unlike the Christian tales, wherein god gave humankind the earth by divine right, we know as Heathens that our world, that fragile bounded space, that age of man with all its comforts, extends only as far as the firelight.

There are giants and monsters and trolls, thurses that make the earth shake and the sea roar, sickness and death; events which may descend and change us irrevocably. We have gods with missing eyes and hands, gods with stitched-up lips, goddesses who mourn for dead sons. We know the ice can be treacherous, and that storms and cold can kill even the mightiest.

We have the stories and the tales, from times before the electric light and the certainties we certainly take for granted. We have the tales of great deeds when kings fared forth to answer ties of kinship, who entered barrows to slay monsters that would threaten their people.

We have the songs of great and terrible battles, where folk were hewn down to lie forgotten in the dust of distant fields, while their sons hauled aloft stones to mark their memory.

We understand then, the ties that bind; ties of blood, but more than that, ties of oath, to the mighty folk who gathered others to them. We comprehend how travellers from distant lands might settle in new soil and become as its true-born children by weaving their *wyrd* with its wights.

This is known.

Or at least, it should be.

For such a knowing is very old. The knowing that the gods have arranged things so that we might thrive. That through our cleaving to these powers, we have established, by act and oath, by piety and pact, a *relationship* with these powers, these wights, these gods. These Beings, whom when we encounter them, are understood by the knowing of their sheer, undeniable Presence.

And this then is where we conceive, not of an Almighty, but a multitude of powers; the kosmos is revealed to be alive, pandaemonic, brimming over with vitality. With this knowing comes an understanding of the reasoning behind *Rta, Maat, Puruṣārtha* – even *order* itself:

> **Order** *(n.) early 13c., "body of persons living under a religious discipline," from Old French* ordre *"position, estate; rule, regulation; religious order" (11c.), from earlier* ordene, *from Latin* ordinem *(nominative* ordo*) "row, rank, series, arrangement," originally "a row of threads in a loom," from Italic root* *ord- *"to arrange, arrangement" (source of* ordiri *"to begin to weave;" compare primordial), of unknown origin.*

This weave, this tapestry, this structure, is a product of *artifice*. It takes *work* to achieve, activity and process. It does not merely happen, but just like the human body requires *constant adjustment in order to maintain the appearance of stability.*

There is that which must be done, that which must be performed, in order to ensure survival. This, then, is the eternal work of the gods; even and especially their death, for only by that most terminal of functions of existence can a new world be born. The cyclic, spiralling paths of existence, their labyrinthine twists and turns, must be explored, no matter their extremity.

This is the essence of survival, which our ancestors knew; a doomed battle which both humanity and gods must face, for death claims us all. Only Memory remains.

This is known.

The war, then, is not a war. The struggle is one of survival, framed by the understanding *that victory is impossible, that it is only achievable by the impossible; by the willing participation in a numinous lived experience which transcends ordinary notions of time and space.*

It is in fact, a rescue mission – the gods reach out to us, we who have forgotten the proper ways and uses of Memory, we who are obsessed with *real* and *unreal*. We who crave *results*, and *things*, who are told we are merely interchangeable, identical cogs in the machinery of existence, rejected and derided if we raise up our faces and ask: *is this all there is?*

We, who in this reductionist, logocentric universe, seemingly ruled by an absent or long dead Absolute, have nevertheless been drawn to the memory of our many and varied gods, to here and now and the knowing which goes beyond the rational, beyond the intellectual.

Despite every dismissal, every derisive smile, we do not believe – *we know that we are experiencing something.* Something that draws us to apparently long-dead tales and half forgotten gods; something that rises up from deep within our bones, whether we be gay, straight, queer, bi, trans, white, black, brown, indigenous, non-indigenous, old or young, healthy as horses, crippled or chronically ill...

On and on, so it goes, this rescue, this extraction from prison. For some it may be swift, others years in the making. For survival lies beneath it all, *a primal recognition that we cannot survive alone – that we are better, as people, together, because safety is an illusion, and we are all a hair's breadth away from suffering. That we are all part of an inextricably linked whole.*

Young and alone on a long road,
Once I lost my way:
Rich I felt when I found another;
Man rejoices in man,

A kind word need not cost much,
The price of praise can be cheap:
With half a loaf and an empty cup
I found myself a friend.

The world is wild, the veneer of civilisation thin – and those with eyes to see can spot the primal forest, even amidst the streetlight and concrete. Earth is a giant, and our youthful arrogance will soon be crushed; by storm, fire, and flood; by melting ice-caps and burning droughts. We shall have to pay attention to our ancestors and their ways sooner than we should like to think.

And even then:

Down we shall go, all of us, into the place of dissolution, into old age and pain and suffering – these are the doors to death. And those who suffer and are oppressed, who are hated and enslaved by the machinery that would squeeze out our very blood, our very blood, for *counterfeit gold*?

Are we not confronted with the necessities of existence? The recognition that this world which has been built, this so-called *civilisation*, has no place for us save as interchangeable blind parts? As slaves? Cast aside, reviled when we can no longer serve or when we disrupt the precious 'norm?'

Do we not feel pain, do we not feel wounds of the soul, the mind, as the failed attempts at cutting us into 'proper' shape ache and contort us with scar tissue?

Do we not feel hunger and thirst, like all human beings, like the god hanging on that Tree?

And does not that ache grow more powerful, that agony swell as our blood quickens? As the pulse beats out its drum-beat, does not the agony of our own negative capability drive us to bite back a shriek?

Do we not struggle against our bonds, to little avail? Feel them bite deep, and deeper still as the blood-flow surges? Our pain, our suffering, our restriction, our terrible knowing of how-things-are. Yet with no excuses: we must survive, we must live, eat, drink, take shelter on this the Longest Road.

There is no escape. *This is known.*

The half wit does not know that gold
Makes apes of many men:
One is rich, one is poor
There is no blame in that.

Cattle die, kindred die,
Every man is mortal:
But the good name never dies
Of one who has done well

Cattle die, kindred die,
Every man is mortal:
But I know one thing that never dies,
The glory of the great dead.

And so those who suffer, who are with little comfort; there is no blame there, for us. No censure. *It is what it is. This is known.*

Has been known, for centuries, perhaps even thousands or millions of years. It is we who have forgotten. We who, all unthinking, have lost our memory of what it is to be human.

But Memory has not lost us. The hall remains, all bright-darkness, smoke and mead; there is shining gold there, lit by the light of the blood pulse, the sheer biological necessity of existence.

Within us, within all phenomena, lies that gold which makes us not apes, but more human than human.

Here then, in a world suffused with the monolithic, the monocultural that seeks to co-opt and reduce diversity, we are confronted by the empty eye of Odin; the blazing monocular intensity of hollow bone and endless death's head smile.

Vision reduced – an expression of the implacable esoteric wisdom, so One Eye takes the singular narrative, the binding noose which throttles the Life from existence, and bears down upon it with terrible fury and endless gravity.

Under that unblinking gaze all is shattered and broken, all is ruptured and set free. The feral, primal understanding at the heart of humanity leaps to meet us, to rescue us at the fundamental level.

And in being rescued, we recognise the Other in ourselves; the countless multitude of ancestors who gather about us and others, who guide our arms and words. It is we then who, filled with the most primordial impulse, Memory singing its golden mead-songs in our veins, become the stranger on the Long Road who offers the lost one half a loaf and the drink they need to carry on their journey.

This is the ancient duty of hospitality writ large.

> **Hospitality** *(n.) late 14c., "act of being hospitable," from Old French* hospitalité, *from Latin* hospitalitem *(nominative* hospitalitas*) "friendliness to guests," from* hospes *(genitive* hospitis*) "guest" (see* host *(n.1)).*

> **Host** *(n.1) "person who receives guests," late 13c., from Old French hoste "guest, host, hostess, landlord" (12c., Modern French hôte), from Latin hospitem (nominative hospes) "guest, host," literally "lord of strangers," from PIE *ghostis- "stranger" (cognates: Old Church Slavonic gosti "guest, friend," gospodi "lord, master;" see guest). The biological sense of "animal or plant having a parasite" is from 1857.*

Only by this primordial attitude of fierce kindness to the Other do we become human, do we allow ourselves to become sovereign, do we become reconnected to our humanity throughout space and time.

Only by allowing ourselves to receive the kosmic Stranger, do we find ourselves once more amongst the familiar, do we find ourselves part of a community which works together for the benefit of all.

And as our ancestors knew, the leader gains strength from those who pledge themselves in service, an interwoven web of pledge and loyalty that brings benefit to all. The sovereign's duty is to their land and people.

So too, with the one who has-the-knowing-of-how-to-Be-and-is-constantly-doing-so. For while gnosis is the knowing, that same knowing radiates outward, for it changes its receiver irrevocably.

For Woden, the Wanderer, the Waytamer, is the Lord of Strangers. The Strangest of the Strange. The Queerest of the Queer. Yes indeed, the most *Ergi* of the *Ergi*.

He whose hall receives all comers, no matter which side they served in life. And so it is with his teacher in the mysteries of *seidhr*; the Lady who knows no boundary, who is Free as Free Can Be. For it is she who gets first-pick of the battle fallen, or did you forget?

This is known.

> ***Rescue*** *(v.) c. 1300, from stem of Old French* rescorre *"protect, keep safe; free, deliver" (Modern French* recourre*), from re-, intensive prefix (see re-), +* escourre *"to cast off, discharge," from Latin* excutere *"to shake off, drive away," from* ex- *"out" (see* ex-*) +* -cutere, *combining form of* quatere *"to shake" (see quash). Related: Rescued; rescuing.*

The mead ferments; the cauldron bubbles, full of blood and honey. The blood seethes in your veins and arteries. Embrace the fury. Shake off your chains and aid your siblings in shaking theirs.

There's work to do, remember?

Our sentence is up.

This is known. **Would you know more, or what?**

Ullr's Gift, MichaELFallson

Arete
Klintr O'DubhGhaill

I was reading a book, a year or two ago, by Don Webb from the Temple of Set. The book was called *Overthrowing the Old Gods*, and in it Webb speaks about the concept of the *Word* and how it relates to the definition of a *Magus*. A *Word* encapsulates an *Aeon* (or something like that) and a *Magus* personifies a *Word*. There was a moment in time, as I sat reading the book (just as I was thinking how foolish and pompous this whole concept seemed) when I was struck, "as though shot with a diamond bullet" by a *Word*.

Arete. That is my Word. I knew I'd heard the Word before but I couldn't remember what it meant or where I'd heard it. *I couldn't even remember what* Arete *meant*! I had to look up the definition of *Arete* online and yet, I still knew, in that instant, that this was *my Word*.

Arete is basically an Ancient Greek synonym for *Virtue* or *Excellence*. The Word is sometimes translated as *Nobility* or *Moral Virtue* but is more traditionally associated with *Fitness*, both in the sense of possessing robust physical health and also in being suitable for one's assigned task. *Effectiveness* or *Efficiency* might be two more good ways of translating *Arete* but neither seems to go quite deep enough. *Arete* is not just efficiency, it is *Maximum Efficiency*. To possess *Arete* is to reach one's highest potential, physically and mentally. To utterly and completely fulfill one's purpose. Not just to be good...but to be *great*!

It almost goes without saying that for a free man to possess *Arete*, by the standard of the ancients, he had to be effective as a warrior regardless of whatever else he happened to do with his time. In both Sparta and Athens, all citizens were soldiers. The Spartans, obviously, took their soldiering a bit more seriously but the Athenians were not exactly lax in that area either. Socrates was an infantryman and a combat veteran who had fought with considerable valor. Plato was also a citizen-soldier, of course, and a competitive wrestler. "Plato" was not even his given name. It was a Wrestling nickname that means something like "Broad-Shouldered." Thus, in its original context, *Arete* implies *Strength, Honor, Courage*, and *Military Efficiency* whenever it is applied to men. *Martial Excellence* might actually be the best simple translation of the Word. In fact, the word *Arete* is derived from the same root as the name of the god *Ares*, just as *Martial* is clearly derived from the name of the god *Mars*.

Oh, yes, *Arete* is most definitely my Word.

Please know that I'm not actually claiming to possess *Arete*. I'm not claiming to be a great warrior or to be excellent in any other way. I'm certainly not proclaiming myself a Magus, or anything foolish like that.

Don Webb:

> *A Magus is a human that has become identified with a concept, an incarnation of it on Earth.*

Yeah...I'm pretty far from being the incarnation of *Arete*. I'm not there...yet...but I want to be. I try to be. It is all I have ever wanted, for as long as I can remember. I want to be great. I am driven by desire to be excellent in everything that I do. Where I cannot be excellent, I strive to be efficient as an absolute minimum. But...to be effective as a warrior? To be strong and physically healthy? To be capable of violence when it is necessary and discipline when it is not? These, to me, seem to be the most fundamental pre-requisites for greatness of any kind.

When I think of *Arete*, I'm reminded of a quote from Arnold Schwarzenegger:

> *For me, life is continuously being hungry. The meaning of life is not simply to exist, to survive, but to move ahead, to go up, to achieve, to conquer.*

This is a feeling I know very well. This *hunger* for greatness is an overwhelming desire to push oneself to become stronger than before. I believe that all great men must have this drive, or else they would never attempt to achieve anything at all. It is in the warriors, though, that I see this hunger most clearly of all. Soldiers and martial artists have always had this is common, the burning need to push themselves, test themselves and become better than they were before. Warriors succeed or fail in this quest, to varying degrees, but almost all of them seem to have the *hunger*.

Another quote, this one from US Navy SEAL Marcus Luttrell:

> *There's a storm inside of us. I've heard many team guys speak of this. A burning. A river. A drive. An unrelenting desire to push yourself harder and further than anyone could think possible. Pushing ourselves into those cold, dark corners, where the bad things live. Where the bad things fight. We wanted that fight at the highest volume. A loud fight. The loudest, coldest, darkest, most unpleasant of the unpleasant fights.*

The Navy SEALs are currently regarded as being among the best warriors in the world. Why? Because they *hunger* for greatness. Because there is a *storm* inside each of them that threatens to consume them if they do not push themselves to be the very best. *Arete* is *Excellence* but this *hunger*, this *storm* is the origin of *Arete*. I cannot claim to possess *Arete* but I most certainly have always had this storm inside of me. I joined the Army, at age seventeen, because I have this *storm* inside of me. I know that *Arete* is my word, not because I am great, but because my heart *burns* for greatness. Weakness, ignorance, and cowardice appear to me as *moral* failings, even more so than cruelty or indifference. Everybody that I respect and admire in this world has the quality of wanting to become better than they are right now, of wanting to be *all* that they can be *and* more. The greatest among us are those who dare to dream of becoming more than human.

> *Where is the lightning to lick you with its tongue? Where is the madness with which you should be cleansed? Behold, I teach you the Superman. He is this lightning. He is this madness.*

– Friedrich Nietzsche

Nietzche's Superman personifies the Will to Power, the inner storm that drives warriors to test themselves. Ares, on the other hand, seems to have represented both the warrior and the outer storm, war itself. Strangely, Ares failed as the personification of *Arete*. The War God came to be regarded as insane, blood-thirsty, and untrustworthy. *Arete* became the name of a Goddess representing *Wisdom* and *Knowledge*, virtues that most people would not associate with Ares or with warriors in general. To a martial artist, though, the association between wisdom and fighting ability might not seem so foreign.

Buddhist Monks at the Shaolin Temple learned Boxing, weapons handling, and an intense physical conditioning program, in addition to practicing Meditation. A less well-known fact is that the students at Plato's Academy practiced Wrestling and Calisthenics as well as Philosophy. Military training and martial arts have always been associated with discipline and character development, perhaps because the skills learned are too dangerous to teach independently of an ethical philosophy. By the same token, the pursuit of knowledge has also often been associated with physical development, in accord with the ancient dictum *mens sana in corpore sano*.

To truly possess *Arete*, then, we can see that strength, courage, and fighting ability are not enough. Martial prowess needs to be tempered by philosophical and ethical training. Academic training should be supported by athletic development. It sounds like a horribly New Age cliché, but both mind and body must be developed to their fullest in order to achieve true greatness. An unstoppable warrior, without ethics or philosophy, is just a dangerous animal. A brilliant scholar, without physical health or self-confidence, is doomed to become the free lunch of some dumb young thug. The great man is neither a mindless beast nor a spineless push-over. Instead, the great man seeks to personify strength and wisdom, courage and self-discipline.

On the other hand, balanced psycho-physical development is not necessarily a pre-requisite for greatness. On the contrary, the inner storm that drives warriors and artists to excellence is neither particularly balanced nor healthy. Major personal weaknesses are unacceptable but an excessive concern with equilibrium may actually prevent the individual from fully exploiting his or her personal strengths and obsessions. A great warrior must have a philosophy but that does not mean all great warriors must also be professional philosophers.

To be a great philosopher, one must also learn how to fight. It's an important part of growing up and an essential step towards understanding human nature. This does not imply, however, that all great philosophers must also be professional soldiers or martial arts experts.

There is a God, from further north, who may represent the ideal of *Arete* far better than Ares ever did. He is a God who personifies both insane blood lust and an unquenchable thirst for wisdom.

You already know who I'm talking about...

Odin.

Odin is the inner storm. Odin is the burning, the river and the drive. Odin is the lightning that licks you with its tongue. Odin is the madness with which you should be cleansed. Odin is the Will to Power. Odin is the insane, obsessive hunger for more strength, more knowledge, more of everything...

> *Wotan is a restless wanderer who creates unrest and stirs up strife, now here, now there, and works magic. He was soon changed by Christianity into the devil, and only lived on in fading local traditions as a ghostly hunter who was seen with his retinue, flickering like a will o' the wisp through the stormy night...[E]very interpretation of intoxication and exuberance is apt to be taken back to classical models, to Dionysus, to the* puer aeternus *and the cosmogonic Eros. No doubt it sounds better to academic ears to interpret these things as Dionysus, but Wotan might be a more correct interpretation. He is the god of storm and frenzy, the unleasher of passions and the lust of battle; moreover he is a superlative magician and artist in illusion who is versed in all secrets of an occult nature.*

– Carl Jung

Odin is my God, the ultimate representation of everything I ever wanted to be. Warrior, Poet, Occultist, Philosopher, and King; Odin is my God – and now I have my Word.

Arete is my Word, what is yours?

Thursjoy, MichaELFallson

Experiencing Thor
Heimlich A. Laguz & Arrowyn Craban Lauer

The Chaos Magical perspective, when filtered through the prism of Heathenry, produces rich new experiences of the divine. For example, the god Thor, so often condemned to the role of the brawny simpleton in the minds of unimaginative contemporary Heathens, attains a whole other dimension in the hands of irreverent reverence.

Thor, very simply, is just as spiritually potent as Odin or any other god. Just as subtle, complex, and fascinating. Folk love to think that a person's brain power is inversely proportionate to their bicep diameter; Thor proves what a shallow prejudice this can be.

Even when Thor is the butt of manipulation and ill-humor we suspect that he acts always with an ironic smirk. He sees through his own role. It is a testament to his enlightened spirit that he can play even the role of buffoon; such acts merely serve to underscore his powers of liberation and release.

Here we present four doorways into the nature of Thor, experiences of his presence that we have been blessed to receive. Perhaps they will provide some kind of indication as to the spirit and practice of Chaos Heathenism. They also demonstrate how joyously the gods respond when we embrace them from a Chaos Heathen perspective.

Thor Says: Invoke with Laughter

This is an account of a Thor-themed ritual offering that my friend Donovan and I performed. One of the most brilliant ritual experiences I've ever had – something only possible in collaboration with a gentleman of his caliber.

I arose early. I packed a lunch of red beans in pasta/tomato sauce, chopped carrot, almonds, and sauerkraut. We ended up mixing these together with surprisingly delicious results when lunch time arrived.

I drove out to Donovan's place. That morning, suddenly inspired, he had made a beautifully carved Mjolnir from wood, a hefty hammer, an offering for us to give. Armed with mead and drinking horn, we drove to a forest by the sea.

We spent the drive talking about our hopes, desires, lives, people we know; about our creative, health, spiritual, hobby, and financial goals.

We walked for an hour or more through exquisite forest, over dizzying ocean cliffs, the sea vast and majestic, the trees all wise and all wit.

We came to our secret location, a gigantic flat rock which perches, secluded and precarious, on the cliff face, overlooking vast ocean vistas. How to find this rock? The almost-hidden trail is marked from the main path by two trees which, if seen from the correct angle, one behind the other, form an Elhaz stave shape ᛉ. Elhaz: perhaps it invokes the sacred space which is open and closed all at once.

We meditated, bare feet; let the epic ocean song wash away our petty conscious thoughts. We knew what we wanted this ritual to be from our conversations in car and forest. To invite Thor to help us renew the momentum of spirit in our lives, to drive out the frosty barbs of negativity and boredom and renew the membrane of magic. We let this hope flow through our beings, through the rocks, the trees, the clouds, the sea.

When it felt right the ritual began, in such a way that we scarcely even noticed that we were in it. We joked and played, laughing (with compassion) about the stiffness and artificiality that some folk fall into on ceremonial occasions – so anxious to get it 'right' that they cramp up and lose the spirit of the thing. Not us; we called and hollered, half serious, half in parody, but we could feel that our deities were warmly inclined to our spirit of joy.

I sang and screeched and howled and Donovan roared. We told snappy tales about Thor's many fine qualities, of his travelling companions, of our desire to uncover the magic in our lives that makes us joyous even amid the imperfect drudgery that seems always ready to swamp our days.

Three brilliant phrases emerged as we seethed and celebrated...

Wyrd Trumps Will

This gem came to me in my meditation. I have in the past (and well after I should have known better) had this idea that if I fill myself with enough magic then with my power-bloated ego I can blast the hard things in my life into halcyon dream-perfection. Clearly a notion that can lead to disappointment!

What crystallized as I meditated was something I've explored several times recently with brilliant people in my life – that we don't get to live a richly magical, spirited life only after we've cleared away all the sources of drudge and struggle.

No, the best way is to call on the magic in the midst of life's hard work, to have the courage and creativity and humor to find magic even amidst the awesome mundanity of dealing with the ignorant, foolish, and petty (at some level that means all of us); in dealing with the unrelenting challenges of work and money and stale repetition and I-never-have-enough-time.

So go with *wyrd*, don't try to fill your will up with numinous force, you'll just waste it in exhausting struggle. Instead work with wind, tide, and wit. Cut with the grain, dance when you are tempted to stomp grumpily. Empty yourself and you cannot be drained – be a conduit, there's an endless supply of magic that just desperately wants to be tapped into idiosyncratic human channels. It might or might not produce what you *think* you need, but there is a good chance it will produce what you *actually* need. Let yourself be curious. Radically curious. Let yourself be bewildered and surprised.

Then in our ritual playfulness a second phrase emerged...

Invoke with Laughter

Chaos Magicians tend to think that laughter is the best way to banish magical moments, spirits, spells, states of mind, anything. Yet in certain senses (not all) this could actually be a very dry, grey, boring, ugly idea. Could it potentially imply that magic has to be pompous, serious, over-stuffed, strained, redundantly effortful – in a word, insincere, in a word, dishonest – in order to be summoned? What an awful notion seems to hide in the injunction to *banish with laughter*!

We, on the other hand, we *invoked* with laughter. We joked about ourselves, people we know, about our gods, and they joked with us and on us, and it was exquisite. Cascading joy flooded the mounting force of our ritual, which had no distinct beginning but just came into tide when it wanted, as we gave it space to do so (a nice example of "*wyrd* trumps will" in action). And Thor is one of the most mirthful figures I can think of, a truly joyous force in the world: who better to call with hilarity?

We talked about ᚦ Thurisaz, its recent recurring *wyrd* appearances in Donovan's life. We agreed that we like this rune, with its scary reputation and its heart of gold. Thurisaz is like ᚺ Hagalaz or ᚾ Nauthiz – it invites a reality check and people are afraid of that and avoid – to their cost, or more accurately, to their loss.

And ᛚ Laguz kept appearing throughout the day, the sea rune, the rune of hidden riches and mystery! Of terror, and fury, and utter confusion, and yet also of "silk and gold and reveries of graciousness" (Nietzsche).

And goats! Thor has a close connection to goats. We celebrated how knowing, collected, assured, adaptable, tricky, durable, flexible, and just plain *weird* goats are. Nobody messes with Goat. Goat is low key. Goat doesn't gab his mouth when he should be silent. Goat doesn't give away his full abilities, doesn't show his hand out of narcissism or insecurity. Goat keeps it real. Goat is permanently, impeccably unflappable. Goat keeps the magic of its membrane in flourishing order. Goat knows that horns are to be worn, not goofily tooted. What a truly awesome role model.

Ritual, not Routine

Then the third phrase came, and it was a verbal crack of thunder as it sprang from Donovan's lips: *Ritual, not Routine*. Yes! Let's not have lives of routine: numb, stupid, clanking, ornery, dogmatic. Repetition can also be playful, flowing, artful, even creative. It can have rhythm and flow and wit. We can move through all the 'must do this' tasks of life with hang-dog heads, or with halos of fire and supple limbs (in a casual, low-key way if you want, of course).

It's all in how you let yourself attach meaning to the things that unfold. Change the meaning, change yourself...well, who knows what sort of brilliant consequences that might have (you might not even notice them)?

Ritual, not Routine applies literally to the art of doing ritual observance – and we were doing ritual, not empty rote motions! It was sacred play. And this goes beyond into all of life. The whole of life is potentially a ritual: improvised, filled with joy, serendipity, learning, healing, growth, courage, and patience in the face of challenge. We forget this at our peril, falling into the factory farm of our own dullness. Yet it takes so little to stay – in the dance, in the joyous.

'Love life' is not an item to be checked off on some to-do list, some roster of accomplishments. And it has nothing to do with the arbitrary turning of events. In this we aligned ourselves with a tradition that stretches from Laozi (and earlier) to Cicero and even to Nietzsche, yet without any self-consciousness or reflective pomposity: that to love this life is wonder, is its own reward, is nourishment complete. That we find love for life when we give love, not when we try to force life into the shape that we ignorantly think is best for us. After all, in an infinitely complex universe, who can really be sure what is best for them anyway?

And to those who disapprove of our light feet: perhaps you need a dose of Nietzsche's *fröhliche wissenschaft,* his gay science, his dancing seriousness and courageous frivolity. Being ponderous and heavy has nothing to do with being profound. Let yourself embrace the vulnerability and power of dedication and play admixed!

We drank toasts of mead charged with lashings of chanted ᚦ Thurisaz runes. We laughed and prayed and affirmed and quaffed. We drenched the hammer and offered it up, our sacrifice. We splashed mead on rock, tree, sky, sea, cloud, every hidden delight of that sacred place. We offered our gratitude liberally.

We ate our lunch happily. We talked to spirits of stone and wood on our walk back through the forest, the mead sending us into buoyant clairvoyance and exuberant inspiration.

We talked and ate into the night, and sang, and played music, and warmed ourselves in the glow of family and dogs and the full moon, and laughed at the limp literalism that sometimes haunts folk that call themselves Heathen, and marveled at the privilege we've been given to flow so easily into the spirit of things (and vice versa).

And I have to re-emphasize – nothing said here takes away the reality of the challenge and difficulty that life presents. If we try to force spirituality into being a magic bullet for the ease of our burdens then chances are good it will not long tolerate our presumptuousness, our pandering to our ego's fear of suffering (which is not a trivial thing, but nonetheless which need not be made the maxim of our actions).

The trick might be to get beyond the mole-vision of bean-counting one's entire life into allotments of effort (lots) and ease (never enough). There is no guarantee that any of us will see out our journey in the way we'd consciously most prefer, but with our eyes fixed on the horizon (and not on our feet) our chances are that much improved, and the toil of the path might be somewhat lessened (and if not then so be it – we are here to learn, so let's not miss whatever opportunities we are given).

All such caveats aside, I want to express my profound gratitude for these fine gifts, these three principles of religious/magical/cultural practice...and for living life, too:

>Wyrd *Trumps Will*
>*Invoke with Laughter*
>*Ritual, not Routine*

I pray I remember, and keep living out my remembrance, of these terrible, wonderful thoughts.

Hail Thor!

– Heimlich A. Laguz

Thor: The Laughing God

"He sent you to talk to me today," he says, tossing his crimson mane and cracking his knuckles. He is huge, thick necked, bursting out of his leathers and pelts. "And talk to me you shall!" He swings a great hammer up onto his shoulder, its bulk swishing through the air like a feather. "Come on then, walk with me kiddo!" Silent, I fall in beside him, scampering to keep up.

"You have to understand, kiddo," he rumbles, "that my power does not come from my muscles, or from eating so many beasts' hearts and livers (though my kingly diet hardly hurts my cause!). Its root lies not in the primeval blood of my mother, Earth, nor in the patrician fury of my father (himself born in part of mighty giant stock)." It is hard to listen; his stumping stride makes the ground shake, and he tosses boulders from his path like so many grains of cat litter.

We stop, suddenly, atop a cliff. We look over vast forests, distant mountains of resplendent white. He sucks in tremendous gulps of air, beats his chest. "This is the air that a god deserves!" he shouts, and his eyes sparkle.

"Fresh air, kiddo. There is no substitute for it. Fresh air and good humor. Good humor!" His words dissolve into guffaws. "When the air is freshest is when it tastes of ozone and rain, and black clouds, and clashing light and sound! Where some tremble, I cannot imbibe enough!"

Then he is silent, lips thin and carved from stone, for the sky is yet clear, pale blue, rarefied. His voice softens, as if following suit. "I laugh when I say this, but I do not joke. Good humor has no substitute. Good humor, kiddo. Laughter is the spring from which my power flows. Laughter can forge mountains and level them, carve river valleys and flood them, birth stars and consume them in a trice. Without laughter I am nothing; laughter is the only thing I am."

He thrusts a finger in my chest; I am driven forcefully to the ground, a dull ache shooting up my tail. "Don't forget," he admonishes fiercely. "Laughter is the greatest love, fury, and force in the universe. There is nothing that is not mirth, and my spirit is the distilled essence of exuberance!"

I have always suspected this to be true. Even Thor's violence stems from boisterous celebration of life, not from malice. The brutality of Odin triumphant in the field, that insouciant will to slaughter – this is not Thor's nature.

No. Thor is superabundance without limit. Confronted with armor, fear, hatred, the grime of miserliness (for surely such is the mean spirit of those he cannot abide), he cannot help but wish to liberate his enemies of their ugliness. He is a heavy handed masseur, not a boorish bully. Every knot of rigidity that he dissolves releases torrents of life into the world, like a kinked hose that is suddenly, violently, straightened.

And therein lies the heart of his friendship with Loki. Oh, the hiss of the anti-Loki brigade! But none can deny that Thor and Loki are boon traveling companions, for so our myths assure us. Two different expressions of the power of laughter, polar opposites that contain a seed of one another. It is just as necessary that they be sworn foes at the end of time as intimate comrades earlier on. Laughter knows no boundary; boundaries are forged by the brittle clutches of seriousness.

Seriousness – that empty armor of lies and madness. That willingness to bind up the world in limitations, abstractions, supposedly moral injunctions. That addiction to the entrapments and blandishments of corporeal power, which is to say, power won not through the good faith of laughter but the poison tongue of the spirit of gravity. Perhaps here lies Loki's fall – who could cling to their sense of humor after an age on the rock, the snake perched above, roped in the guts of their son?

The power won through seriousness is a brittle illusion, made to shatter, and the price paid for it is too high. It is always too high. But there are always fools willing to delude themselves into thinking otherwise. Eventually they turn to stone and arrogance, and as Thor demonstrated in his duel with Hrungnir, the Thunder God is more than adept at breaking heads that have become too big for their bodies.

"Don't forget it," he says again. "You cannot get anywhere without laughter as your companion. That's why I love these high altitudes – high spirits fly about the summits of the teeth of the world! We are natural siblings and companions." He swings his hammer, that potent symbol of fecundity, of new life, of pumping vigor.

"Laughter, little one, laughter! Who do the dour vultures of the halls of power hate the most? The servants of mockery and lampoon! Those that clutch at the illusion called 'control' cannot bear to have the skins of their bad consciences pricked. And am I not a thorny god?"

The lesson is ended like that, abrupt and complete. I open my eyes and gaze at the predawn light outside. I see that it is good.

– *Heimlich A. Laguz*

Creative Destruction: The Hammer of Healing

Thor seems to be the most popular of all the Northern gods. Which is probably part of the reason that I have always avoided him. It is in my nature to seek less obvious paths. I also do not tend to court deities; more often they enter my life unbidden. And usually it is goddesses and not gods that come to me.

Naturally, I had a pretty shallow understanding of this god. At a distance he seems simple, even vulgar and brutish. Not exactly my style. Mystery, uncanniness, a bit of audacity, and a trace of the trickster are the traits that usually charm me. But things change...

2009 was a rough year for me. The first day of it saw me transitioning out of a 12-year relationship, which filled me with excitement, immense sorrow, and paralyzing fear. Striking out on my own was challenging, especially in such an unsteady economy. Then my freelance work dried up over the summer, leaving me almost destitute – something that has never happened in the 6 years I have been working for myself. I was ripe with anxiety; a deep terror struck at my foundation.

Not surprisingly, I developed a debilitating lower back injury. It was brutal and kept me from the computer and in much pain. I don't do painkillers, so I faced it like a woman. I prayed and prayed, nurtured, and nourished the best I could. I sought guidance through dreams and conscious communication with the divine influences in my life. I did a lot of healing through laying on of hands.

One morning as I was laying in bed, my hands humming over my abdomen, I heard a clear voice ring through my mind. It said simply...*Invoke Thor*. I had been humbled so deeply by this point that I had only a moment of What?! before I did just as I was asked.

Immediately a figure appeared at the right side of my bed in my mind's eye. He was tall and muscular with long reddish-blond hair that was braided at the temples, and a full mustache but no beard. He was poised as though rooted in a deep well of strength, embedded in the foundation of Being. His eyes were sparkling and a smile played over his lips.

I have no idea where this vision of him came from, and it is admittedly different to what I would have conjured consciously if I was asked. What I do know is that I had this immediate feeling of deep kinship, a profound affection and trust that was beyond sibling-like in nature. It filled me with delight.

He was holding what seemed to be a glorified sledgehammer. It was intricately carved in swirling patterns from hilt to head.

After these initial impressions I was a bit stumped as to what to do or ask. He sensed my question and showed me an image in my mind. I saw the parts of my back that were in pain and they looked like mountains of black ice. In a flash I grasped his intention, which scared the shit out of me! But at this point what did I have to lose?

He waited patiently for me to ready myself, then raised his hammer as I tried fruitlessly to keep from cringing. With a roar of laughter he brought it down and smashed some of those mountains of ice. They scattered into dust and an ocean wave of exhilaration washed over me. I also started laughing. He continued bringing his hammer down in a great arcs and occasionally sweeping it through me like some barbaric croquet mallet, all the while laughing and roaring. His raw joy was infectious.

He came to me like this every morning for three days. On the third day I was completely healed. There was no pain at all in my back or hip.

I have called on him many times since. Sometimes he uses his hammer to smash through my blockages, sometimes he just has me lean against him like a great oak tree, our roots extending deep into the earth. A quiet peace coursing through me slowly, like rising sap. Relief from fear and stress that comes from taking the long view of life as a tree or deity might. Confidence anchored in knowing my strength.

Not long ago I was directed to a story in "*Gylfaginning*" where Thor, while staying at a farmer's house, kills his goats to make a meal of them for himself, his companions, and the family who dwell there. In the morning he waves his hammer over the goats' skin and bones to bring them back to life. What a strange vision! I ask him to try this on me sometimes when I am feeling out of alignment. His hammer, like a giant magnet, seems to pull me into balance again. I can literally feel my muscles relaxing, my vertebrae shifting, life-force freely coursing from sacrum to skull.

These experiences have brought me to a different view of healing. Sometimes violence is necessary to break down blockages. Sometimes force and aggression are needed to invoke energy from stagnancy. The magic is in the intention. It must be done with joy, a love of life, and much laughter.

– *Arrowyn Craban Lauer*

Thor Says: "Let Go!"

So long as I live, my ego is indestructible. It is a condition of being a finite being of the sort we call *human* that an ego is part of the complex called Self (albeit only a part, and not even the greatest).

I have often advocated for the destruction of the ego. Then, realizing this brought me little peace, I advocated for its curtailing, hemming in, restricting. In short, advocated for controlling and regulating the ego. I could not see how ironic it was that activities such as controlling and regulating (and destroying for that matter) are all very much par for the ego's course. No wonder I have struggled with myself despite the rich spiritual life I have been gifted.

Thor gave me a valuable lesson. I kneeled, and he stood behind me. "You want to be free of the ego's insanity?" He asked. "You want to stop trying to force reality to fit your lazy wish-fulfillment childishness by sheer force of thinking and emoting?" (he knows that I have found such mental activity to bring nothing but suffering and pessimism).

"So!" he cried, and struck my head clean from my shoulders with his hammer.

But immediately my head grew back, good as new.

"Again!" He cried, and Mjolnir's reverse sweep decapitated me again. A new head immediately popped out of the gaping cavity of my neck.

"And again!" He was laughing now, his hammer swishing back and forth as though light as a switch of birch. With each swing, he sent my head flying. Yet by the time the backswing was on its way, a new head had appeared, ready to be knocked off again.

Finally, his point made, Thor stopped. "So," he declared, "now you see that as soon as the ego is in any way abolished (short of physical death), it reappears. Its roots run deep, and at a certain point cannot be destroyed without ending your life." I realized that the addiction to ego is like an addictive relationship to food (what we might call compulsive overeating). A food addiction is trickier than, say, a drug addiction, because you cannot quit food as an aid to overcoming the addiction. You have to manage a stable relationship with food, while constantly placing your hand in the wolf's maw.

Now, how then to deal with the ego, its endless complaining, whining, raging, resenting, fearing, overthinking, superstition, paranoia, and all the rest? How, if not by trying to either control or abolish it?

"Just hand it over to me, or whoever you wish to hand it over to," Thor says, reading my mind. "Just say, 'Thor, I'm handing this over. I'm letting go.' You can trust me that I'll put your ego in a nice safe place, and you can get on with developing all the other parts of your psyche that have been atrophied in the shadow of your ego's unruly canopy."

Just hand it over? Just hand it over. Mind turns to powerless worry? Hand it over. Mind turns to self-righteous pomposity (designed to inflate a feeling of well-being with little merit of effort)? Hand it over. Even the need to always let go…can be let go.

Like all human beings, I am lopsided, uneven in my psychic anatomy. It is very hard to straighten a crooked spine when the load that bent it is still on your shoulder. Better to give it to the Divine so that your posture can be healed. The gods want us to be hale in order to better serve and celebrate them. They want to help. But we have to ask (know you how?).

How do we ask? The simplest formula I have heard is the prayer that goes, "God – help." And then the trick is not to immediately look for the magical solution of all your problems. Causality doesn't work like that. Let that go. And the need to let it go. And then in the next moment, whatever comes up – let it go. And that too. And that objection. And that digression. And that worry that you digressed. And so on.

Thor reminded me of his Marvel Comics incarnation. The comic book Thor flies, but not through force of will, not through effortful thinking, not through having a specific flying power.

No, how he flies is by whirling his hammer violently, around and around, until it builds up tremendous centrifugal force. Then he throws it, which actually amounts to releasing its circular momentum into a straight line. Just as it leaps away, he grabs the strap on the end of the handle and the hammer carries him with it.

So! This, Thor told me, is the ideal model for how to proceed. If we want to advance, if we want to fly, the way to do it is not through direct effort. No, instead we build momentum, or find momentum, or tap into momentum. When the time comes to move, we do not provide the power ourselves, we just channel the energy we have invoked through right action, self care, sensitivity, intuition, and all the rest.

If we over-think this at all then it will not work. Thor is a god of action (this is what makes him such a profound mystic). Over-thinking, egoism whether self-aggrandizing or self-destroying, has a way of subtly creeping back into the mind. Vigilance but also self-compassion are necessary. It will never totally subside, but it can become more and more easily sated and salved – and therefore gradually takes up less space that could otherwise be held by happiness, laughter, play, and power.

So! Whirl the psychic hammer – do not try to somehow force forward. Instead, when the time is right just – let go, and catch the strap. The inner Mjolnir will do the rest. Our job is not to be big, strong, heroic, and striving. Our job is to make ourselves available for forces much more powerful and playful.

Hail Thor!

– Heimlich A. Laguz

Sunna, MichaELFallson

On *Participation Mystique*
Heimlich A. Laguz

Consider *participation mystique*, a term coined by anthropologist Lucien Levy-Brühl and used extensively by Carl Jung. In such a state, our beliefs and the objects of our beliefs are experienced as one undifferentiated mass. Thus, for example, we can experience an inanimate object (or even living things like trees and animals) as having intentions, feelings, thoughts, spirit, and other qualities of consciousness.

This stands in contrast to what some would call anthropomorphism (thus revealing their allegiance to nihilism, which I will discuss shortly). In *participation mystique* correspondence is identity; there are no symbols, only literalism.

This mode of relationship enables us to experience the living magic of the cosmos (for surely *participation mystique* is a vehicle for the riches of imagination), but it also enables some very backward and hackneyed thinking, for example paranoia, denial, and superstition. The world is mystical, but if we are immersed without reflection in that world then we can get into trouble. For we then lack perspective on the sense or otherwise of our beliefs and deeds.

At the other extreme from so-called 'primitive' mysticism we have 'modern' nihilism: when all our attributions, projections, and beliefs are radically withdrawn from the world around us, are seen purely as products of our isolated consciousness. Consequently we risk experiencing nothing as satisfying, comforting, joyous, or meaningful. *Participation mystique* enables the very possibility of communication, by conjuring for us a 'theory of mind for the Other' and therefore implying the existence of relationships. That possibility is lost in nihilism, which is stuck in an endless, narcissistic, self-examining regress.

Nonetheless, great self-understanding and insight can come from the reflectiveness of nihilism. Once we withdraw our raw and undifferentiated acceptance of our experience of the world, we can develop subtle perception and deep appreciation of complexity. We can assess the implications of our thoughts and deeds, evaluate them, and refine them.

So if the supposedly premodern consciousness of *participation mystique* has reverence but not sense; and if the supposedly modern consciousness of nihilism has insight but wallows in the despair of abstraction, what are we to do?

Contra Levy-Brühl, who saw *participation mystique* as being culturally "primitive," I do not believe that these two modes of consciousness are mutually exclusive. Rather, throughout history their symbiosis ebbs and flows in complementary tides. They exist in each of us, all the time, and weave around one another in complex and subtle patterns. Both can be active in a single belief or action, engaging together like multifaceted computer programs interfacing over the Internet; like two chess masters of equal ability but totally opposed styles and methods; like Odin's ravens Thought (nihilism) and Memory (mysticism).

Participation mystique invariably collapses. Either its own irrationality causes it to dismantle (consider the Protestant Reformation of an insane Catholic church); or it is so flawlessly absorbed in the "world of its concern" (c.f. Martin Heidegger's work) that it becomes vulnerable to a sudden dramatic change of game (as happened to many indigenous cultures when rapacious European invaders turned up with guns, grog, and the Cross). Eve always ends up eating the apple and, though it can be unpleasant, the fall into ego consciousness is a necessary potentiality on the horizon of sacred oneness.

The Faustian fall into the clutches of the Devil's isolated ego leads to a different kind of disaster than those which haunt *participation mystique*. Once we forget that our actions have consequences in the causal web that binds everything together, we begin to do incredibly stupid things. For example, burn dangerous quantities of fossil fuels, divide the world into 'good' and 'evil' on the basis of skin color or religious identity, or base our society on disposability, unsustainably exponential growth, and other illusions. We layer abstractions upon abstractions, until stratospherically arbitrary conventions such as legality and economics conjure plenty in the midst of poverty and poverty in the midst of plenty.

Nonetheless, with the self-reflection of nihilism we are afforded an opportunity to, as Jung would say, withdraw our projections from the world. We can begin to recognize that *our emotions, attributions, beliefs, thoughts, and feelings about the world are distinct from the objects in the world to which they pertain.*

This is similar to what Edmund Husserl called the *phenomenological turn*. He correctly intuited a strong streak of *participation mystique*, of absorption in objects without reflection, in all the sciences (it continues today). In response, he called for a phenomenological revolution – to go "back to the things themselves" – to the projections which are the meat of all human experience.

A simple example (cribbed from Heidegger): we all have an intuitive idea of what this 'life' thing is that biology studies, and that intuition implicitly guides the very shape of all biological study. But try to draw out that intuition into a clear, explicit statement that does not, in some fashion, already presuppose the shape of the field of study! Not so easy to do, least of all if you are a biologist. Husserl warned that often our implicit understandings quietly but fatefully determine the way we experience and interpret reality. Modern research on cognitive bias – on the dangers of the tendency thumbnailed by Robert Anton Wilson as "the prover proves what the thinker thinks" – is a powerful contemporary scientific exploration of this problem.

So Husserl invokes this turn, away from the world, to the phenomena themselves. In the process he puts the question of reality 'as such,' 'in truth,' aside. Which is in a sense nihilistic (or at least a kind of epistemological agnosticism). Yet it allows us to clarify how our unconscious beliefs frame and occlude the experiences we have. This in turn opens us, enables us to experience reality with a lot more open-mindedness, wonder, curiosity, acceptance, and equanimity. At least, it does if we set it to good use and do not allow it to become a hall of mirrors *ala* postmodern philosophy (which indeed partly emerged as a successor to Husserl's ideas).

If we do not stop at a narrow and cramped state of nihilism (withdrawal of meaning from the world into the perceiver), but instead use that state to clarify how we relate to the world, then we find ourselves drawn, as Husserl was, to appreciate both the forest *and* the trees. Thus, instead of being stuck with *only* mysticism, or *only* nihilism, we are given the gift of a bigger picture and a rapprochement of what seemed at first to be fundamentally irreconcilable modes of consciousness.

For Jung this all has a psychological dimension. Psychological well-being is achieved once we have systematically withdrawn all our projections from the world, grasped them *as projections*, as objects themselves ("to the things themselves!" we again hear Husserl cry).

This gradually enables us to see how our experience is shaped by our expectations, habits, and unconscious beliefs. Through this process we come to realize that it is not the world, not events, not other people that make us happy or unhappy, but rather our ability to achieve peace within ourselves; we become less dependent on the arbitrary whims of fate in order to feel whole. Of course, we then have to reintegrate ourselves so that the breach of psyche and cosmos is resolved into a new, far more robust relationship between mind and world.

(This is not to say that negative life events character somehow magically 'shouldn't' have a traumatic consequence, but to rather say that the person who achieves something close to Jung's ideal of *individuation* is able to accept, cope with, and resolve negative situations more effectively and with less suffering, gaining in the process more power to positively impact the world).

Jung saw this process of withdrawal and rebirth in the symbolism of alchemy. He felt that the alchemists – sometimes purposefully, sometimes instinctively – used the state of *participation mystique* as a framework within which to experience their psychological withdrawal, transformation, and reintegration. Their medium? The myth-laden operations of their paraphernalia. Here we see the brilliance of alchemy: it distills the best of nihilistic, detached consciousness by establishing it within an environment of mystical literalism!

(Psychotherapy is almost identical, except that it substitutes the *temenos* of the therapeutic relationship for the retorts, alembics, and chemicals of the pseudo-scientist. The analogy was certainly not lost on Jung).

So: we begin by being immersed uncritically in the world, unable to separate our consciousness, our emotions and beliefs, from that which is around us – other people, other places, other things. Then we separate and become self-conscious – we detach ourselves from the world around us in order to come to self-awareness. Finally we reintegrate, so that our newfound perspective serves to open and enrich our experience, while imparting a fresh sense of inner wholeness.

In this way we can enjoy the mystical sense of all existence as a sacred and interconnected whole without the blinders that we suffered prior to our quest for self-awareness. And naturally this is actually a recurring cycle, without alpha or omega.

The three stage model (withdrawal, transformation, reintegration) can be seen in the three stages of alchemy. We begin with the *Prima Materia*, the raw stuff to which we apply our Art. Then we enter stage one, *nigredo*: blackening, death – the detachment of self from world. Our gestation produces stage two, *albedo*: whitening, in which we are emptied out until we are pristine, unsullied by the world; but also isolated, disconnected. Finally comes stage three, the *rubedo*: reddening, where our pristine nature is redeemed to the world, and vice versa. Thus the lead becomes gold.

It is significant in this connection that Mercurius, the arch-patron of alchemy, *is both* Prima Materia *and the Philosopher's Stone*; that is, he is both lead and gold. We begin with the lead, we finish with the gold, but Mercurius shows them to be the one thing. We complete our alchemical or psychological journey back where we started, yet at the same time everything is totally different. In this sense, alchemy depicts a spiral movement: our circular orbits nevertheless also describe an ascending path, with the Self or the Stone as the axis of the spiral. The same holds for any sound process of spiritual or psychological development.

The Philosopher's Stone, the goal of alchemy, is that which is wrested from the chaos of the world, refined in isolation, and then reintegrated with the world from which it was wrenched in such a way that it transforms the world where once the world dominated it. In a sense, this psychological redemption touches all of objective reality, for they are one even as they are distinct.

It is from Jung that I draw the analogy of the Self to the Stone – snatched from the blindness of naive projection, refined in the isolating reflection of the therapy room (or other life experiences), and then returning to the world in such a way that it is connected with, but no longer dissolved into, everything around it. It no longer needs to attack or defend or justify itself or anything of the sort. It is its own singular foundation *and yet simultaneously* it is utterly integrated and one with the universe as a whole.

In an inspired vision Woden appeared to me, younger than he ever has – no beard, and two eyes. He led me through a forest to a clearing. In the clearing was a phoenix (a symbol of the Philosopher's Stone, of the goal of psycho-spiritual wholeness and perfection).

Woden explained that it is a mistake to think the phoenix dies and is reborn. Rather, he said, if you look closely you can see an almost invisible membrane around it: its egg. The phoenix can expand and contract this membrane at will. When its egg is expanded it contains the whole universe, and thus we perceive the phoenix and think it alive. But when need be, the phoenix can contract the egg until the bird is tightly enclosed. Then it seems to us to have disappeared, to have died, only to be 'reborn' when the phoenix is ready to 'participate mystically' through projection once again, which is to say, only when it again expands its membrane to encompass the world around.

This is the psychological and spiritual model which Woden, in his almost Mercurial form, encouraged me to pursue. The eternal phoenix, neither born nor unborn; in the world, loving the world, but not owned by the world. Shamanistic but not superstitious; realistic but not cynical.

That the three-part process of withdrawal, transformation, and reintegration is common in premodern cultural imagery suggests that *participation mystique* was never as absolute as Levy-Brühl proposes; otherwise it would never have been posed as a problem or questioned at all. Jung and Levy-Brühl were blindsided by the disowned shadow of the European colonial gaze. That the threefold process here discussed is so resonant even in modern times suggests that nihilism does not hold total sway even in this, its ascendant age. We can have hope: the ancient ways still retain their healing power.

Yet none of the foregoing means anything if we do not act on our hope. Meditate. Keep a journal. Get psychotherapy. Advocate for social justice. Take a stand for nature. Commune with like-minded seekers. Reflect. Pray. Make art. Find the divine in small things and hidden places. Be your own alchemist. This is the purpose for which we were made.

For when we invert the alchemical way – when we run things inside out and try to observe *participation mystique* within a cocoon of nihilism – then we expose ourselves to danger, reducing ourselves to mere armchair practice and idle talk. We may sound like we have undertaken the necessary work but the truth is we are just exposing ourselves to the worst aspects of both mysticism *and* nihilism, under the spell of our laziness, fear, hurt, arrogance, self-hatred, and all the rest. We might even make ourselves worse off than when we began, for we risk flagrant hypocrisy as well. Alchemy was considered a dangerous art, and these are some of the pitfalls of proceeding incorrectly.

I have made such mistakes too readily in my life. Now is the time, now is *always* the time, to undo the ills of armchair 'wisdom' and roll up my sleeves; to challenge my excuses and strive for something better.

Join me.

Portrait of an Owl, Arrowyn Craban Lauer

Academic Sources
Sweyn Plowright
Additional suggestions by Rig Svenson & Heimlich A. Laguz

In this chapter we provide a list and brief discussion of the main historical sources that have inspired and informed Heathenism. We have tried to keep it as concise and affordable as possible, while still covering all of the areas of interest. The purpose of the list is to allow Heathens to see for themselves where the earliest information comes from, and be able to make informed decisions about their Heathenism.

Information on the sources can also be found online and in the books we mention here. Some care needs to be taken with online scholarship, as it can be quite inaccurate. However, a fairly complete collection of these sources can be gathered from online bookstores for less than the cost of a night on the town.

Tacitus

Written by the Roman noble Tacitus around 98CE, *De Origine et situ Germanorum* (*Of the Origin and Location of the Germani*), is commonly known as *The Germania*. It describes the tribes, laws, lands, and customs of the people inhabiting Northern Europe. It is not a first-hand account, but a work of documentary research, gathering information from many of the reports from the Roman incursions in the area, as well as talking with traders and Germanic mercenaries in Rome. There are many affordable, even free, translations available in the online bookstores. **Search: Tacitus,** *Germania.*

Flavius Josephus

Josephus was a 1st-century Jewish military historian who first fought against the Romans, then worked for them as an interpreter. He chronicled many of the military campaigns of the time, and wrote in some detail about the Germanic soldiers, and their increasing presence in the Roman army. Free translations available online. **Search: Flavius Josephus.**

Procopius

Procopius of Caesarea had a legal background and wrote about recent and current military history during the rule of Justinian in the 6th Century. Many of his accounts were first hand, so he could almost be seen as a war correspondent.

Some of the campaigns were against Germanic tribes, and he includes some interesting details about them, although it should be remembered that from his Roman point of view he tended to look down upon the tribes as uncivilised. Available from online bookstores in paperback, and in electronic formats for under a dollar. **Search: Procopius, Wars of Justinian.**

Ahmad ibn Fadlān

Ibn Fadlān was a diplomat attached to the ambassador from the Caliph of Baghdad to the Volga region in the 10th century. There he met and described the Volga Vikings (the Rus) and their customs. His descriptions are some of the earliest of Vikings, who he says were tall and covered in tattoos of "tree patterns." It also contains a detailed account of a Viking funeral. Free part-translations are available online. One full translation, listed below, can be found second hand in online stores. **Search: ibn Fadlān.**

The Rune Poems

There are three surviving poems that illustrate each rune with a verse based on the rune's name. The "Anglo-Saxon Rune Poem" was written in Old English about the Anglo-Saxon 33-rune row. The "Old Icelandic Rune Poem" and "Old Norwegian Rune Poem" were written about the Scandinavian 16-rune row.

The three poems are quite different, but when seen together they can provide insights into the possible meanings attached to the Elder 24-rune row.

All three poems with original language and modern English translations are included in Sweyn's *The Rune Primer*, available in online bookstores. **Search: Rune Poems, Futhark, *Rune Primer*.**

Gesta Danorum

Written by the Danish chronicler Saxo Grammaticus, this book covers the history of the people of Denmark as he knew it. It covers the mythical history of the Heathen ancestors and gods, and moves forward to the better-known history until Saxo's time in the late 12th century.

It contains a wealth of information on customs, laws, and institutions of government. However, it does seem to have a significant Christian bias in parts. Some affordable translations are available in online bookstores. **Search: Gesta Danorum, Saxo Grammaticus.**

Poetic Edda

Also known as the *Elder Edda*, this is perhaps the best known of the sources. It contains in verse form much of the mythology that is known from Viking times. It was preserved mainly in a document known as the *Codex Regius* written in Iceland in the 13th century.

It includes the *Hávamál*, words of wisdom from Odin, which in turn contains the *Rúnatáls þáttr Óðins*, which describes Odin's finding of the runes.

The work is divided into multiple sections, the mythological highlights of which include:

Völuspá – The Prophecy of the Seeress
Hávamál – Sayings of the High One
Vafþrúðnismál – Vafthrúdnir's Sayings
Grímnismál – Grímnir's Sayings
Skírnismál – Skírnir's Journey
Hárbarðsljóð – The Poem of Hárbard
Hymiskviða – The Poem of Hymir
Lokasenna – Loki's Quarrel
Þrymskviða – Thrym's Poem
Völundarkviða – The Poem of Völund
Alvíssmál – All-Wise's Sayings

Two well-known and affordable translations are one by Lee Hollander, and a more recent one by Carolyne Larrington. Some of the text in the original language can be found online. **Search: *The Poetic Edda.***

Prose Edda

Also known as the *Younger Edda*, this is a compilation of mythological stories written down by Snorri Sturluson around the year 1220. Amongst the tales there is useful information on poetry, kennings, and other insights into Heathen literature interspersed.

The work is divided into four sections:

Prologue – Introduction
Gylfaginning – The tricking of Gylfi
Skáldskaparmál – The language of poetry
Háttatal – List of verse-forms

Recent translations include one by Jesse Byock, and one by Anthony Faulkes. Original language texts are harder to find. **Search: *The Prose Edda* or *Edda.***

Sagas

Many of the Icelandic sagas are available from Penguin Classics. They give a fascinating glimpse of a time when Heathenism was still alive in many parts of Scandinavia. **Search: Saga, Guta, Vinland, Grettir, Njal, Eirik, Eyrbyggja, Volsunga, Gautrek, Harald, Odd, Yngling, Egil, Laxdaela, Hrafnkel.**

Anglo-Saxon Works

Several sources written in Old English describe the world of the Germanic Heathen times. Most notable would have to be *Beowulf*, also the *Battle of Maldon*. Bede's history contains an account of the settlement of England by the Heathen Germanic tribes.

Riddles were a favourite art form in Anglo-Saxon literature; the *Exeter Book* is the largest source for these. Several books can be found with the translations.

Anglo Saxon Poetry, by S. Bradley, is available in electronic form. It is comprehensive and affordable, but translations are rather flat prose.

The Anglo-Saxon World: An Anthology by Kevin Crossley-Holland is also affordable, with a good selection of works in a reasonable translation. Many translations of *Beowulf* on its own are available, and it is worth getting a couple to compare. **Search: Anglo-Saxon Literature, Old English Poems, *Beowulf*, Widsith, Deor, Bede, *Battle of Maldon*.**

Germanic Archaeology

This is an ongoing field of study. Interesting insights have come from finds of physical artifacts, as well as linguistic and genetic evidence. The easiest way to find articles is by online search, however, some care must be taken that the articles are genuine academic research. **Search: Germanic, archaeology, linguistics, finds, artefacts.**

Recommended Academic Books

Some of these are not cheap, but they discuss the sources with a deep knowledge of their context and limitations. Many can also be found second hand online.

Anglo-Saxon England	Lloyd & Jennifer Laing
Anglo-Saxon Military Institutions on the Eve of the Norman Conquest	C. Warren Hollister
Anglo-Saxon Paganism	David Wilson
Aspects of Anglo-Saxon Archaeology: Sutton Hoo and Other Discoveries	Rupert Bruce-Mitford
Barbarians to Angels: The Dark Ages Reconsidered	Peter S. Wells
Both One and Many: Essays on Change and Variety in Late Norse Heathenism	John McKinnell
Chronicles of the Vikings	R.I. Page
Complete Fairy Tales	Jacob and William Grimm
Dictionary of Northern Mythology	Rudolf Simek
Edda and Saga	Jónas Kristjánsson

Freyja, the Great Goddess of the North	Britt-Mari Näsström
Gods and Myths of Northern Europe	H.R. Ellis Davidson
Handbook of Nordic Mythology	John Lindow
Ibn Fadlān's Journey to Russia: A 10th-Century Traveler from Baghdad to the Volga River	Richard Frye
Leechcraft: Early English Charms, Plant Lore, and Healing	Stephen Pollington
Lords of Battle	Stephen S. Evans
Myths and Symbols in Pagan Europe	H.R. Ellis Davidson
Nordic Religions in the Viking Age	Thomas A. DuBois
Norse Mythology: A Guide to the Gods, Heroes, Rituals, and Beliefs	John Lindow
Norse Myths	R.I. Page
Of Ghosts and Godpoles	Þorbert Línleáh
Roles of the Northern Goddess	H.R. Ellis Davidson
Runes and Their Secrets: Studies in Runology	Edited by Gillian Fellows Jensen, Marie Stokluind, Michael Lerche Nielsen, and Bente Holmberg
Runes, Magic, and Religion: A Sourcebook	John McKinnell & Rudolf Simek, with Klaus Düwel
Runic Amulets and Magic Objects	Mindy MacLeod & Bernard Mees
Scandinavian Mythology: An Annotated Bibliography	John Lindow
The Early Germans	Malcolm Todd
The Lost Beliefs of Northern Europe	H.R. Ellis Davidson
The Poetic Edda	trans. Carolyne Larrington
The Poetic Edda	trans. Lee Hollander
The Sword in Anglo-Saxon England	H.R. Ellis Davidson
The Tradition of Household Spirits	Claude Lecouteux
The Viking Art of War	Paddy Griffith
The Viking Way: Religion and War in Late Iron Age Scandinavia	Neil Price
The Vikings	Else Roesdahl
The Vikings and their Origins	David Wilson

The Well and the Tree   Paul Bauschatz
Wilder Man: The Image of the Savage   Charles Freger
Women in the Viking Age   Judith Jesch

Sources for Inspiration

Any and all of these can be sniffed out on the Internet, some more easily than others. *All of these materials must be viewed with a highly critical mind*, especially those authors who surreptitiously try to pass off their own personal opinions as objective facts of history, archaeology, or practice.

Books & eBooks:

Heathenism

True Helm, Sweyn Plowright
   A personal exploration of themes of Northern Warriorship and Heathen mysticism, applied to modern life. It includes a retelling of the legend of Wayland the Smith.

Drinking from the Well of Mimir, Bil Linzie
Uncovering the Effects of Cultural Background on the Reconstruction of Ancient Worldviews, Bil Linzie
Investigating the Afterlife Concepts of the Norse Heathens: A Reconstructionist's Approach, Bil Linzie
Germanic Spirituality, Bil Linzie
   Bil Linzie is an American Heathen reconstructionist, and one of the deepest thinkers in our community. Despite some flaws (such as his unreasoning rejection of the idea that Heathens should cultivate personal relationships with the gods), all of his work is highly, highly recommended. These books are free ebooks that can be found easily via Google.

The Real Middle-Earth, Brian Bates
   Bates is an English psychologist who attempts to delve into the archaic Heathen worldview itself. Occasionally plays loose with historical evidence, but on the whole an excellent phenomenology of Heathen consciousness.

Our Troth, Volume 1, The Troth
Our Troth, Volume 2, The Troth
   The Troth is a major non-racist Heathen organization that puts out a lot of excellent, scholarly, material. These books provide a comprehensive grounding in Heathen religion and practice.

Bright From the Well, Dave Lee
   A speculative and inspiring amalgam of spiritual reflection, fiction, and magick.

The One-eyed God, Kris Kershaw

Odin's Way in the Modern World, Wayland Skallagrimsson

Rune Magic

The Rune Primer, Sweyn Plowright
   Sweyn's very simple, clear, demystifying introduction to the runes. The single best starting place for those interested in rune magic because it provides a solid base in skepticism and critical thinking to balance the florid speculation that runs rampant among most authors on rune magic (even those that say they're above such things!).

Taking Up the Runes, Diana L. Paxson
   Paxson's encyclopedic guide to the runes; among other things valuable because she summarizes and compares the views of the main contemporary rune magic authors.

Helrunar, Jan Fries
   Fries' idiosyncratic, free-wheeling guide to rune magic. Sometimes plays fast and loose with historical evidence, but usually openly so the reader can make informed decisions for themselves. A fun and inspiring text, well worth reading. Be sure to get the most recent edition, as there are several versions.

Futhark, Edred Thorsson
   A classic text on contemporary rune magic. Probably required reading, but be aware that although Thorsson presents himself as a rigorous reconstructionist (and takes other authors to task for not being reconstructionists) he is nevertheless sometimes guilty of directly or implicitly trying to pass off his own inventions and interpretations as fact.
Runelore, Edred Thorsson
   The sequel to *Futhark;* similar comments apply.
The Rune Caster's Handbook, Edred Thorsson
   There is no truly excellent handbook on runic divination but this not a bad starting point, though Thorsson's invention of the bright rune/murk rune dichotomy is a significant shortcoming.

The Stanzas of the Old English Rune Poem, Gary Stanfield
   Stanfield is a *hard* reconstructionist and his analysis and translation of the "Old English Rune Poem" reveals bountiful gifts of insight and understanding into the runes' multidimensional meanings. As with every author, his conclusions warrant consumption with a pinch of salt at times, but on the whole Stanfield has set the standard for serious Heathen runology with this book. A shame it only covers one of the three main rune poems. Bonus: the book is free as a PDF download from http://runicwisdom.info/rwtoc.htm

Chaos Magic

Liber Null & Psychonaut, Peter Carroll
   Peter Carroll's classic guide to Chaos Magic, including an excellent curriculum of practice. A foundational text.
Liber Kaos, Peter Carroll
   More excellent Chaos Magical material.

Condensed Chaos, Phil Hine
   Hard to find in print (although less developed prototypes of the text still float about online as ebooks). A wonderfully playful, down to earth, practical guide to doing magic.
Prime Chaos, Phil Hine
   Hine explores multiple aspects of contemporary magical practice in this valuable, insightful tome. Hard to find.

Visual Magick, Jan Fries
   The definitive guide to practicing magic. A short, simple, hands-on book that is endlessly inspiring and creative. The single best starting place for anyone wanting to learn how to work magic. Fries does not himself identify as a Chaos Magician, but his approach resonates strongly with the chaos current nonetheless.

S.S.O.T.B.M.E Revised: An Essay on Magic, Ramsey Dukes

Prometheus Rising, Robert Anton Wilson

T.A.Z.: The Temporary Autonomous Zone, Hakim Bey
   The seminal text on the intimate relationship that can obtain between anarchism and Chaos Magic.

Hinduism & Buddhism

The Origins & Development of Classical Hinduism, A.L. Basham
Am I a Hindu?: The Hinduism Primer, Ed Viswanathan
The Myths and Gods of India, Alain Danielou
Shiva: The Wild God of Power and Ecstasy, Wolf Dieter-Storl
The Gods Drink Whiskey, Steven T. Asma
Confessions of a Buddhist Atheist, Stephen Batchelor
The Inner Journey: Views from the Hindu Tradition, M. H. Case (editor)

Hellenismos

Five Stages of Greek Religion, Gilbert Murray
The Greek Way, Edith Hamilton
Kharis: Hellenic Polytheism Explored, Sarah Kate Istra Winter

Gnosticism & Early Christianity

The Jesus Mysteries: Was the "Original Jesus" a Pagan God?, Timothy Freke and Peter Gandy
Jesus and the Lost Goddess, Timothy Freke and Peter Gandy
The Laughing Jesus, Timothy Freke and Peter Gandy

Left Hand Path

The Satanic Bible, Anton Szandor LaVey
The Church of Satan, Michael Aquino
Pacts with the Devil, S. Jason Black and Christopher S. Hyatt
Tantra without Tears, S. Jason Black and Christopher S. Hyatt
The Devil's Party: Satanism in Modernity, Per Faxneld and Jesper Aa. Petersen
    Includes some interesting information about early Satanism in Scandinavia and Continental Europe.

General Magic

Seidways, Jan Fries
    The definitive book on trance magic. Bursts with so many ideas for magical practice that it would take several lifetimes to explore them all! A freewheeling, hilarious, bizarre, and essential magical text, flaws and all (it misses the historical form of *seidhr* in some respects, but totally nails the spirit). Be sure to get the most recent edition.

Tranceformations, Diana L. Paxson
    Paxson's comprehensive practical guide to developing trance magic skills. Less flamboyant than *Seidways,* but more structured.

The Book of Lies, Aleister Crowley
    Verses of poetic wisdom combining numerology, Tantra, and deep mystical insight. It is full of wit, double or triple entendre, and the signs of an education sadly rare in this world.

Pronoia is the Antidote to Paranoia, Rob Brezsny
    A quirky almanac in honor of what could be called The Spirit of Optimism. A wonderful source of inspiration, humor, and (ir)reverence.

The Three Minute Meditator, David Harp
    A very practical, empowering, concrete guide to learning to meditate.

Urban Voodoo, S. Jason Black and Christopher S. Hyatt

Protection & Reversal Magick, Jason Miller
Defensive magick with good reason and logic locked behind it. You won't find wishing for karma. You'll discover proven methods in this unique defense manual.

The Cosmic Serpent, Jeremy Narby
A mind-blowing exploration of ayahuasa, neon serpents, DNA electromagnetic waves, animism, and extraterrestrial language as the seeds of life on earth. This is perhaps a sensationalist characterization for what is a remarkably sober book that explores some very wild territory. If you are an alien and/or a snake then this is the book for you (we trust you know what we're talking about, and if not, you'll enjoy reading it anyway).

Philosophy & Psychology

Owning Your Own Shadow, Robert Johnson
Inner Work, Robert Johnson
Johnson is a Jungian psychologist. His books are short, profound, and intensely practical. *Owning Your Own Shadow* is a great guide to becoming a whole person; *Inner Work* offers exceptional tools for dream interpretation and active imagination practices.

Collected Works, C. G. Jung (especially *Psychological Types, Psychology & Alchemy, Alchemical Studies,* and *Mysterium Coniunctionis*)
Memories, Dreams, Reflections, C. G. Jung
Modern Man in Search of a Soul, C. G. Jung
The Red Book, C. G. Jung
Jung is often watered down, misunderstood, and slandered by the well-meaning but poorly-informed; hence there is no substitute for reading his works. Start out with the more accessible texts (*Modern Man in Search of a Soul* and *Memories, Dreams, Reflections*), then move into the more challenging material. Reading Jung is like attending an intense spiritual boot camp, especially when combined with the Jungian techniques that Johnson provides in *Inner Work* (above). *The Red Book* is an illuminated manuscript Jung created to document his own spiritual-psychological initiatory journey. A truly remarkable magical text, almost certainly *the* grimoire of the 20th Century.

Alchemical Active Imagination, Marie-Louise von Franz
Alchemy: An Introduction to the Symbolism and the Psychology, Marie-Louise von Franz
Projection and Recollection in Jungian Psychology, Marie-Louise von Franz

Von Franz was a long-term colleague of Jung's. Her work is much more accessible without sacrificing any depth, and she often does a better idea of expounding on Jungian psychology than Jung himself. All of her books are highly recommended.

Basic Writings, Martin Heidegger (edited by David Krell)
Being and Time, Martin Heidegger

Heidegger's work is extremely obtuse and difficult to understand, however his books do reward the persistent reader, and his ideas have been extremely valuable to at least one of this book's authors. We note that Heidegger's collaboration in the early days of the Nazi regime is indefensible. We also note, however, that as far as we can determine his philosophy is antithetical to any sort of totalitarianism, proving once again that a thinker who lacks solid spiritual (and ethical!) practice risks failing the promise of their inspiration.

Thus Spoke Zarathustra, Friedrich Nietzsche
The Gay Science, Friedrich Nietzsche

Horribly flawed and deeply brilliant, Nietzsche is a challenging, provocative thinker whose complex, poetic writing warrants many readings. Read the Kaufman or Hollingdale translations of these books; the 19th century public domain translations (found everywhere online) are **utterly worthless**.

On Equilibrium, John Ralston Saul

The *Elhaz Ablaze* camp is divided on this author. Some of us see him as an advocate for reflection, animism, and practical reason; others of our number think him a muddle-headed, tin-hat romantic. Read it and decide for yourself.

The Power of Myth, Joseph Campbell

Also a documentary made by Bill Moyers, this book is an excellent introduction to Campbell's brilliant and insightful ideas about mythology.

A Blue Fire, James Hillman

A great anthology of essays by the Jungian analyst who invented the concept of polytheistic psychology.

The Myth of the Eternal Return, Mircea Eliade
   A classic text on the psychology, structure, and process of myth and ritual practice. Hugely influential, and rightfully so, as with everything Eliade wrote.

My Voice Will Go With You, Milton Erickson (edited by Sidney Rosen)
   Inspiring, confounding, remarkable tales of psychiatrist Milton Erickson's clinical work, highlighting his sophisticated, playful, creative, and loving use of trance and hypnosis to help his clients achieve incredible transformations and healing. Erickson comes across like an avatar of Odin in his aspect as a healer.

A History of Western Philosophy, Bertrand Russell

In Search of the Warrior Spirit, Richard Strozzi-Heckler
   Documents an experiment with teaching meditation and related disciplines to the US Army Special Forces.

The Warrior Ethos, Steven Pressfield

The True Believer, Eric Hoffer

The Compleat Witch (aka The Satanic Witch), Anton Szandor LaVey
   Amateur psychology, seduction, and manipulation.

The Mystery Method, Eric Von Markovik
   Read alongside *The Compleat Witch.*

On Killing, Dave Grossman

The Gift of Fear, Gavin de Becker

The Secret Life of Nature, Peter Tompkins
The Secret Life of Plants, Peter Tompkins & Christopher Bird

Plant Intelligence and the Imaginal Realm: Beyond the Doors of Perception into the Dreaming of Earth, Stephen Harrod Buhner
The Secret Teachings of Plants: The Intelligence of the Heart in the Direct Perception of Nature, Stephen Harrod Buhner
Ensouling Language, Stephen Harrod Buhner

Does it Matter?, Alan Watts
Tao: The Watercourse Way, Alan Watts
Watts' playful, profound approach to both Eastern and Western thought warrants reading and re-reading. His recorded lectures are also worth seeking out (search Youtube, especially for Watts' mind blowing eulogy for Jung).

Mutual Aid, Peter Kropotkin
A classic text on community and reciprocity whose implications extend far beyond its anarchist roots.

Physical Culture

Arnold: The Education of a Bodybuilder, Arnold Schwarzenegger
One could do a hell of a lot worse than using the beginner's routine from this book. Also, it turns out Arnie is much more interesting and intelligent than you'd probably expect.

Bruce Lee: The Art of Expressing the Human Body, John Little

Beyond Brawn, Stuart McRobert
Essential reading for hard-gainers.

The Spartan Health Regime, Anthony Bova
Poorly spelled but possibly the best all-around introduction to old school physical culture and ancestral nutrition ever written.

Dinosaur Training, Brooks Kubic
A manifesto for old-school strength training, written by a former Wrestler and Power Lifter turned Lawyer and Author.

Dinosaur Bodyweight Training, Brooks Kubic
Dinosaur Training for pure calisthenics enthusiasts.

Never Gymless, Ross Enamait
The definitive guide to progressive bodyweight strength training with minimal equipment.

Infinite Intensity, Ross Enamait
    All round strength and conditioning for Boxers and combat athletes. Takes up where *Never Gymless* left off.

Convict Conditioning, Paul Wade
    A highly detailed guide to *progressive* bodyweight strength training. This is the book to read if you need to get super-strong in a small space with limited equipment. Practical, inspiring, and extremely challenging.

Practical Guide to Physical Education, Georges Hebert
    One of the foundational texts of *Methode Naturelle,* which went on to form the basis of *Parkour* and much of modern Military PT.

Functional Training for Sports, Michael Boyle
    A first rate textbook on professional level strength and conditioning, applicable to any sport or martial art.

The Centurion Method: The Complete Age of Iron Edition, Craig Fraser, Lucy Fraser, & Paul Waggener
    A deeply problematic text but possibly the first book ever to approach physical fitness training from an Occult Philosophy/Left Hand Path point of view. A partial answer to the question, 'Why are there so many fitness books recommended in a work on Chaos Heathenism?'

Nutrition

Nutrition is a highly effective means of regulating mind and emotions. *This is functional inner alchemy!*

In Defense of Food, Michael Pollan
The Spartan Health Regime, Anthony Bova
Nutrition and Physical Degeneration, Weston A. Price
The Metabolic Typing Diet, William L. Wolcott and Trish Fahey
Nourishing Traditions, Sally Fallon
Seven Weeks to Sobriety, Joan Mathews Larson
The Vegetarian Myth, Lierre Keith
The Primal Blueprint, Mark Sisson

Martial Arts

Combat Sports in the Ancient World, Michael B. Poliakoff
The Martial Arts of Ancient Greece, Kostas Dervenis and Nektarios Lykiardopoulos
The Wrestler's Body: Identity and Ideology in North India, Joseph S. Alter
By the Sword, Richard Cohen
Viking Weapons and Combat Techniques, William R. Short
Master of Defence, Paul Wagner
The Martial Arts of Renaissance Europe, Sydney Anglo
The Bartitsu Compendium, Tony Wolf (editor)
Championship Streetfighting: Boxing as a Martial Art, Ned Beaumont
Kill-as-Catch-Can: Wrestling Skills for Streetfighting, Ned Beaumont
Tao of Jeet Kune Do, Bruce Lee
Mastering Jujitsu, Renzo Gracie and John Danaher

Fiction & Off-Topic

Some of these books are specifically re-tellings or re-visionings of Germanic myth, ancient history, or speculative voyages into occultism and magic; others are just good fun.

Days in Midgard: One Thousand Years On, Stephen T. Abell
The Light Bearer, Donna Gillespie
Rhinegold, Stephan Grundy
Liber Malorum, Sean Scullion (editor)
Elric series, Michael Moorcock
Conan series, Robert E. Howard
Wyvern, A. A. Attanasio
Last Legends of Earth, A. A. Attanasio
The Dragon and the Unicorn, A. A. Attanasio
The Silmarillion, J. R. R. Tolkien
The Lord of the Rings, J. R. R. Tolkien
Mercurius, Patrick Harpur
Fight Club, Chuck Palahniuk
The Song of Troy, Colleen McCullough
Masters of Rome series, Colleen McCullough
Gates of Fire, Steven Pressfield

Rome Inc., Stanley Bing
The Hyperion Cantos, Dan Simmons
The Nantucket Series, S.M. Stirling
The Emberverse Series, S.M. Stirling
The Domination/Draka Series, S.M. Stirling
Starship Troopers, Robert A. Heinlein
A Song of Ice and Fire, George R.R. Martin (as if everyone isn't reading this already)
The Way of Wyrd, Brian Bates
Brisingamen, Diana L. Paxson
Written in Venom, Lois Tilton
The Odin Brotherhood, Mark Mirabello
American Gods, Neil Gaiman
The Quiet Soldier, Adam Ballinger
The Dream World of H.P. Lovecraft, Donald Tyson
Fiction written by H. P. Lovecraft
The Mists of Avalon, Marion Zimmer Bradley
Imajica, Clive Barker
Steppenwolf, Hermann Hesse
Siddharta, Hermann Hesse
His Dark Materials series, Philip Pullman

Magazines

Hex Magazine

Hex explored Heathenry from a household point of view, weaving academic, magical, culinary, historical, literary, and personal threads into a lovely whole. No longer producing new issues but back issues are still available. Visually stunning as well as featuring inspired articles.

Odroerir Magazine

Great ezine about reconstructionism. Sadly only a couple of issues came out.

Idunna Magazine

The official magazine of The Troth, usually has great content.

Gods & Radicals

Pagan anarchist magazine at the cutting edge of radical pagan politics.

Gratitude

Matthew Hern:

I want to thank my brother and my wife, T. S., Henrik Zoltan, Tibeta, and Vera K – for love, magic, and friendship. Thanks for help on the Path and inspiration: Ian Read, Ingrid Fischer, Dave Lee, David J. Jones, Jon Sharp, Christopher "Wednesday" Smith, Steve Davies, Ariman, Michael Kelly, Annabel Lee, *und ein tiefer dank an* Michael Moynihan. For the Vajra in the Chaos to Sven Kreyenfeld-Kuniß and Maarten Schoon.

My deep thanks go to Heimlich A. Laguz and Arrowyn Craban Lauer for great friendship and generosity, as well as their Great Dagazian Minds, which teach old spiritual lessons that Heathenism forgot: compassion, vulnerability, creativity on the one hand; and fire, passion, and power on the other hand. They don't exclude each other!

Thanks to the Elhaz Fellowship, Sweyn and Klintr especially, for our *Freigeist* debates back in the day that gave birth to this book, which is necessary in this post-truth world of constant shallowness. Thanks to Jóhannes von Necromantie for his thoughtful comments on the Elhaz Ablaze website, too. I thank Dave Lee for being my teacher, supporter, and friend since 2010.

You are our Chaos Stars – like you we still have Chaos in ourSelves to give birth to a dancing star!

Heimlich A. Laguz:

Thanks to every visitor to the *Elhaz Ablaze* website, and to my fellow creators, who are not just collaborators; they are kin (Klintr has seen me at my worst and we're still friends, which I find incredible). Special thanks to Donovan and Jóhannes von Necromantie, without whom *Elhaz Ablaze* would be much less than it is (and I would be much less for lack of their friendship). To S. N. Goenka for *Vipassana*, and to Minerva for leading me to that gift. Heart-felt hails to Odin and Loki! I honor Arrowyn Craban Lauer, numinous ring-breaker that she is, and my parents for embracing my Quixotic temperament.

Arrowyn Craban Lauer:

I am grateful for the blood of trees, the swoop of wings, the glint of bone, the sparkle in my lover's eye, and the honey on his tongue.

MichaELFallson:

I am grateful to my loving wife and children who continue to tolerate my *wyrdness* and to my ancestral family who do keep me tru as I exist between the nine worlds. I offer many thanks to the Old Ones for the trees and the sea and the animals and the runes as well as for the unique opportunity to be a part of this timely publication.

Mark Morte:

Mark hails outsider artists and Occultnix everywhere, particularly Jean Dubuffet of the Art Brut movement.

Klintr O'Dubhghaill:

Gratitude section, huh? Gratitude is hard...probably because it interferes with my carefully cultivated self-image as a cynical, self-interested, self-sufficient bastard...but I guess I'll give it a shot.

There are relatively few things that I'm truly grateful for in this world; among which are beer, blowjobs, and really good books. I'm grateful to my buddy Heimlich for having turned me on to a few of the right books at the right moments during some rather important transitional phases in my life. I'm additionally grateful to him for having encouraged me to write, for having read my drivel, for encouraging me again to continue, for having done the vast majority of the grunt work on this particular project, as well as the original *Elhaz Ablaze* site...and for having put up with my self-involved bullshit in the meantime.

I'll have to buy Heimlich a few beers next time I see him. No blowjobs, though, I'm not that grateful.

Sweyn Plowright:

When I think of what I am grateful for, I remember the books that I read at a young age. The first would be Charles Darwin's *On the Origin of Species*. Many works by Isaac Asimov & Arthur C. Clarke, both fiction and scientific. Carl Sagan of course, who I quote in *Learning Logic*. Without the intellectual grounding of these giants, and the sense of wonder they conveyed, real spiritual growth and understanding would not have been possible.

Lonnie Scott:

Gratitude. A feeling that pulls a mind back to the seeds that began the growth now harvested. My own gratitude reaches back to Paul Peterson who put me on a Runic and Heathen path 20 years ago. My gratitude knows the joy of *Liber Null & Psychonaut* put in my hands by Chuck Smith. Paul and Chuck both rest now in the Halls of their Ancestors. May their memory live on! My gratitude goes to Heimlich A. Laguz for bringing *Elhaz Ablaze* to life. There I found my feet on solid ground. Also to Jason Miller for his Strategic Sorcery course that opened many doors. I must show gratitude to Rick Wilson for his endless kindness in sharing Runic and Heathen knowledge. I'm grateful for the wisdom and lessons of Marcus Katz in the ways of Tarot and divination. My gratitude goes to Fiona Benjamin for the divination that ushered me back to the hearth of Heathenry when I felt lost. Further gratitude to Lothar Tuppan for his guidance and wisdom on one hand, and his friendship on the other. Finally, my gratitude goes to The ADF, The Troth, The Rune Gild, and all of you out in Midgard courageous enough to seek the mysteries.

VI:

What am I grateful for? Mostly?
Not being a corpse. And cats.

Within the context of not being a corpse, well, then we're talking about the finer things in life.

Gratitude

Whisky. The warmth of a lover. Fine friends, family, good food, and interesting books.

As a crippled magician, I may not be able to ride, be a doughty fighter, be able to manage a flock, or shower folk with wealth. But, I have some small faculty with words – those shapes of sound, those glyphs of ink.

And if word follows word, and gives word to me? Then I'm grateful for that, too.

For the rhythm and the rhyme. For the sacred spaces in between.
For the hearthfire of the heart, about which we all warm ourselves.
For the breath, for the light in the blood; for the nodding head, the glance that speaks of shared, inner knowing.
For the tree that, in death, carries these words to you, its body crushed and stained.
(Everything has a use, a worth, a way to be anew. Even, and especially, the dead.)

To those who thought my words were worth sharing, worth sliding onto leaves to nestle next to other ideas? Those who read them, think on them? To you I'm grateful, too.

And finally, I'm grateful to be able to ask, and answer, the ancient question: "Would you know more, or what?"

About the Creators

Matthew Hern

Matt Anon is a mystic and writer, who is very interested in ecstatic experience, magic, religion, intense music, beauty, weirdness, and travel as pilgrimage. He studies different perspectives and applications of exploring mysticism and doing magic and develops his own philosophy rather than following the worn-out paths of others. Matt has a Masters Degree in Religious Studies and Anthropology and currently writes his PhD thesis about occult philosophy in the Renaissance at Delhi University in India. His main research areas are esotericism, occultism, Tantra, and New Religious Movements. He's also a Fellow of the Rune-Gild and a member the Apophis Club.

Heimlich A. Laguz

Laguz has been practicing magic – runic, chaos, and otherwise – since 1996, and has described itself as a Heathen since 1999. An INFJ personality, Laguz is motivated by an endless thirst for growth and mystery, typically with the intention of being able to thereby also support the growth and healing of others. Laguz's academic and career foci lie in arts philosophical, psychological, and therapeutic. Laguz also has a passionate interest in progressive politics and has been a dedicated advocate for a range of social justice causes. Laguz loves to make music, meditates daily, and venerates various deities with vigorous devotion. As the image suggests, Laguz readily patrols the limits of its comfort zone.

Arrowyn Craban Lauer

I started drawing when I was three years old. It just felt natural to want to capture what I was perceiving and try to hold it in place on paper, in dirt, on cloth, or in skin. I didn't realize at the time that I was continuing a tradition of countless of generations of my ancestors. I think that through the process of eye to mind to hand to pencil to paper to eye I am in essence trying to get a grip on the crazy flux of earthly existence. Trying to interpret, and understand, and then influence the flow of life. And my reasons haven't changed since I was three – I just have more words now.

In my life travels I have studied herbal medicine & healing traditions from all over the world; cooking & fermentation; art & mythology; tattooing & handcrafting; primitive skills & folk ways; music, love, & nature worship; esoteric arts & magic.

Many years ago I was told in a dream that everything I needed to learn about this world I could learn from my ancestors. This set me on a path of enquiry to find out just who they were and what they knew about life.

I am a creatrix by trade and a lifelong practitioner of Chaos Magic.

MichaELFallson

MichaELFallson was born in Darlinghurst, in Sydney, Australia, in 1968. He was raised in remote bush and rural settings from the age of 2. He studied fine art at the National Art School 18 years later, graduating with a major in printmaking. His band Beastianity was created around this time and continues to produce songs in order to unite Stray Aliens throughout the world.

He was encouraged by his grandfather to look to and rely upon the plants and animals, as well as the seen and unseen forces and symbols of nature, to inspire his visual and musical works.

He gives thanks and praise for the Australian bush, his wondrous wife Melf, the Old Ones and the Runes who guide and protect his children, family, and dearest kin eternally.

With 25 years experience in acute and forensic settings, Michael currently works within a rural Child and Adolescent Psychiatry service and has a role as a local consultant in first episode psychosis.

Chaos is his life in Love.

Mark Morte

Mark Morte is a New Zealand-born, Australian-based, and internationally-renowned Psychonautik Clown. He has been contributing his darktistic talents to underground comics, music, and film for close to 40 years. His inspired artwork is displayed in Sweyn Plowright's *True Helm: A Practical Guide To Northern Warriorship* and his groundbreaking comic character Moribund was a regular in the infamous *Eddie* magazine, highlighting the absurdity and harshness of inner-city Sydney's 1980s street scene in first person. Mark is an integral member of Beastianity and continues to write, perform, and crowd incite in a collection of occult-themed extreme electronic and black/death metal groups.

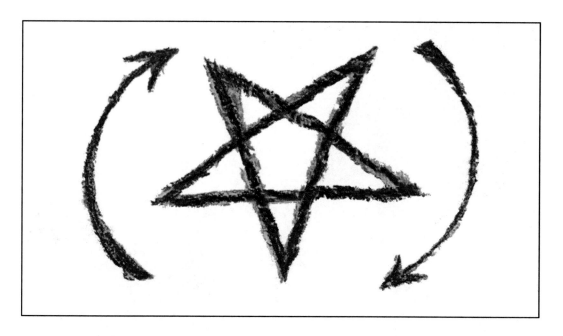

Klintr O'DubhGhaill

Klintr O'DubhGhaill has been an Army Reserve Paratrooper, a published Poet, a Bouncer, a Film and Philosophy Student, an amateur Cage Fighter, and a professional Personal Trainer. He is currently a full-time Dad and part-time Martial Arts Instructor, with pretentions of one day becoming a novelist.

Sweyn Plowright

Sweyn has been known in Heathen circles for a number of years, and has been a contributor to *Elhaz Ablaze* since 2008. His Heathen interests began with Runes after reading Tolkien's works in 1972.

He was asked to lead the Rune-Gild South Pacific Region for the decade of the 1990s, leaving in 2000 to establish a non-hierarchical study network called Rune-Net. He has contributed articles to several Heathen journals over the years, and published the successful handbook *The Rune Primer* in 2006.

His academic studies have included Physics, Maths, Psychology, Statistics, Linguistics, and Logic. His other interests include motorcycling, martial arts, and music. He has performed in the band Beastianity along with some of the other contributors to this book, and has released a solo album on CD.

Lonnie Scott

Lonnie Scott is an author, teacher, and Heathen born and raised in the land of the Mad Gasser.

Lonnie has explored many aspects of the occult, with an emphasis on Tarot, runes, meditation, trance, Paganism, and Heathenism, for over 20 years.

He's an award winning Tarot Professional voted Tarosophist of the Year 2014 by the Tarosophy Tarot Professionals Association. He is also a Professional Hypnotist, Meditation Coach, and NLP Practitioner.

Lonnie has been influenced by Jason Miller's Strategic Sorcery Course, *Ár nDraíocht Féin* (ADF), The Troth, The Tarosophy Tarot Professionals Association, The Rune Gild, Rune-Net, and various local networks. Lonnie is also a martial artist perfecting tapping out before passing out, and dodging sticks and knives. He hopes one day to appear in a *Star Wars* film, and sing the Seventh Inning Stretch at Wrigley Field.

VI

Craig 'VI' Slee lives in the NW of the UK. Writer, Odinsman, Bearded Frothing Madman, he's been Heathen longer than he has been anything else. He likes fine whisky and loves cats.

Index

Please note that the index does not include references to sources listed in the "Academic Sources" and "Sources for Inspiration" chapters of this book.

93rd Current, 9
Abell, Steven T., 148
Adorno, Theodore, 27
Advaita Vedanta, 132
Aesir, 26
Ain Soph Aur, 130, 133, 137
Albedo, 225
Alchemy, 10, 74, 75, 76, 82, 84, 127, 128, 134, 224, 225, 226
Aletheia, 80, 81, 82, 83, 84, 85, 86, 87, 88, 89, 90, 92
ALU, 93, 151, 152, 184, 185
Anarch, 38, 39
Anātman, 133
Ancestors, 11, 13, 19, 22, 29, 30, 34, 35, 36, 37, 39, 40, 44, 45, 49, 50, 51, 52, 53, 54, 57, 58, 59, 61, 66, 70, 84, 89, 99, 101, 102, 104, 105, 106, 107, 109, 110, 112, 113, 114, 117, 148, 184, 189, 191, 193, 194, 196, 197, 231
Ancient Greece, 41, 44, 45, 80, 96, 98, 126, 201
Ancient Rome, 44, 45, 80, 91, 98, 104, 190, 229, 230
Anima Mundi, 127
Ansuz (rune), 154, 155, 162, 184
Anti-modernist, 11
Antinomian, 72
Aquino, Michael, 131, 132, 134, 178, 180, 181
Archery, 99
Arendt, Hannah, 147
Ares, 202, 203, 204
Arete, 201, 202, 203, 204, 205
Asgard, 31, 161, 163
Astrology, 10
Atman, 132
Auden, W. H., 79
AUM, 137

Axis Mundi, 175
Babalon, 130
Bacon, Sir Francis, 105
Bagby, Benjamin, 148
Balance, John, 28, 123
Baldr, 85, 86, 191
Baugi, 160, 161, 163
Bede, 232, 233
Being, 15, 18, 19, 24, 78, 80, 81, 112, 128, 131, 152, 183, 184, 191, 211, 215
Belief, 12, 18, 29, 36, 40, 55, 61, 71, 73, 74, 77, 83, 86, 87, 101, 102, 103, 106, 107, 110, 111, 112, 113, 114, 115, 116, 118, 141, 142, 144, 150, 151, 164, 169, 175, 221, 222, 223, 224
Beowulf, 148, 232, 233
Berzerker, 6, 45
Bigotry, 17, 18, 35, 103, 113, 114
Bindrunes, 47
Bingen, Hildegard von, 135
Blavatsky, Helena, 9, 10, 33, 122, 132, 178
Bodyweight strength training, 95
Body-wisdom, 17
Böhme, Jakob, 24
Book of the Law, 23, 125, 130
Boxing, 95, 98, 203
Brahman, 132
Bronze Age, 44
Bruno, Giordano, 10
Buddhism, 16, 18, 21, 44, 45, 48, 73, 103, 115, 121, 122, 125, 131, 132, 136, 173, 175, 203
Buddhism, *Dzogchen*, 173
Byock, Jesse, 232
Calisthenics, 95, 96, 97, 98, 99, 204
Capitalism, 13, 18, 21
Carroll, Pete, 10, 27, 111, 136
Catholicism, 22, 70, 71, 222
Ceremonial Magic, 9, 125, 126, 174, 182

261

Chaos Heathenry, 7, 9, 11, 12, 17, 18, 21, 22, 26, 28, 54, 55, 69, 74, 75, 76, 78, 79, 80, 82, 83, 84, 87, 88, 91, 92, 117, 174, 176, 207
Chaos Magic(k), 9, 10, 12, 13, 21, 25, 32, 47, 49, 73, 74, 83, 84, 87, 110, 111, 122, 129, 133, 135, 136, 141, 142, 143, 164, 168, 169, 170, 174, 176, 177, 182, 183, 184, 209
Chaos Theory, 9
Chaotopia, 137, 174, 183
Chemognostic sacrament, 31, 129
Chi, 33
Christ, Jesus, 45, 70, 71, 76, 190, 191
Christianity, 11, 12, 18, 22, 25, 29, 34, 35, 45, 48, 70, 71, 72, 76, 78, 82, 83, 84, 87, 89, 90, 91, 101, 105, 106, 107, 109, 122, 124, 132, 134, 135, 181, 183, 184, 190, 192, 205, 231; see also Creationism
Christopherson, Peter "Sleazy," 9
Coil, 9, 123
Coincidentia oppositorum, 134, 181
Collective Unconscious, 71, 76, 77, 127, 128, 146, 158
Colonialism, 29, 71, 89, 226
Common Law, 104, 105, 106, 107
Connected Breathwork, 33
Creationism, 109, 111
Crossley-Holland, Kevin, 233
Crowley, Aleister, 9, 10, 11, 23, 27, 32, 101, 114, 122, 123, 124, 125, 126, 130, 131, 132, 133, 164, 171, 175, 178, 180
Dagaz (rune), 21, 148, 152, 162, 174
Daoism, 77, 136; see also Laozi
Davidson, H. R. E., 102, 119
Deep Mind, 127, 143, 146
Descartes, Rene, 62, 132
Devil, 48, 222; see also Satan, Set
Dionysus, 205
Divination, 52, 54, 142
Does not matter, need not be, 144
Dogma, 11, 70, 74, 75, 77, 83, 84, 102, 110, 112, 117, 118, 137, 150, 175, 176
Dorneus, Gerardus, 128
Druidism, 47
Durkheim, Emile, 22

Ebner, Margaretha, 135
Edda, Poetic, 11, 84, 231, 232
Edda, Prose, 11, 148, 158, 232
Ego, 14, 17, 18, 71, 73, 77, 78, 131, 134, 136, 141, 142, 143, 144, 146, 147, 151, 155, 176, 180, 181, 182, 209, 212, 217, 218, 222
Egyptian Lore, 45, 47, 48, 74, 125, 130, 131
Eight Lectures on Yoga, 122, 124
Ein Skopudhr Galdra (music project), 159, 163
Elhaz (rune), 19, 49, 91, 92, 161, 178, 208
Eliade, Mircea, 11, 22, 179
Elric, 155
Emerson, Ralph Waldo, 11, 124
Enantiodromia, 72, 83, 90, 91
Enlightenment (era), 10, 11, 29, 39, 103, 104, 107, 109, 110, 128,
Enlightenment (mode of consciousness), 27, 122, 137, 175, 180, 182
Ergi, 35, 197
Erickson, Milton, 165, 166, 167
Eros, 10, 27, 74, 205
Essentialism, 90
Europe, 11, 41, 43, 44, 102, 119, 229
Evola, Julius, 37, 38
Faulkes, Anthony, 232
Faust, 155
Fehu (rune), 162
Fencing, 95, 98
Ficino, Marsilio, 10, 25, 126, 130
Fire + Ice, 36, 40, 174, 175, 185
Folkism, 12, 28, 29, 113
Franz, Marie-Louise von, 74, 83
Free Masonry, 9
Freestyle shamanism, 171
Freki, 157
Freud, Sigmund, 22, 121, 181
Freyja, 36, 86, 130, 159, 164, 191, 197
Fries, Jan 77, 127, 145, 155, 171
Frigg, 191
Fundamentalism, 29, 102, 109, 112, 118, 122
Futhark, 35, 36, 37, 147, 148, 151, 157, 177, 230

Futhark, Elder, 148
Futhark, Younger, 35, 148
Futhork, Anglo-Saxon, 148
Fylgja, 30, 32
Galdor, 147, 148, 149
Gebo (rune), 23
Geertz, Clifford, 13
Genealogy, 14, 50
Geri, 157
Giants, 84, 85, 86, 87, 88, 91, 122, 192
Ginnung, 25, 27, 177
Ginnungagap, 177
Gnosis, 12, 13, 49, 124, 129, 136, 150, 158, 187, 191, 197
Gnosticism, 87, 105
Godwin, Joscelyn, 10, 126, 135, 175
Goenka, S. N., 16, 157
Goethe, Johann Wolfgang von, 155
Golden Dawn, 9, 122, 136
Goldsworthy, Andy, 81
Grammaticus, Saxo, 231
Grof, Stanislav, 33, 129
Guénon, René, 37
Gunnlod, 161
Gylfaginning, 216
Gymnastics, 95, 97, 98
Hagalaz (rune), 157, 159, 210
Hamingja, 34, 39, 184
Hamr, 33
Havamal, 116, 188, 189
Heaney, Seamus, 148
Heathenry, 9, 10, 11, 12, 13, 17, 18, 19, 21, 22, 25, 26, 28, 29, 30, 35, 36, 38, 39, 41, 47, 48, 49, 51, 54, 69, 70, 71, 72, 73, 74, 76, 77, 78, 79, 80, 81, 83, 86, 88, 89, 90, 91, 101, 102, 103, 104, 105, 106, 107, 109, 110, 111, 112, 113, 114, 115, 116, 117, 118, 125, 131, 135, 141, 142, 143, 148, 150, 152, 153, 155, 158, 169, 170, 171, 175, 177, 184, 187, 207, 211, 229, 231, 232
Hegel, G. W. F., 181
Heidegger, Martin, 15, 18, 80, 81, 92, 222, 223
Hel, 33, 60, 139, 161, 163, 191
Helm of Awe, 30, 155
Hermes, 34

Hevajra, 121
Hilmarsson, Hilmar Örn, 102
Hinduism, 32, 40, 44, 45, 95, 96, 97, 98, 121, 124, 130, 131, 132, 135, 184
Hollander, Lee M., 232
Holy Guardian Angel, 32, 129, 133
Homophobia, 17, 35
Hospitality, 7, 49, 154, 196
Hughr, 31
Huginn, 31
Humility, 73
Humor, 35, 73, 77, 164, 166, 171, 176, 207, 209, 213, 214
Husserl, Edmund, 223
Hypnosis, 48, 51, 57, 165, 170
Ibn Fadlān, Ahmad, 101, 230
Ibn Gabirol, 130
Illuminates of Thanateros, 177
Illusion of separateness, 61, 130
Inclusiveness, 28
Indo-European, 16, 18, 23, 30, 43, 44, 45, 86, 95, 96, 97, 98, 99, 183
Indra's Web, 183
Irony, 18, 73, 77, 132, 141, 147, 148, 156
Isa (rune), 123
Islam, 69, 87, 104, 109, 136; see also Sufism, *Tariqat*
Isolate Intelligence, 78, 132; see also self-deification
James, William, 11
Johnson, Robert, 88
Jord, 84
Jormangand, 61
Josephus, Flavius, 229
Jujutsu, 98
Jung, Carl Gustav, 11, 22, 30, 38, 71, 73, 74, 76, 88, 92, 127, 128, 129, 143, 167, 177, 205, 221, 222, 223, 224, 225, 226
Jünger, Ernst, 39
Kabbalah/Qabalah, 125, 130, 134, 135
Kali, 21, 130, 174, 177
Kampfringen, 98
Kaun (rune), 35
Kelly, Michael, 25, 30, 32, 34, 134, 136, 174
Kepler, Johannes, 127, 132
Kettlebells, 95, 97

Ki, 33
Kia, 9, 74, 177; see also *Zos Kia Cultus*
Kuhn, Thomas, 111
Laguz (rune), 38, 162, 173, 185, 210
Landvættir, 30
Laozi, 211
Larrington, Carolyn, 232
Lateralus, 19
LaVey Anton, 136, 181
Leary, Timothy, 129
Lee, Dave, 33, 130, 137, 174, 176, 183
Left Hand Path, 72, 131, 134, 137, 173, 174, 178, 179, 180, 181, 182, 184
Levy-Brühl, Lucian, 221, 222, 226
Liber Null & Psychonaut, 47
Liberation Theology, 190
Ljóssalfar, 30
Locke, John, 107
Logic, 24, 103, 114, 115, 152, 181
Loki, 35, 48, 159, 191, 214
Lyke, 33
Maat, 193
Macleod, Mindy, 150, 152
Mandala, 173
Mantra, 77, 115, 144
Marvel Comics, 218
McNallen, Stephen, 113
Mead of inspiration, 86, 90
Meditation, 16, 23, 28, 48, 49, 51, 54, 56, 57, 114, 115, 116, 124, 125, 157, 159, 164, 168, 209
Mees, Bernard, 150, 152
Meister Eckhart, 24, 25, 135
Mercurius, 225
Merswin, Rulman, 135
Mesmerism, 9
Metagenetics, 113
Metzner, Ralph, 129, 181
Mimir, 90
Mirandola, Giovanni Pico della, 10, 25
Mjolnir, 217
Modernity, 11, 12, 81, 83, 88, 89, 90, 92, 103, 104, 105, 109, 122, 132
Morphic fields, 113
Morrison, Jim, 7
Muninn, 31, 189

Myne, 31
Mystery, 15, 17, 18, 23, 37, 40, 41, 48, 69, 70, 71, 72, 73, 74, 75, 76, 77, 78, 79, 80, 81, 82, 83, 84, 87, 90, 91, 92, 123, 131, 134, 137, 144, 145, 146, 147, 148, 152, 170, 173, 174, 175, 176, 185, 210, 215
Nauthiz (rune), 210
Navy SEALs, 45, 203
Necronomicon, 47
Neopaganism, 11, 17
Neoplatonism, 9, 126, 174
Nettesheim, Agrippa von, 10
Neuro-Linguistic Programming, 48
New Age, The, 32, 47, 109, 113, 114, 115, 117, 128, 136, 204
Newton, Sir Isaac, 127, 132
Nietzsche, Friedrich, 92, 168, 170, 203, 210, 211
Nigredo, 225
Nine Noble Virtues, 71
Nirvāna, 131, 133, 137
Norns, 183
"Nothing is True, Everything is Permitted," 13, 176
Nuit, 129, 130, 131, 133, 134, 137
Objectification, 80, 86
Occultism, 9, 17, 21, 37, 40, 47, 48, 79, 122, 125, 131, 177, 178, 181
Odianism, 175
Odin, 13, 20, 21, 22, 23, 24, 25, 26, 31, 34, 35, 36, 69, 70, 71, 77, 78, 82, 84, 85, 86, 87, 90, 92, 149, 154, 155, 156, 157, 159, 161, 164, 165, 167, 170, 171, 174, 175, 181, 189, 191, 196, 204, 205, 207, 213, 222, 231
Odin, Bolverkr, 26, 158, 159, 160, 161, 162, 163
Odin, Father of Victory, 191
Odin, High One, 188, 191
Odin, Woden, 23, 154, 155, 156, 197, 225, 226
Odin, Wotan, 23, 205
Óðr, 22, 31, 159
Olcott, Henry, 9
Olympic Games, 98
Önd, 32, 33
Orientalism, 122

Orlog, 105
Orridge, Genesis P., 9, 134, 179
Orthodoxy, 12, 71, 76, 141
Orthopraxy, 12, 71, 141
Othala (rune), 148
Ouroborus, 61
Owning Your Own Shadow, 88
Pagan, 41, 47, 48, 51, 71, 99, 115
Pammachon, 98
Pankration, 98
Paradigm, 176
Participation mystique, 221, 222, 223, 224, 226
Pascal, Blaise, 121
Patanjali, 122, 124
Patriarchy, 71
Pauli, Wolfgang, 129
Pennick, Nigel, 24, 37
Perdurabo, 123
Phenomenology, 22, 74, 76, 223
Philosopher's Stone, 225
Philosophia perennis, 23, 37, 38, 122, 134
Physical culture, 95
Picatrix, 126
Plato, 38, 132, 201, 203
Pleroma, 137
Postmodernism, 9, 12, 13, 21, 26, 28, 30, 36, 111, 174, 176, 223
Prana, 32, 123
Pranayama, 123, 125
Prima Materia, 225
Procopius, 230
Pronoia, 129
Psychick TV, 9
Psychological Reconstruction, 49
Psychological Types, 71
Psychotherapy, 16, 28, 164, 167, 224, 226
Puruṣārtha, 193
Quantum physics, 9, 127, 128, 129
Quarternity, 92
Race/Racism, 12, 17, 28, 29, 35, 38, 48, 62, 71, 80, 113, 122, 147; see also bigotry
Raidho (rune), 145
Rational Heathenism, 11, 101, 103, 108, 113, 114
Rational Paganism, 118

Ravindra, Ravi, 23, 24, 134
Read, Ian, 21, 22, 23, 28, 30, 31, 36, 110, 175, 185
Reconstructionism, 18, 48, 49, 89, 152
Reich, Wilhelm, 33
Reichenbach, Karl, 33
Relativism, 13, 111, 176; see also postmodernism
Renaissance, 9, 98, 126
Right Hand Path, 131, 132, 137, 180
Rilke, Rainier Maria, 92
Rinpoche, Sogyal, 173
Ritual, 29, 74, 82, 99, 102, 117, 141, 142, 146, 149, 152, 153, 154, 156, 157, 158, 163, 164, 166, 171, 179, 185, 207, 208, 209, 210, 211, 212
Romanticism, 10, 11, 12, 22, 29, 63, 101, 117, 136
Rosicrucianism, 9
Rta, 193
Rubedo, 134, 225
Runa, 22, 37, 40, 77, 78, 82, 87, 134, 174, 176, 185
Rúnatáls þáttr Óðins, 78, 231
Rune Gild, 21, 29, 78
Rune poems, 91, 116, 230
Rune yoga, 117
Runes, 12, 19, 21, 22, 23, 29, 30, 33, 35, 36, 37, 38, 40, 47, 48, 49, 52, 54, 69, 70, 77, 78, 82, 87, 91, 92, 93, 114, 116, 117, 119, 123, 134, 141, 142, 143, 144, 145, 146, 147, 148, 149, 150, 151, 152, 153, 154, 155, 156, 157, 159, 161, 162, 165, 171, 173, 174, 175, 176, 177, 178, 184, 185, 191, 208, 210, 211, 230, 231
Runic Amulets and Magic Objects, 150
Said, Edward, 22
Sàl, 33
Samadhi, 25, 124, 125, 181
Satan, 47, 132, 134, 155, 179, 180; see also Devil, Set
Satanic Bible, 47
Satanism, 129, 132, 136, 178
Schwarzenegger, Arnold, 202
Science, 10, 11, 18, 28, 29, 44, 49, 57, 76, 80, 107, 110, 111, 113, 123, 126, 128, 223

Seidhr, 49, 155, 197
Self-Deification, 180; see also Isolate Intelligence, Temple of Set
Self-love, 19
Set/Setian/Temple of Set, 131, 132, 134, 174, 178, 179, 201
Shaivism, 23, 184
Shakti, 121, 184
Shaolin, 203
Shiva, 20, 23, 121, 180, 184
Sigil magic, 27, 47, 121, 123, 134, 143, 144, 145, 146, 147, 148, 150, 153, 158, 171
Simultaneous oneness and difference of all things, 76
Skaldskaparmal, 158
Sleipnir, 68
Social justice, 190, 226
Soul-Lore, 30, 33, 34, 184
Spare, Austin Osman, 9, 121, 147, 177, 178, 182
Spiritualism, 9
Steuco, Agostino, 38, 134
Stick Fighting, 98
Sturluson, Snorri, 101, 148, 232
Sufism, 37, 69, 87, 136
Suñyatā, 132, 133, 137, 173
Superstition, 10, 18, 30, 37, 104, 218, 221
Suso, Henry, 135
Suttung, 86, 160, 161, 162
Swarup, Ram, 40, 41
Tacitus, 101, 229
Tantra, 16, 18, 37, 49, 73, 121, 129, 130, 179, 184
Tariqat, 69, 71
Tarkovsky, Andrei, 40
Tarot, 51, 52, 114
Tauler, Johannes, 135
Technocracy, 61, 80, 83, 84, 86, 88, 89, 90, 91, 110, 136
Temple of Set, 129, 131, 132, 134, 174, 179
That, or something better, 144
The Fool of the Sacred Chao, 173
The Incredible String Band, 122
Thee Temple ov Psychick Youth, 27, 47
Thelema, 9, 134, 175
Theosophy, 9, 33

Thor, 11, 25, 35, 84, 159, 171, 207, 208, 210, 212, 213, 214, 215, 216, 217, 218, 219
Thorsson, Edred, 26, 30, 36, 78, 141, 142, 146, 175, 179
Thoth, 34
Thurisaz (rune), 210, 211
Tolkien, J. R. R., 11, 148
Tool, 19
Track & Field, 95
Unio Mystica, 132, 180
Universalist, 28
Unsubstantiated Personal Gnosis, 158
Unus Mundus, 128, 129, 131, 135
Uruz (rune), 185
Vafthrudnir, 84, 85, 86, 90
Vafthrudnismal, 84, 85
Vajrayana, 121
Veritas, 80, 81, 82, 83, 85, 86, 87, 88, 89, 90, 91, 92
Viking, 13, 26, 29, 35, 36, 48, 106, 107, 230, 231
Vinculum amoris, 127, 132
Vipassana, 16; see also meditation
Visual Magick, 127, 145, 171
Vivekananda, 11, 124
Void, 23, 25, 27, 124
Voltaire, 107, 113
Voudoun, 33
Vulnerability, 18, 72, 83, 84, 91, 154, 211
Watchmen, 28
Watts, Alan, 92
Webb, Don, 131, 132, 184, 201, 202
Weber, Max, 11
Weightlifting, 95, 97
Werewolves, 44
Western Martial Arts, 95
Whitman, Walt, 21
Wicca, 47, 48, 101, 114
Wiedergaenger, 33
Wights, 30
Wilber, Ken, 181
Will to Power, 176, 203, 205
Wilson, Robert Anton, 31, 128, 175, 223
Wode, 31, 32, 40
World Tree, see *Yggdrasil*
Wrestling, 95, 96, 98, 201, 204

Wyrd, 29, 30, 36, 40, 49, 50, 58, 78, 79, 85, 87, 89, 104, 144, 145, 146, 153, 158, 161, 170, 171, 173, 182, 183, 190, 192, 209, 210, 212
X-Men, 28

Yggdrasil, 24, 69, 181
Ymir, 77
Yoga, 23, 25, 32, 95, 96, 122, 124, 125
Zen, 136
Zos Kia Cultus, 9, 177

CPSIA information can be obtained
at www.ICGtesting.com
Printed in the USA
FFOW01n1654040618
47052478-49391FF